College Student-Athletes

Challenges, Opportunities, and Policy Implications

A volume in
The David C. Anchin Research Center
Series on Educational Policy in the 21st Century: Opportunities, Challenges, and Solutions
Bruce Anthony Jones, *Series Editor*

UNIVERSITY OF SOUTH FLORIDA
College of Education
David C. Anchin Center

MISSION STATEMENT
David C. Anchin Center

The mission of the David C. Anchin Center is a statement of faith in the educators of today and a commitment to excellence in the schools of tomorrow. Through our mission statement, initiatives of the Center fall under three broad programmatic categories: (1) Research and Service (2) Communications and Information Dissemination, and (3) Policy Advocacy on Behalf of Research Based Best Practices in Education.

College Student-Athletes

Challenges, Opportunities, and Policy Implications

edited by

Daniel B. Kissinger
University of Arkansas

Michael T. Miller
University of Arkansas

Sponsored by

UNIVERSITY OF
SOUTH FLORIDA
College of Education
David C. Anchin Center

INFORMATION AGE PUBLISHING, INC.
Charlotte, NC • www.infoagepub.com

Library of Congress Cataloging-in-Publication Data

College student-athletes : challenges, opportunities, and policy implications /
edited by Daniel B. Kissinger, Michael T. Miller.
    p. cm. – (Educational policy in the 21st century)
  Includes bibliographical references.
  ISBN 978-1-60752-140-2 (pbk.) – ISBN 978-1-60752-141-9 (hardcover)
1. College sports–United States. 2. Education, Higher–Aims and objectives–United
States. 3. College athletes–Education–United States. I. Kissinger, Daniel B. II. Miller,
Michael T.
  GV351.C65 2009
  796.04'30973–dc22

                                                                          2009019537

Printed in the United States of America

CONTENTS

PART I

ENTERING THE COLLEGE ENVIRONMENT

PART II

TYPES OF STUDENT-ATHLETES AND THEIR IDENTITIES

PART III

CHALLENGES WHILE ENROLLED

PART IV

INSTITUTIONAL DIMENSIONS TO STUDENT ATHLETES

COLLEGE STUDENT-ATHLETE

Challenges, Opportunities, and Policy Implications

Our editors, Kissinger and Miller, brought together an eclectic group of scholars to create the first volume in this educational policy series to offer an in-depth analysis of the experience of the student-athlete before, during, and after the college experience. The volume provides an excellent explication of the strengths, challenges, and weaknesses in the research literature on college athletics. The timing for this volume could not be better. In the wake of Barack Obama's presidential win, there is a renewed interest in higher education that promises to be different from the previous eight years of the George W. Bush Administration—particularly as this concerns issues of student access and achievement. Now more than ever, institutions of higher education will have to ensure that they provide academically rich experiences for students that result in their college completion and transition into successful livelihoods. New student-related policies will have to be developed and old ones reviewed so that they reflect the advent of this reality.

The volume helps answer many pressing policy questions regarding the role of athletics in higher education in the 21st century. How do institutions of higher education maintain a focus on academics and balance this focus

College Student-Athletes: Challenges, Opportunities, and Policy Implications, pages ix–x
Copyright © 2009 by Information Age Publishing

with the desire to advance top-ranked athletic programs and fulfill the *esprit de corps* needs of students, faculty, administrators, university donors, business, and the larger community? How do we ensure that the institutional pursuit of being number one does not interfere with the primary academic, social, and interpersonal needs of incoming and active student-athletes? At what point does the highly competitive and increasingly profit-driven field of athletics corrupt the philosophical spirit of higher education, which is ideally more grounded in collective purposes?

This compelling volume is a must-read for students, practitioners, and academicians who are in the field of college sports. But it is also required reading for anyone interested in policy issues of student recruitment and retention, and for those who are interested in institutional strategies for making life better for all students on the college campus in a way that is consistent with attaining and sustaining the ideal mission of higher education.

Congratulations to editors Kissinger and Miller on the completion of a volume that is comprehensive, thorough, and extraordinarily succinct on a topic that is woefully underrepresented in our research on higher education.

Bruce Anthony Jones
Series editor

FOREWORD

Gary M. Miller
University of South Carolina

The inception of collegiate athletics many years ago began a trend that has evolved into the big-time athletic programs that are present today. The issues faced in the early years were similar to those faced by today's collegiate athletes. However, in the early days, there was not the concerted, systematic effort put forth by institutions to enhance the educational efforts of the individuals participating in organized intercollegiate athletics on their campuses.

I listened to a talk that Dr. Richard Lapchick gave to one of my classes in which he described the disappointment his father, Joe Lapchick, experienced when he realized his collegiate basketball players were not attending classes at St. John's University. In the presentation, Dr. Lapchick discussed how his father began study halls for these athletes and indicated that he believed that was the first time a coach had set mandatory study halls for student-athletes.

Over the years, institutions and the governing bodies for intercollegiate athletics have placed specific expectations for academic success for student-athletes. In response to these expectations, programs for assisting student-athletes in meeting educational requirements have emerged on campuses across the United States. In addition to academic support efforts, programs such as the National Collegiate Athletic Association's Champs/Life Skills

Program have been developed to assist student-athletes in gaining knowledge and skills relevant to various developmental areas of their lives.

Whether one is at a National Association for Intercollegiate Athletics institution or a National Collegiate Athletic Association Division I campus, the student-athletes on the campus are a unique subculture within the institution. A positive interface has emerged as individuals overseeing athletic programs, support personnel, and academics have begun to work together on behalf of student-athletes. It appears that efforts have evolved from having one "coach" responsible for the academic and developmental aspects of student-athletes to models that provide systematic, comprehensive, organized, campus-wide services to enhance the campus life of student-athletes. The progression has been exciting to observe. I can recall meeting Mr. Harold White, an assistant coach who was the single person responsible for the academic tutoring of athletes at the University of South Carolina in the mid-1970s. He just about "did it all." Eventually, he became a founding member of the National Athletic Academic Advisors' Association, a group whose members are now heavily involved in providing academic and personal support services for student-athletes at campuses across the United States.

As a handful of academics began examining the issues facing student-athletes, individual professional organizations have developed and some already existing professional groups have seen networks emerge as interest in researching and studying student-athletes has evolved. As a result, numerous articles have been published and books written addressing this subculture.

It is promising for helping professionals to become involved in these efforts and the diverse issues addressed in this book. The contributors provide current and useful information for individuals currently working with and those who plan to work with student-athletes on our campuses in the years ahead.

CHAPTER 1

THE CONTEMPORARY COLLEGE STUDENT ATHLETE AS A SUBPOPULATION

Daniel B. Kissinger
Michael T. Miller
University of Arkansas

Intercollegiate athletic programs combine opportunities to extend success-ful scholastic athletic careers and gain a post-secondary education that can facilitate student-athletes' successful transition into the professional work-force. Participation in college athletics also brings a unique set of personal, academic, and athletic challenges related specifically to their role as a stu-dent-athlete. These factors have led scholars and researchers from a broad range of academic disciplines to characterize student-athletes as a distinct subpopulation of college students.

BRIEF HISTORY

College athletics first appeared on American campuses in the 1800s in the form of extracurricular activities (Rudolph, 1990). Soon thereafter, athlet-

College Student-Athletes: Challenges, Opportunities, and Policy Implications, pages 1–7
Copyright © 2009 by Information Age Publishing
1

ics on campus began to serve a different purpose; that is, as a vessel for uniting the intellectual core of the campus with a greater sense of community. Since the occurrence of the first intercollegiate athletic event, an 1852 boat race between the Yale and Harvard crew teams, intercollegiate athletics have become a focal point for institutional pride. However, history shows that athletics have also served as beacons for criticism by constituents of higher education institutions who question the legitimacy of athletics within the broader academic mission of higher education. Today, thanks in part to the near saturation of sports media coverage, athletic-related triumphs and problems once relegated to the campus or local news can quickly evolve into a story capable of generating national media headlines. When troubling situations do arise, higher education institutions often move quickly to limit negative exposure and outcomes. One strategy is to draw upon the institutional good will engendered by their athletic programs. In some instances, however, this practice belies a more self-protective posture; that is, the utilization of athletic programs to hide or divert attention from more serious institutional problems (Sperber, 2000). On the other hand, intercollegiate athletic programs have evolved into a formidable and often central tenet of an institution's identity. Along with higher education's increased use and reliance on athletic programs to generate publicity and income, entertain communities, and recruit quality students (athletes and nonathletes) to their institution, there has been an increase in cross-disciplinary research dedicated to more fully developing an understanding of the college student-athlete experience as a whole. To that end, it is the goal of this text to provide the reader with a glimpse into the unique challenges, barriers, and opportunities encountered by college athletes that are, for the most part, integral to their success yet are far removed from the consciousness of the average college sports fan.

THE COLLEGE STUDENT-ATHLETE

Concern about the well-being of college athletes can be found as early as 1905, when President Theodore Roosevelt threatened intercollegiate athletics with federal intervention unless reforms were made to limit football injuries. While the revolution of sports equipment (from protective gear to playing surfaces) has substantially reduced injury concerns, substantive arguments remain concerning the potential exploitation (McCormick & McCormick, 2006), academic potential (Kramer, 1996; Shulman & Bowen, 2001), and the personal and psychological development and health of student-athletes (Ferrante, Etzel, & Lantz, 1996; Harris, 1993; Parham, 1993). The notion of college student-athletes as a specialized group, however, can be traced to Clark and Trow's (1966) view that this subpopulation emerged as a result of the generational differences and expectations that were confronting higher education at the time. Their vision subsequently laid the groundwork for today's contemporary view of the college student-athlete.

Clark and Trow's (1966) initial classification of students was segmented into four primary categories: (1) academic students (attach greatest importance to ideas), (2) vocational students (career preparation), (3) collegiate students (social and extracurricular activity engagement; learn from social relationships), and (4) nonconformists (individualism over others). (Sedlacek, Walters, and Valente, 1985, provide a thorough interpretation of the Clark and Trow classification and subsequent research.) Although students would not be completely categorized in any one area, they would hold preferences that would most closely align themselves with one of the four domains. The college student-athlete of the time would have been situated prominently in descriptions of collegiate students, where the primary motivation for college attendance was related to engagement in the college experience, including sports, Greek chapters, and other largely social groupings. In the mid-1990s, Miller and Nelson (1996) provided the first serious revisiting of the Clark and Trow subculture work. Miller and Nelson concluded that although the labels may well still be appropriate, the description of those students within each were radically different, with highly engaged students in areas of technology replacing the 1960s beatnik as the nonconformist. Today, profiles of student-athletes are cited as a distinct subpopulation of college students with their own issues and needs (Birky, 2007; Gohn, 2004).

CHARACTERISTICS AND STEREOTYPE

Understanding the increasingly prominent role and influence of intercollegiate athletics across the higher education spectrum requires a broadening of one's view of college athletes. Outside the athletic realm, for instance, there remains a limited awareness of the resiliency needed by student-athletes to effectively navigate the normal developmental events associated with the college experience in conjunction with the unique challenges inherent in the student-athlete experience. There is, however, an ever-expanding, empirically driven effort to understand the student-athlete. Parham (1993) suggested that college athletes experience a set of six distinctive challenges: (1) balancing athletic and academic responsibilities; (2) balancing social activities with the isolation of athletic responsibilities; (3) balancing athletic successes and/or failures with emotional stability; (4) balancing physical health and injury with the need to continue competing; (5) balancing the demands of relationships with entities such as coaches, teammates, parents, and friends; and (6) addressing the termination of one's college athletic career. Arising from these basic assumptions are numerous factors that must be considered when examining the contemporary student-athlete. As a result, those working with student-athletes should adopt a proactive approach in order to ensure the student-athlete's personal, academic, and athletic needs are being addressed.

One of the ongoing arguments remains the core conceptualization of the college athlete as a student-athlete. Constituents of the institution, including fellow students and faculty, may consider the term student-athlete as misleading, believing instead that the primary identification of a student-athlete lies with their athletic goals instead of with the academic challenges and rewards associated with higher education. It may be particularly surprising to many, then, that established stereotypes of college athletes as dumb jocks lacking the intellectual constitution and academic motivation to succeed in higher education are incongruent with the literature regarding the academic accomplishments of the contemporary student-athlete (McCormick & McCormick, 2006). Moreover, recent research suggests that student-athletes, despite the various challenges they encounter, are generally pleased with their college experience (Potuto & O'Hanlon, 2007). Generally speaking, however, there is little in the way of empirically based attempts to correlate the broad range of constituents who, to varying degrees, impact the contemporary student-athlete experience. This text represents an effort to better understand the contemporary college student-athlete through a critical examination of the varied constituencies both within and outside of the higher education environment that factor into the student-athlete equation, from recruitment to graduation.

The purpose of this volume is not to debate the legitimacy of college sports, but rather, the aim is to provide an in-depth discussion of the state of the contemporary college student-athlete. As a result, the authors of this text have been selected to explore specific questions regarding the personal, academic, and policy issues student-athletes encounter as a result of participating in athletics. The volume concludes with a discussion of the state, federal, agency, and institutional policy implications of hosting voluntary college student athletic participation in higher education. This introductory chapter serves to provide the reader with some basic, foundational information on college students who participate in athletics, and concludes with a brief outline of future research directions.

OPPORTUNITIES FOR EXPLORATION

Those interested in the scholarship of college student-athletes have many areas of possible research. Although much of the research and exploration on this subpopulation of the general student body has taken place within the context of sports and entertainment, there are several key areas that are particularly important in the context of the academy. These dimensions, explored throughout this text and in need of further study, are important for several reasons. First, most policy and action through legislation has sought to control environmental variables that impact student-athletes, not the behaviors and actions of the athletes themselves. Second, higher education institutions are first and foremost centers of intellectual insight, and in theory, the entertainment function is a secondary purpose, at most. However, athletic entities within higher education have increasingly been properly placed in "entertainment" categories, yet they still hold a fundamental responsibility to the college student who chooses to participate in athletic team competitions. Third, there is a need to protect college student-athletes from exploitation that can result from a situation that is highly profitable with low labor (student-athlete) costs. Outlined here are some of the major areas that have a particularly timely need for study, discourse, and dialogue both within and outside of the higher education community.

1. **Transitions.**   How do secondary school students make the decision about which college to attend, how do they decide on whom to trust with their academic and athletic futures, and equally important, how do institutions socialize these students into their environments? Many colleges and universities begin their orientation of student-athletes with disability testing, and from those results, create highly individualized programs that rely heavily on academic advisors. This may create barriers between student-athletes and other students on campus. Additionally, some of the strategies that are effectively used with the general student body, such as early warning signs in enrollment, social structure and network development, and intellectual and academic engagement, could be applied to the subpopulation of student-athletes.

2. **Psychological development and maturation.**   A continuous area of study within the collegiate environment is the maturation and psychological development of college students. This has grown from basic explorations about why students succeed, to the more philosophical discussions about learning and developmental competencies and the desired behaviors and actions of college students. This concern has been demonstrated by college administrator attempts to develop an appreciation for volunteerism through service learning programs. In a similar discussion, institutions need to be able to intentionally describe the desired psychological state of students as they graduate from college, including such domains as a student's capacity for making informed, rational decisions about politics, purchasing, and societal behaviors. Such discussion transcends all subpopulations of

students, and is particularly relevant with student-athletes. Questions about student-athlete behaviors, including substance use and abuse and behavior, have been relegated to the discretion of individual coaches, and almost all too frequently, newspaper headlines. Institutions and a variety of agencies, including the NCAA, need to become more aware of the emotional intelligence and psychological emotional health of student-athletes and build programs and protocols that foster positive reactions and learning, rather than simply relying on athletic performance to dictate a reward structure.

3. **Intellectual capacity.** There is little to no research that documents well the intellectual capacity of student-athletes. There are frequent and popular allusions to the academic ineligibility of student-athletes, inferring that athletic prowess is negatively correlated with intellectual ability. To the contrary, many student-athletes spend a tremendous amount of time and display substantial ability to learn, deconstruct, and reconstruct elements related to athletic ability, including health and wellness, opposing team tendencies, responsiveness, motivational and interpersonal relationship skills, and even mathematics related to performance. Research needs to explore how to balance athletic commitment with prompting and developing intellectual curiosity, and how this balance might be situated in often adversarial environments that foster competition between the two.

4. **Role of stress and stress response.** College students typically experience inconsistent levels of stress while enrolled and pursuing a degree, fluctuating between new experiences and transitions, to time and self-management issues. Many of the experiences of student-athletes, however, are heightened in terms of stress, as coaches, administrators, and teammates rely on the athlete to perform at a certain level. The consequences for not performing are much more severe than individual self-perception, and can include the employment and welfare of coaches, the treatment and attitude of other students and teammates on campus who might treat the athlete poorly, and even the collective psyche of an entire campus, community, or state. How athletes learn to deal with this stress in a healthy and productive way is an important element in the services that institutions can provide to their student-athletes.

5. **Health and mental welfare.** In addition to the physical demands of participating in college athletics at any level, there are tremendous mental issues surrounding how athletes see themselves, how they situate and process the idea of their future beyond athletics, and how they balance the competing demands of intellectual discourse and athletic competition. Institutions have responsibility for the mental and physical health of student-athletes and generally do an

exceptional job of helping athletes perform at their very physical best. College athletic programs are often not, however, conducive environments for openly exploring issues related to one's mental health.

Explored throughout this book are a wide number of topics and issues that could be the focus of academic or athletic accrediting bodies, a federal oversight committee, and/or those scholars and administrators in higher education who have the capacity and motivation to support college athletes. This discussion seeks to expand the current scholarship on college students, and the authors are to be commended for their willingness to begin opening the process of exploration, celebration, and the identification of what the collective academy needs to engage to promote healthy and successful students in all programs.

REFERENCES

Clark, B., & Trow, M. (1966). The organizational context. In T. Newcomb & E. Wilson (Eds.), *College peergroups: Problems and prospects for research* (pp.). Chicago: Aldine.

Ferrante, A. P., Etzel, E., & Lantz, C. (1996). Counseling college student athletes: The problem, the need, 1996. In E. F. Etzel, A. P. Ferrante, & J. W. Pinkney (Eds.), *Counseling college student athletes: Issues and interventions* (2nd ed., pp. 3–26). Morgantown, WV: Fitness Information Technology.

McCormick, R. A., & McCormick, A. C. (2006). The myth of the student-athlete: The college as employee. MSU Legal Studies Research Paper No. 03-18. *Washington Law Review, 81*, 71–157.

Miller, M. T., & Nelson, G. M. (January 1996). *Student cultures on campus: Priorities for a decade of research.* Paper presented at the International Conference on American Cultural Studies, Honolulu, HI. (ERIC Reproduction Service Document No. ED412780)

Parham, W. (1993). The intercollegiate athlete: A 1990's profile. *The Counseling Psychologist, 21,* 411–429.

Potuto, J. R., & O'Hanlon, J. (2007). National study of student-athletes regarding their experiences as college students. *College Student Journal, 41*(4), 947–966.

Rudolph, F. (1990). *The American college and university.* Athens: University of Georgia Press.

Sedaleck, W. E., Walters, P., & Valente, J. (1985). Differences between counseling clients and nonclients on Clark-Trow subcultures. *Journal of College Student Personnel, 25*(4), 319–322.

Shulman, J. L., & Bowen, W. G. (2001). *The game of life.* Princeton, NJ: Princeton University Press.

Sperber, M. (2000). *Beer and circus: How big-time college sports is crippling undergraduate education.* New York: Henry Holt.

CHAPTER 2

COLLEGE STUDENT-ATHLETES

Tracing Historical Research Trends in Higher Education

Darla J. Twale
Karen Abney Korn
University of Dayton

In order to learn more about college student-athletes, we must follow a trail of quality research through the last half-century. College athletics in primitive forms began in the 19th century, but understanding players became a ripe field of research only a few decades ago. The purpose of this chapter is to trace historically the trends in research on college student-athletes in an effort to determine future areas of study, beginning with a brief history of sport in higher education.

The need for student physical activity to complement mental stimulation and other co-curricular activities dates to the Harvard gymnasium of 1826 (Brubaker & Rudy, 1997). Harvard and Yale spiced early team competitions with crew matches as early as 1852 (Betterton, 1988), and Fordham defeated St. Francis Xavier College and Amherst downed Williams in the first baseball matches in 1859 (Betterton, 1988). However, organized sports,

College Student-Athletes: Challenges, Opportunities, and Policy Implications, pages 9–19
Copyright © 2009 by Information Age Publishing

9

campus athletic clubs, fraternity intramurals, and intercollegiate athletics emerged after the Civil War. Rutgers and Princeton boasted the first "football" match in 1869, a soccer precursor to the game now played (Brubaker & Rudy, 1997).

By 1880, as new sports were added and existing ones evolved into the more established and popular versions played today, college athletics programs sported training programs, paid coaches, alumni support, and team management (Brubaker & Rudy, 1997). College sports as big business emerged, which ultimately resulted in a push for winning teams, competitive scholarships, higher revenues, larger stadiums, and highly sought-after players and coaches (Brubaker & Rudy, 1997). What once sufficed as "free" publicity for a college's academic prowess shifted irreversibly to the school's national reputation as a sports superpower. Athletics as a public relation ploy attracted a different kind of student to higher education (Veysey, 1965). However, Jenks and Riesman (1977) contended that opening college admission to the academically underqualified or the working class who can play sports renders an appreciable negative effect on the athletically challenged and females who would never be considered varsity material. By the same token, coaches sought out players in places that admissions counselors never ventured, inadvertently increasing campus diversity for lower classes and minorities (Jenks & Riesman, 1997).

HISTORY OF RESEARCH ON STUDENT-ATHLETES

At the turn of the 20th century, when college sports appeared to careen out of control, measures were taken to minimize physical injury, regulate football, and establish oversight committees. During this time, college athletics offered all students a means for unprecedented frenzied expression, which prompted spirited behavior aimed toward the "game." However, this became problematic when emotions spilled into the classroom, and administrators had to respond (Brubaker & Rudy, 1997; Veysey, 1965). Ward (1908) called for the regulation of college athletics following scandals, poor sportsmanship, and win-at-all-cost attitudes. Schoonmaker (1930) noted college football revenues were spent on the institution and the athletic program rather than on the athletes who were bringing in the crowds, thereby exploiting student-athletes and their educations in favor of winning games.

Athletics also played an important role for many different types of institutions, including historically black colleges and universities (HBCUs). Football competition among HBCUs dates to 1892, and the boon to black student culture and school spirit appeared a must to attracting potential students to campus, especially women who wished to participate in sports competition. Corruption, scandal, and criticism of HBCU college sports emerged by the

1920s, affecting the goals set forth for the education of blacks, including indifference to athletes' academic eligibility. Outgrowth of the "Talented Tenth" movement appeared to fall on deaf ears as the spirit of sport outpaced the lure of the lab and library for students (Miller, 1995).

Savage (1930) studied intercollegiate athletics only to report little had changed as a result of any previous call for reforms. His research suggested that amateur standards be implemented and athletics take on a more co-curricular approach and complement classroom learning rather than be purely extracurricular. Research reported decades later revealed similar abuses thought to have been remediated earlier in the century (Brubaker & Rudy, 1997). Additional research in the first half of the 20th century found (1) college athletics to be less profitable than originally estimated especially in scholarship monies, and (2) graduating athletes had nowhere else to display their physical talents when they graduated. Therefore, the research suggested that colleges might refocus their efforts on developing athletes' intellectual ability as opposed to their physical prowess, which offered few, if any, long-term health gains (Brubaker & Rudy, 1997). In fact, the establishment of the Harvard gymnasium as a laboratory to study physical prowess prompted Harvard's athletic director to exploit the nature of sport into the emerging scientific realm as researchable material (Veysey, 1965). Savage concluded that colleges' recruitment and treatment of athletes essentially subvert and run contrary to the reasons why men obtain an education in the first place.

Harmon (1940) discussed meshing the sports programs with the more important academic program in terms of admission requirements, meeting instructor grade standards, and student demonstration of successful classroom performance before demonstrating athletic field competence. Reeder (1942) studied the academic performance of college athletes and found little or no difference between them and their nonathletic peers on admissions criteria and rates of probation and eventual dismissal. Perhaps that is why a decade later there still remained a need to eradicate problems with players, coaches, and game-fixing by establishing admission standards, continuance policies, and declarations of majors and degree pursuits for student-athletes (Semler, 1952). In fact, Tunis (1961) advocated for greater moral education of college students and regarded the role of college athletics as negatively affecting all student morals. Koch (1971) labeled collegiate sport regional conference play as simply cartels of major institutional sports programs competing against themselves for ever increasing resources. Delany (1997) chronicled the effect of commercialization of college sports on the institutional support of student-athletes.

McLaughlin's (1986) review of empirical research indicated contradictions between student-athletes' field participation and academic and career pursuits. In Astin's (1979) landmark study on college students, athletic involvement stood out as only a minor variable explored. Findings indicated that athletic involvement was negatively associated with smoking, and positively associated with drinking and overall satisfaction with college.

Attention to improving the collegiate career of college student-athletes through established research agendas appeared distant, at best, given the negative publicity it had drawn for decades. In their first attempt to bring order to numerous higher education research studies of which some included the student-athlete, Pascarella and Terenzini (1991) suggested that the student-athlete can benefit from the development of critical thinking skills. However, varsity athletics have become prized for their athletic ability at the expense of academic opportunities. They cited other studies that investigated the relationship between educational attainment and athletics; however, these studies do not take into account different types of athletic engagement and precollege differences. In an analysis of career choice and development, Pascarella and Terenzini's review of research indicated that college athletes involved in career maturity is lower among revenue sport athletes compared to nonathletes. While they conceded that athletic participation may benefit social mobility from lower to higher socioeconomic levels, evidence on whether it influenced occupational status remains ambivalent.

Parham's (1993) research on college student-athlete stressors included challenges posed by academics; social and leisure activities; and repercussions from athletic success, potential injury, and college career denouement. Problems faced by male and female college athletes differed. Females especially were prone to eating disorders, stress fractures, and sexism. Athletes of color faced additional prejudices than white athletes. Parham noted that high self-esteem was a critical factor needed to aid athletes as they coped with these stressors. Strong emotional reservoirs and support from others helped to nurture athletes through crisis. Poor coping mechanisms lead to a host of high-risk behaviors such as substance abuse, addictions, academic ineligibility, violence, and dismissal. Poor coping also manifested itself in student-athletes' contingency career plans should the big leagues not be interested.

In 2001, *New Directions for Student Services* dedicated an issue in the new millennium to student services for college student-athletes (Howard-Hamilton & Watt, 2001). Over time few journals dedicated complete issues to the study of college student-athletes. However, in their much anticipated second edition of *How College Affects Students*, Pascarella and Terenzini (2005) synthesized and summarized 1990s research, some of which dealt with college student-athletes. They concluded that sports participation did not necessarily promote leadership and that revenue sports players tend to embrace diversity more than their nonrevenue counterparts. Additional studies that they highlighted focused on retention and graduation rates, critical thinking, cognitive development, and moral development. Most results remained mixed and inconclusive, thus suggesting more future studies on college student-athletes would be necessary.

Based on what research has been conducted thus far, we posed the following research questions: (1) Who is conducting research on college student-athletes? (2) What type of research has been conducted more often? (3) What changes or trends in researching college student-athletes appear over time? (4) What topics are being researched on college student-athletes? and (5) What trends can be found in the higher education mainstream journals specifically?

METHOD

We used quantitative content analysis to paint a picture of what topics have been researched on college student-athletes, by whom, through what method, and published in mainstream scholarly journals from 1970 through 2008 (a process described by Stage & Manning, 2003). We catalogued research articles only, thus overlooking literature reviews, theoretical and analytical works including exposés, essays, anecdotes, commentaries, critiques, design models, and discussions of outreach programs, courses, or support services. We omitted research articles in the database on coaches, NCAA presidents, athletic trainers, athletic administrators, mascots, alumni giving to athletics, non-American college athletes, and faculty and college student attitudes toward athletes, thus focusing exclusively on student-athletes.

Because of the range of publications, we classified journals into several categories such as higher education, the social sciences, health- and sports-related areas, and law. Those journals identified as higher education mainstream publications were *Journal of Higher Education, Review of Higher Education, National Association of Student Personnel Administrators, Research in Higher Education, Journal of College Student Development,* as well as journals devoted to community colleges, such as *Community/Junior College Quarterly Review,* counseling, *Journal of College Counseling,* and administration, *Administrative Science Quarterly.* Social science publications ranged from *Social Science Quarterly* and *Journal of Psychology,* to *Economics of Education Review* and *Race, Ethnicity, and Education.* Health journal examples spanned *American Journal of Sports Medicine, Journal of Drug Education,* and the *American Journal of Health Education.* Some of the scholarly sport journals included *Sociology of Sport Journal, Journal of Physical Education, Recreation, and Dance,* and *Physical Educator.* While not necessarily focused in one category, several journals published on minority and gender issues related to college student-athletes, such as *Journal of Black Studies, Journal of Ethnic Studies,* and *Sex Roles.* We developed a special category of legal topics found mainly in the *Journal of College and*

University Law. Cataloged separately, these articles were later merged with the qualitative entries.

Our rationale for our schema was that the presence of research on college student-athletes in top- and second-tier journals indicated several points: (1) The research was peer reviewed; (2) the results from the study were likely to merit the attention of media such as the *Chronicle of Higher Education*, faculty contemplating research and teaching athletes as well as graduate students in higher education administration programs, athletic directors, and college/university presidents who regulate policy in college sports; and (3) the range of topics covered would likely span college admission, academics, broadly defined health issues, legal and financial issues, social and psychological development, and career matters.

Trustworthiness of the journals fortified by the quality of their peer reviewers and editorial boards factored into our sampling process as we expected those articles appearing in identified journals to be of high quality. Furthermore, one place to note indications of the importance of significant issues in a discipline or field is to read its supporting literature. We were especially interested in which trends and topics appeared in the higher education journals, only suggesting that these topics are viewed as critical by the gatekeepers of these fields.

Using a standard ERIC search with key descriptors such as college, student, athlete, and athletics, we identified 357 research articles published between 1970 and 2008. Few research articles on college athletes appeared before the 1970s so they were incorporated into the literature review as augmenting the historical background. Given our criteria for inclusion and exclusion, the final analysis covered 204 usable entries. We focused the content analysis on the gender of the first author, decade in which the research was published (1970s through 2000s), type of research performed (quantitative, qualitative), focus of the journal (higher education, social sciences, health, sports, law), and general topic of the article as a means to determine over time the trends in research on college student-athletes (Love, 2003; Pitt, 1975).

RESULTS AND DISCUSSION

Who is conducting research on college student-athletes? According to the data, the first author on 204 published research articles between 1970 and 2008 was male ($n = 141$; 66%). Articles on college student-athletes first authored by men grew from eight publications in the 1970s to 28 the next decade, 51 throughout the 1990s, and 54 articles thus far in the 21st century. Female first authorships ($n = 58$; 34%) began with eight in the 1980s, grew to 17 in the 1990s, and has thus far reached 33 publications on college student-athletes this decade. While women appeared unlikely to be conducting published research on college student-athletes prior to the 1980s, they indicated their interest and made their presence known during the current decade. In conclusion, women were as likely as men to publish research in higher education, health, and law journals, more likely than men to publish research in the sport journals, and much less likely than men to be featured in the social science journals.

Topic choices varied by gender, with men selecting more topics in academics, social skills, and finance. Women had a greater affinity for research in the areas of health and body image, addictions and abuses, bias and discrimination, and psychological identity. Men and women were equally likely to employ quantitative as qualitative methods. With more women involved in sports as a result of Title IX and a concomitant increase in college sport programs for women, it followed that as more women entered faculty positions, they studied their own concerns and areas of interest to them and continued to build momentum garnering space in the journals. By contrast, scholarly study of men's sports and male college athletes came far later than their presence on the playing field or discussion in the literature.

What type of research has been conducted more often? Of the 204 articles chronicled, 64% were quantitative ($n = 130$), 16% were qualitative ($n = 31$), and 20% appeared in legal journals ($n = 42$). Legal articles were merged with the qualitative ones for a total of 36%. Over the decades studied, more quantitative research has been conducted, specifically 44% in the 1970s compared to 75% in this decade. While qualitative research designs have become more acceptable to manuscript reviewers and increased slightly over time, their proportion has slowed in comparison to quantitative designs. With an increase of qualitative methods being used and securing space in scholarly journals, it was surprising to learn that research on college student-athletes has remained mostly quantitative. College athletes are an easily identified group that has been studied from various perspectives, so we wondered why researchers have not taken the opportunity to ask and answer research questions that address the how and why of being a college student-athlete.

What changes or trends in researching college student-athletes appear over time? With 4% of the articles appearing in the 1970s ($n = 9$), 18% in the 1980s ($n = 37$), 37% in the 1990s ($n = 68$), and 44% published in the 2000s ($n = 90$), clearly, research on college student-athletes has risen steadily and exponentially since the 1970s. Based on the distribution, higher education journals have consistently increased the space devoted to the college student-athlete from two articles in the 1970s to 48 in this decade. By contrast, social science and the law journals have allotted declining space to student-athlete issues over time. Apparent increases in health and sport journals that coincide with the educational momentum toward wellness indicated a consistent pattern in sport journals beginning in the 1980s through the present and an increase for health journals commencing in the 1990s.

What topics are being researched on college student-athletes? The two most popular topics over the span of analysis were academic issues including performance, eligibility, graduation rates, and grade point averages ($n = 43$, or 21%) and bias and discrimination with regard to gender, race, and sexual orientation ($n = 39$, 19%). In more recent decades, body image, physical health, and mental health register prominently in the research literature ($n = 28$, 14%) as well as research on college student-athletes' difficulties with substance abuse and addiction, that is, steroid use, alcohol, smokeless tobacco, and gambling ($n=24$, 12%). Additional research addressed a college student-athlete's social skills ($n = 21$, 10%) and psychological identity ($n = 18$, 9%) in terms of self-worth, self-confidence, adjustment, competence, role conflict and strain, and moral development. Another group of research topics included problems with finances ($n = 8$, 4%), preparing for a career after college ($n = 7$, 3%), college selection processes ($n = 7$, 3%), and other individualized topics ($n = 9$, 4%). What appeared to be problematic in the early days of collegiate sport in the 1930s, that is, academics, remained a major concern at the close of the century.

Over time, popular topics on college student-athletes come and go reflecting significant events and trends in other parts of society. While academic issues and discrimination were researched in the 1970s, psychological identity concerns rose during the 1980s. Discrimination and bias reemerged in the 1990s as did research on addictions and substance abuse among college student-athletes. Prominent topics of the new century focused on health issues, body image, and social skills. While the greatest number of articles revolved around academic topics, proportionally this contingent has declined in comparison to other topics.

What trends can be found in the higher education mainstream journals specifically? Most of the classified research articles appeared in the largest grouping, higher education–related journals ($n = 81$, 40%), followed by the legal journals ($n = 42$, 20%). Journals devoted exclusively to sports carried 16% of the research articles ($n = 32$), the social science classification published 15% of the research on college athletes ($n = 30$), and health-related journals added 7% ($n = 14$), with others ($n = 5$, 2%) unable to be specifically classified. It appeared that social science journals devoted more space proportionally in their journals to college student-athlete academic issues than the higher education journals, but over time that has declined. Health journals allotted space for the addiction/substance abuse articles while sport journals published slightly more research on health and body image than the health-related journals. Higher education journals dedicated space in their publications to a wide variety of topics including academics, social skills, psychological identity, and body image.

IMPLICATIONS

The data indicate several interesting situations that are likely to affect future research on college student-athletes. First, women appear to be researching issues that pertain to female athletes. As more female academics conduct research, they attend to issues essential to their gender and have targeted their manuscripts to specifically focused journals. While women academics may have had difficulty gaining entrance into the social science journals decades ago, they appeared to be welcome in the sports, health, and higher education journals. Journals that target women's issues in particular did not appear in the data, indicating that these journals did not venture into this field or academics are not sending them there for review.

Women academics have found the study of student-athletes a field to be mined. Many of the issues facing college females in general have a negative impact on female athletes in particular, rendering this research area quite lucrative. Based on the fact that momentum has increased for publishing on issues that face female athletes, more articles first authored by women scholars are likely to appear in refereed journals. Female scholars continue to study issues that pertain to women with increasing fervor.

Second, college athletes represent a unique subset of college students, many of whom enter college and remain there at risk. While each campus may attract similar students, certain cadres of students exhibit difficulties that require targeted campus social, personal, and career services. Discovering exactly what is needed demands more action research approaches to keep pace with athletes' needs on individual campuses. National quantitative studies highlight aspects of trends inherent in the bigger picture but may do little to illuminate perplexing, recurring problems on one campus or among different types of institutional classifications. Research approaches may do well as customized studies that employ more qualitative methods that solve problems campus by campus. Sharing that renegade data at conferences, through ERIC, or in edited texts may be helpful at illustrating various approaches to addressing issues faced by college student-athletes (e.g., Pascarella & Terenzini, 1991, 2005).

Third, the data indicated that information on college student-athletes has garnered more space in scholarly journals, particularly prevalent in higher education journals and in health and sport science publications. While some journals devote space to other topics, the sport science publications allot more space to the specialized topics related to athletes and athletics. The wide variety of publications suggests that a diversity of topics is reaching a diverse audience of campus professionals as well as auxiliary groups in the health fields. Indications show that more specialized fields are sponsoring journals such that greater opportunity may exist to publish additional research on emerging problems faced by college student-athletes.

The early literature on college student-athletes failed to explore research topics on male athletes to the extent that research has been conducted on female athletes over the last several decades following their entrance into campus sports. Given that men played collegiate sports for decades before academic scholars thought to conduct research that would address issues that have plagued campus athletics and athletes, female scholars sought to address the needs of campus athletes more judiciously. Because college sports appeared more important to the enterprise than the college student-athlete, organized campus athletics rather than the athlete took center stage. Failing to study the unique personal character and development of the earliest athletes—*their* academic struggle and *their* life during and after college—renders our collective knowledge of the college student-athlete underwhelming. The data indicate more is being done even though an earlier plan for studying athletes would have perhaps placed them at less risk than the data now show them to be. As more scholars conduct research and more journals publish the results, perhaps we will continue to expand our knowledge base, share and build upon these findings, and resolve some of the issues that continue to vex the college student-athlete and the support personnel that address their needs.

REFERENCES

Astin, A. (1979). *Four critical years.* San Francisco: Jossey-Bass.

Betterton, D. (1988). *Alma mater.* Princeton, NJ: Peterson's Guide.

Brubaker, J., & Rudy, W. (1997). *Higher education in transition* (4th ed.). New Brunswick, NJ: Transaction.

Delany, J. (1997). Commercialism in intercollegiate athletics. *Educational Record, 78,* 39–44.

Harmon, J. (1940). Educational principles in administering intercollegiate athletics. *Education, 60,* 513–516.

Howard-Hamilton, M., & Watt, S. (Eds.). (2001). *Student services for athletes.* New Directions for Student Services #93. San Francisco: Jossey-Bass.

Jenks, C., & Riesman, D. (1977). *The American revolution.* Chicago: University of Chicago Press.

Koch, J. (1971). The economics of "big-time" intercollegiate athletics. *Social Science Quarterly, 52,* 248–260.

Love, P. (2003). Content analysis. In F. Stage & K. Manning (Eds.), *Research in the college context* (pp. 83–96). New York: Brunner-Routledge.

Miller, P. (1995). To "bring the race along rapidly": Sport, student culture, and educational mission at historically black colleges during the interwar years. *History of Education Quarterly, 35,* 111–133.

Parham, W. (1993). The intercollegiate athlete: A 1990s profile. *The Counseling Psychologist, 21,* 411–429.

Pascarella, E., & Terenzini, P. (1991). *How college affects students.* San Francisco: Jossey-Bass.

Pascarella, E., & Terenzini, P. (2005). *How college affects students* (2nd ed.). San Francisco: Jossey-Bass.

Pitt, D. (1975). The critical analysis of document evidence. In G. Lewis (Ed.), *Fist fights in the kitchen* (pp. 319–331). Pacific Palisades, CA: Goodyear.

Reeder, C. (1942). Academic performance. *Journal of Higher Education, 13,* 204–208.

Savage, (1930). Ohio report on athletics. *Journal of Higher Education, 1,* 330–333.

Schoonmaker, F. (1930). Pity the poor athlete: Problem of amateurism. *Harper's Magazine, 161,* 685–691.

Semler, C. (1952). Intercollegiate athletics and secondary schools. *Education Digest, 17*(8), 18–20.

Stage, F., & Manning, K. (Eds.). (2003). *Research in the college context.* New York: Brunner-Routledge.

Tunis, J. (1961). Education and ethics: The effect of organized sports on the moral tone of the nation. *Journal of Higher Education, 32,* 247–251.

Veysey, L. (1965). *The emergence of the American university.* Chicago: University of Chicago Press.

Ward, A. (1908). Regulation of athletics. *Education, 28,* 300–305.

PART I

ENTERING THE COLLEGE ENVIRONMENT

CHAPTER 3

RECRUITMENT, ADMISSION, AND RETENTION OF FIRST-YEAR STUDENT-ATHLETES

Victoria L. Sanders
Henry A. Gardner
Jeffery Jones
East Stroudsburg University of Pennsylvania

Many high school athletes spend their entire high school career focused on receiving an athletic scholarship in their respective sport. The prospect of being recruited by a college or university, for most, is considered validation that they have competed at a level in their particular sport that merits such attention. In their mind, achieving a full or partial scholarship at the collegiate level is akin to taking the first step in reaching their ultimate goal of playing professional sports. While the reality is that most will never receive an athletic scholarship, nor have the opportunity to play beyond the collegiate level, the grand illusion remains that achieving an athletic scholarship is a rite of passage into the next level, professional sports.

College Student-Athletes: Challenges, Opportunities, and Policy Implications, pages 23–36
Copyright © 2009 by Information Age Publishing
23

In September 2002 the National Association for College Admission Counseling (NACAC) prepared a "Statement on Recruitment and Admission of Student Athletes." Recognizing that there are questionable practices used in recruiting student-athletes, the NACAC took a firm stance to protect both students and institutions. They noted the importance of athletics in the educational enterprise, and noted in very strong terms the need to create balance for student-athletes with their athletic, social, and academic priorities. There is intense competition for a limited number of outstanding athletes; this often results in pressure to modify admission standards and procedures. When modifications of standards and procedures in the admission process occurs, the institution and the student suffers (NACAC, 2002). In the admission process the overriding consideration must be for the academic experience of the student-athlete. Because of their strong beliefs regarding this issue, the Executive Committee of the NACAC provided its membership with a set of guidelines to be followed by high school counselors and college admission representatives when recruiting and advising student-athletes about college selection and attendance.

Of the nearly 305 million people who currently populate the United States, there are only 17,000 professional athletes. The National Collegiate Athletic Association (NCAA), in a study conducted by Nicole M. Bracken in February 2007, concluded that of the three major sports, basketball, baseball, and football, the estimated probability of competing in interscholastic athletics beyond high school is:

Men's Basketball
- Less than one in 35, or approximately 3.0%, of high school senior boys playing interscholastic basketball will go on to play men's basketball at a NCAA member institution.
- Less than one in 75, or approximately 1.2%, of NCAA male senior basketball players will get drafted by a National Basketball Association (NBA) team.
- Approximately three in 10,000, or approximately 0.03%, of high school senior boys playing interscholastic basketball will eventually be drafted by an NBA team.

Women's Basketball
- About 3.3%, or approximately three in 100, of high school senior girl interscholastic basketball players will go on to play women's basketball at an NCAA member institution.
- About one in 100, or approximately 1.0%, of NCAA female senior basketball players will get drafted by a Women's National Basketball Association (WNBA) team.

- Approximately one in 5,000 or approximately 0.02%, of high school senior girls playing interscholastic basketball will eventually be drafted by a WNBA team.

Football
- About 5.7%, or approximately one in 17, of all high school senior boys playing interscholastic football will go on to play football at an NCAA member institution.
- About 1.8%, or approximately one in 50, of NCAA senior football players will get drafted by a National Football League (NFL) team.
- Approximately eight in 10,000, or approximately 0.08 percent, of high school senior boys playing interscholastic football will eventually be drafted by an NFL team.

Baseball
- Approximately three in 50, or about 6.1%, of high school senior interscholastic baseball players will go on to play men's baseball at an NCAA member institution.
- Less than 10 in 100, or about 9.4%, of NCAA senior male baseball players will get drafted by a Major League Baseball (MLB) team.
- Approximately one in 200, or approximately 0.45%, of high school senior boys playing interscholastic baseball will eventually be drafted by an MLB team.

After extensive research conducted during the 1990s, Art Young, Director of Urban Youth Sports at Northeastern University's Center for the Study of Sports, concluded that only 1 out of every 50,000 high school athletes will ever become a part of a professional sports team. Yet, the mindset of many high school athletes, especially those who participate in the "glamour sports" of basketball, football, and baseball, is that a career in pro sports is a reality. This belief is especially true of African American youth who grow up in deprived socioeconomic communities. The prevailing attitude of instant stardom by the offer of a scholarship opportunity has derailed the lives of many amateur athletes. The glorification of the lifestyle of professional athletes, such as owning expensive cars, living in expensive houses, and a glamorous social life, continues to cloud and dominate the thinking of many interscholastic/intercollegiate athletes. Far too many complete four years of college eligibility degreeless and unprepared to function in a society that does not reward former athletes who lack formal skills.

The impact of participating in intercollegiate athletics on the personal lives of student-athletes transcends all aspects of the student's life. Research has suggested that there is great benefit to the general admission and recruitment process at colleges who have well-established sports programs.

This can be explained partially by the visibility that sports programs bring to colleges and universities via print, radio, and television media. Furthermore, a good sports program can have a great economic impact on the overall health of a university. Many colleges and universities spend large amounts of their overall athletic budget in the areas of scholarships, equipment, travel, facilities, and coaches. The economic impact to the university is minimal to the revenues that are generated by fielding successful programs. The exposure, depending primarily on how well a sports program competes, can equate to millions of dollars in free advertising.

Research has also suggested that with the exposure derived from winning NCAA championships in the areas of basketball and football, administrators can expect an increase in the number of admission applications received during that particular year. Jaren Pope, assistant professor of agricultural and applied economics at Virginia Tech, conducted a study with his brother Devin Pope, an assistant professor at the Wharton School of the University of Pennsylvania. The effect of increases in admission applications was substantiated in their research as they examined data from 1983 to 2002 on application numbers and applicant SAT scores at 330 schools.

In their findings they identified that teams who advanced to the NCAA Sweet 16 may expect a 3% increase in the number of applicants received during the following year. The University of Kansas, winners of the 2008 NCAA National Basketball Championship, were predicted to realize a 7–8% increase in applications (Ezarik, 2008). Their research also suggests that private schools can expect the largest increase in admission applications.

George Mason University, located outside of Washington, D.C., had one of the largest enrollment increases ever recorded. Several years ago they competed in the NCAA Final Four Basketball Tournament. They not only experienced large increases in their fundraising but also experienced a 22% increase in the number of admission applicants the following year. "The number of admissions inquires rose 350%," said Robert Baker (Sauer, 2008), director of George Mason's Center for Sport Management. Baker, in a study he conducted titled "The Business of Being Cinderella," found that NCAA championship success and increased student enrollments contributed to an increase of 25 points in SAT scores, which led to increased student retention rates.

Between 1999 and 2007, Gonzaga University, a private school that participated in the national tournament, experienced an increase in new enrollments from 4,500 students annually to 7,000 students. This increase in enrollment has been directly tied to their visibility during national tournament competition.

In a study titled "The Impact of College Sports Success on the Quantity and Quality of Student Applications" conducted by the Department of Agricultural and Applied Economics at Virginia Tech University (1996), the following conclusions were made regarding NCAA Championship success and percentage increases in student applications the following year:

NCAA Men's Basketball

Make the tournament	1%
Make the Sweet 16	3
Make the Final Four	4–5
Win the championship	7–8

NCAA Football

Make the Top 20	2.5%
Make the Top 10	3
Win the championship	7–8

As part of the enrollment process, in addition to meeting the NCAA requirements for eligibility, student-athletes must also meet the regular admission process of the attending university. One of the most misguided assumptions by prospective student-athletes regarding admission to a university is that they are automatically eligible for admission based on NCAA eligibility. Often, student-athletes fail to recognize that admission requirements are completely separate from NCAA requirements.

According to NCAA rules, student-athletes who decide to attend a Division II member institution must meet the minimum core grade point average of 2.0. The minimum SAT score is 820 (verbal and math sections only) and the minimum ACT sum score is 68. In addition to the minimum grade point average and test score requirements, student-athletes are required to pass 14 core courses for Division II eligibility. The 14 core courses consist of 3 years of English, 2 years of mathematics (Algebra I or higher), 2 years of natural/physical science (1 year of lab if offered by high school), 2 years of additional English, mathematics, or natural/physical science, 2 years of social science, and 3 years of additional courses such as foreign language or non-doctrinal religion/philosophy.

Could the gap between the academic credentials of the student body and student-athlete be increasing? Philip Smith (2001), former Dean of Admissions at highly selective Williams College, argued that athletic recruiting is a substantial form of affirmative action in higher education. In order to ensure success on their playing fields, admissions directors are setting aside specific numbers of places for recruited athletes and going lower on the academic ladder to fill them (Fiske, 2001). Shulman and Bowen (2001) documented the lengths that prestigious small liberal arts colleges who compete on the Division III level will go to in order to recruit athlete-students to their institutions. Shulman and Bowen's data show that recruited athletes as a whole are entering selective colleges with weaker academic credentials than their peers; for these students it is no surprise when their academic performance is below that of students who entered the institution with higher academic credentials. The most disturbing data showed that even when these students have comparable standardized test scores and academic credentials, they (athletes) consistently underperform in the classroom.

The Pennsylvania State Athletic Conference (PSAC) is considered to be one of the most highly regarded athletic conferences in all of Division II athletics. Located in the state of Pennsylvania, the PSAC is comprised of 14 member institutions. Based on current data, "The number of student-athletes designated by the conference as 'Scholar-Athletes'—those who have attained a cumulative grade point average of 3.25 or better—has increased nearly every year since that standard was adopted in 1995–96. The impressive number of yearly designees reached 1,420 in 2006–07. Furthermore, the most recent figure is nearly double the total of those in the mid-1990s and is almost one-third of the total population of PSAC Division II student-athletes" (Adair, 2007).

Although the admission process into PSAC institutions varies from university to university, the requirements for admission are more stringent than the eligibility requirements for NCAA competition. As member institutions continue to show increases in the number of applicants each year, the more likely it is that the enrollment requirements will tighten. As is the case with both public and private institutions in Division I of the NCAA who experience a surge in the number of applicants during championship years, Division II institutions who are championship participants can now afford to become more selective in their admissions processes.

RETENTION

With the increase in enrollment and the knowledge that the student-athlete may be at an academic disadvantage, the academic retention of the student-athlete should become a primary focus for the attending college or university. According to Swail (2004), retention is a major and ongoing issue and problem for colleges and universities, and half of all students who enter college do not graduate. This trend within institutions is particularly troubling for student-athletes who have multiplied pressures for performance and time demands.

In a recent *Chronicle of Higher Education* article (Hoover, 2008), David Kalsbeek, senior vice president for enrollment management and marketing at DePaul University, discussed what he believed to be the pitfalls of college retention programs.

- **Obfuscation of outcomes**. Kalsbeek said that administrators often steer discussions of retention away from graduation rates and toward more noble-sounding results, like improving "educational attainment." The problem, he said, is that college officials then tend to divert their focus from a clear, quantifiable measure of success.
- **Socialism of strategy**. On many campuses, officials argue that all faculty and staff are responsible for retention, and that "retention is everyone's responsibility" is a catch phrase. But unless someone, or some office, has responsibility for retention strategies, those approaches are not likely to succeed.
- **Obsession with outliers**. Colleges tend to devote too much time and resources to students who are the most at risk of failing, Mr. Kalsbeek said. He urged administrators to focus not on "outliers," but on reaching students in the mainstream.
- **Perseveration on persistence**. Student success is often measured in terms of "persistence," that is, the percentage of a cohort of students who continue from one academic year to the next. Yet the measure may mask problems particular students are having.
- **Assuming attributes are achievements.** One might guess that a college with a high graduation rate has a sound retention program, while a college with a lower graduation rate has a less effective one. The truth may not be so simple, said Mr. Kalsbeek, who described graduation rates as "institutional attributes" that indicate the demographic profile of a particular college's students. "Graduation rates are largely a function of what an institution is, not what it does.

Many of senior student affairs and academic affairs officers and their respective staffs across the country are concerned with the reality of decreasing college retention and graduation rates, which have, for the most part, become a national concern. Freshman student-athletes face great pressures to succeed both academically and athletically once they are recruited, signed, and matriculated. The reasons for these concerns include:

- Low psychological coping strategies
- Mental and physical health factors
- Family stability and financial readiness
- Peer pressure from the neighborhood
- Misleading promises from college athletic recruiters
- Poor study skills
- Lack of academic motivation to succeed
- Inadequate preparation for college
- Delusions of instant stardom

Numerous articles help explain why freshman athletes, upon matriculation to a college or university, may face greater odds of persisting than might their nonathlete peers. Lubker and Etzel (2007) noted that the first year of college is difficult for virtually all students, for social and academic reasons. They went on to argue that the impacts of college transition and sport disengagement can cause tremendous difficulty for first-year student retention. Person and LeNoir (1997) noted that the integration within an academic community is hugely problematic for most students, and this is compounded for student-athletes.

Tinto (1993, 1997) noted that there are five conditions that stand out as being supportive of retention. They are:

1. Institutional expectations
2. Effective advising about institutional requirements and programs of study
3. Academic, social, and personal support
4. Involvement of students as valued members of the institution
5. Active student involvement in learning

According to Tinto, high expectations are a condition for student success; no one rises to low expectations. The faculty and staff expectations of a student's performance has the potential to greatly impact the student's perception of ability to succeed. Institutions must provide academic, social, and personal support to help students find success, and this support can be provided in many forms including mentoring programs, summer bridge programs, or simply day-to-day meaningful and personal contact with faculty and staff. Students must believe they are valued members of the institution. The most important factor for student persistence and graduation is that the institution is perceived as a setting that fosters learning.

Stansbury of Villanova University highlighted Garret's (2000) research centered on comparing traditional measures, noncognitive variables, and sports participation in predicting academic success for male student-athletes. Garret focused on research conducted in the late 1980s, which found that athletic participation provided a positive impact on the development of leadership and interpersonal skills for student-athletes. Hood, Craig, and Ferguson (1992) found that students who begin their college careers with typically low academic scores are more likely to have difficulty succeeding in college without some sort of academic assistance. Pascarella and Terenzini (2005) found that, when comparing athletes to nonathletes in particular schools, the athletes had significantly lower scores in reading comprehension and mathematics at the end of their freshman year. Garret found that while sport type did not have an effect on academic success rates, other variables might play a more important role in providing for the best possible academic situation for any student-athlete. Garret suggested that boosting the academic self-concept of student-athletes will positively impact student persistence and success. Garret also recommends that institutions provide workshops and sessions that teach study skills and strategies necessary to succeed in college-level classes in order for the student-athlete to make a smoother transition from high school to college life.

Simmons and Van Rheenen (2000) in an article published in the *Journal of College Reading and Learning* make an interesting point in their discussion of the variables that affect a student-athlete's performance in the classroom. They argued that negative stereotypes of athletes can lead to lower expectations by faculty members, and this may inadvertently reinforce the need to focus on athletics rather than academics. Across the country and especially at larger institutions where athletics is a major part of campus life, this assessment may well be true. Regardless of gender, student-athletes are seen as the jocks of the school, a stereotype and self-fulfilling prophecy that too often makes student-athletes relegate themselves to the low level that is expected of them by faculty, staff, and other students. Simmons and Van Rheenen's research examined other noncognitive variables including motivation, exploitation, commitment, social status, self-handicapping excuses, and the relationships between academics and athletics. They determined that there was a strong correlation between grade point average and commitment and exploitation. They found that student-athletes with strong commitments to athletics, along with athletes who felt they were being exploited by the university, had significantly lower grade point averages than those students who focused more on academics than athletics. This research concluded with the recommendation that academics and athletics be used to complement and reinforce each other. Student-athletes must continue to grow in the academic realm if they are to persist and be able to participate in demanding athletic programs (Stansbury, 2003).

What are colleges and universities doing to ensure positive retention of student-athletes? East Stroudsburg University of Pennsylvania (ESU), one of 14 institutions in the Pennsylvania State System of Higher Education, has a total of 22 intercollegiate athletic teams and approximately 700 student-athletes. In an effort to address the issue of student-athlete retention, each student-athlete with a declared major is assigned a faculty advisor. In addition, student-athletes who remain in undeclared status for their freshman and/or sophomore years have an academic advisor as well as academic support services available through the university's Department of Academic Enrichment and Learning. More specifically, in an effort to ensure student-athlete use of university support programs, the institution employs a faculty advisor in intercollegiate athletics specifically charged with the responsibility of providing student-athletes academic advising and personalized attention.

Over the last 10 years, East Stroudsburg University's campaign to expand academic advising and support programs in an effort to promote academic excellence and increase retention rates among the student-athletes has greatly enhanced the retention of freshman student-athletes, lending credence to the proposition that the retention of freshman student-athletes is more greatly enhanced when every effort to foster retention is executed within the institutional environment.

A snapshot of the persistence rates for freshman student-athletes at East Stroudsburg University over the last 5 years is provided below.

Entering Cohort Year	Returning	Persistence		
		Overall	Athlete	Nonathlete
2002	2003	76.32%	83.18%	75.73%
2003	2004	76.61%	82.75%	76.04%
2004	2005	76.33%	82.03%	75.75%
2005	2006	76.65%	82.50%	76.11%
2006	2007	76.41%	81.23%	75.96%

Source: ESU Office of Institutional Research (2007)

Another model of a student-athlete retention program comes from Cecil College, the Student-Athlete Academic Success and Retention Program, which has the following goals:

1. Develop and improve study skills necessary for college-level academic success.
2. Bring about self-discovery and self-realization that is so often lacking in the educational process.
3. Improve retention, graduation, and transfer statistics.
4. Provide guest speakers to discuss specialized topics.

Person and Lenoir (1997) described three distinct retention models that facilitate a positive approach to helping student-athletes remain focused toward successful completion of academic and athletic goals. Those models consist of (1) hiring a full-time or part-time program coordinator or student affairs educator to provide academic support services including advising, counseling, career development, tutorials, faculty mentoring, and other supportive activities; (2) hiring a faculty coordinator who is advised by a board consisting of one or more faculty and administrative representatives who work with students through a system of set performance criterion;

and (3) hiring a program director to administer a pre-college summer program, academic support services, career development services, and graduate school preparation.

RECOMMENDATIONS

Curtis, a professor of sports administration at Lynn University in Boca Raton, Florida, presented an interesting concept regarding student-athlete academic success as it relates to task orientation and goal setting. Curtis (2006), a former college student-athlete, noted that loyalty to teammates trumps devotion to academics. He described today's student-athlete as cynical about education because they often have sports agents whispering promises and dreams in their ears and some boosters all too ready to fill any empty hands. Curtis states that rather than fighting with student-athletes in an effort to mold them all into a single, preconceived model of the university student, we should embrace the differences that make student-athletes unique on the college campus. Curtis discussed how student-athletes set goals and how they approach the task of goal setting. With two types of goal orientation, task orientation, and ego orientation, it has been noted that an individual who is driven by a sense of task orientation considers successes to be met with the development of new skills or the improvement of a personal ability level. On the other hand, an individual who is driven by a concept of ego orientation views success as dependent upon one's superiority over others. Competitive athletes are most often driven by ego orientation. Athletes have been trained to win by setting easily definable goals; winning over other people equals success, losing to other people equals failure. It must be recognized that the classroom is generally not the best place for ego-based goal orientation. Most successful students are driven by task orientation. For successful students, the development of new skills and self-improvement, often for its own sake rather than for some external benefit (such as winning over someone else), are the factors that drive goal setting. Researchers such as Valente (2004) demonstrated that a focus on task orientation as a way of setting goals has promoted the most effective motivational patterns conducive to achievement and academic success. However, student-athletes generally do not operate in this way. Student-athletes compare their success to how everyone else is doing—who is the leading scorer, who runs the fastest, throws the farthest, who is the MVP? Athletes placed in an environment in which there is little or no competition generally will be simply unmotivated to achieve (Roberts, 2002). Lynn suggests that as part of the advising process for student athletics, student-athletes should be helped to modify their goal orientation in the classroom from the familiar ego orientation to the more appropriate task orientation. As academic advisors to student-athletes we must learn how to advise these students to clear their mind from distractions such as pressures from their teammates, coaches, fans, and others. Athletes must rid themselves of the cognitive interferences that impede their ability to concentrate on the task at hand such as passing an exam or reading an assignment. As academic advisors and mentors it is our responsibility to help the student-athlete learn how to become task-oriented goal setters.

The University of Minnesota (2008) provides recommendations that may benefit institutions and the athletes they recruit in reaching academic goals of persistence, progress, and success. These recommendations have been implemented at the University of Minnesota with statistically significant, positive results.

- Formalize, standardize, and streamline data collection of student-athletes' academic performance by creating a centralized database that can be used by relevant units across the institution.
- Examine the potential for an extensive and comprehensive Summer Bridge program to help student-athletes successfully transition into the academic and social rigors of life on a college campus.
- Increase access to academic programs relevant to student-athletes as a way to increase their interest and motivation, leading to better academic outcomes.
- Intensify efforts to track, engage, and provide opportunities to former student-athletes who have left the institution without graduating but who have accumulated enough credit hours so that graduation is well within reach.
- Strengthen efforts to more fully integrate intercollegiate athletics with the broader university community by eliminating unnecessary barriers and creating structures and opportunities that promote a culture of integration.

The focus of any initiative must be on improving the academic experiences of student-athletes. Successful initiatives will include integration of the athlete into the campus community with a focus on outcomes that will lead to degree attainment. Implementation of an institutionalized retention program for student-athletes, along with the incorporation of recommendations similar to those prescribed by the University of Minnesota, will help ensure that campuses focus on both the athletic and academic achievements of the student-athlete.

REFERENCES

Adair, W. (2007). *The Pennsylvania State Athletic Conference, rules and regulations.* Lock Haven: Pennsylvania State Athletic Conference.

Curtis, T. (2006). Encouraging student athletes' academic success through task orientation goal setting. *Journal of College and Character, 7*(3), 8–15.

Ezarik, M. (2008). Admissions score: sports success and college applications. *University Business, 12*(5), 52.

Fiske, E. (2001, January). *Gaining admission: Athletes win preference. New York Times.*

Hood, A. B., Craig, A. F., & Ferguson, B. W. (1992). The impact of athletics, part-time employment, and other activities on academic achievement. *Journal of College Student Development, 33*, 447–453.

Hoover, E. (2008). Enrollment expert gives top 5 reasons why student-retention strategies fail. *Chronicle of Higher Education, 55*, A26.

Lubker, J. R., & Etzel, E. F. (2007). Adjustment experiences of first year students: Disengaged athletes, non-athletes, and current varsity athletes. *NASPA Journal, 44*(3).

NACAC Executive Committee. (2002). *NCAA statement on recruitment and admission of student athletes.* Indianapolis, IN: National Intercollegiate Athletic Association.

NCAA Research Staff. (2007). *NCAA study of eligibility and recruiting.* Indianapolis, IN: National Collegiate Athletic Association.

Pascarella, E. T., & Terenzini, P. T. (2005). *How college affects students: a third decade of research.* San Francisco: Jossey-Bass.

Person, D. R., & Lenoir, K. M. (1997). Retention issues and models for African American male athletes. In M. Cuyjet (Ed.), *Helping African American men succeed* (pp. 79–91). San Francisco: Jossey-Bass.

Pope, J., & Pope, D. (in press). The impact of sports success on the quantity and quality of student applications. *Southern Economic Journal.*

Roberts, G. C. (2002). *Motivation in sport and exercise: Conceptual constraints and convergence.* Champaign, IL: Human Kinetics.

Sauer, S. (2008, March). Eight per cent. *The Sports Economist.* Retrieved June 1, 2008, from www.thesportseconomist.com

Shulman, J. L., & Bowen, W. G. (2001). *The game of life: College sports and educational values.* Princeton, NJ: Princeton University Press.

Simmons, H., & Van Rheenen, D. (2000). Non cognitive predictors of student athletes academic performance. *Journal of College Reading and Learning, 30*(2), 167–181.

Stansbury, S. R. (2003). *Evaluating academic success in student athletes: A literature review.* Philadelphia: Villanova University, Department of Education and Human Services.

Swail, W. S. (2004, November). *The art of student retention: A handbook for practitioners and administrators.* Paper presented at the Texas Higher Education Board Policy Institute 20th Anniversary Recruitment and Retention Conference, Austin.

Tinto, V. (1993). *Leaving college rethinking the causes of student attrition.* Chicago: University of Chicago Press.

Tinto, V. (1997). Classrooms as communities: exploring the educational character of student persistence. *Journal of Higher Education, 68*(6), 559–623.

Valente, L. (2004). What can we learn from the student athlete? *Phi Kappa Phi Forum, 84*(4), 14.

CHAPTER 4

THE RECRUITING PROCESS

The Experiences of Student-Athletes

Paul M. Hewitt
University of Arkansas

From the time she was five years old, everyone knew that there was something special about Cyndi. She was cute, bright, and she moved with a grace that did not fit her young years. As she grew, she began to excel in any physical activity she tried. No matter what the activity, she always caught the immediate attention of the adults who where watching the game. When she turned 11 she began to focus on softball and began to pitch. Soon she began to dominate her age group and began to play for highly competitive traveling teams. At the age of 14 she joined a women's "B" team to play in the ASA (Amateur Softball Association) National Championships. At the conclusion of the tournament her team had finished third and she was named as a Second Team All-American. At the conclusion of her senior season in high school she had been named All-District for four years as well as Player of the Year multiple times. Her final newspaper article headline read, "A Legend's Farewell." It was not a question of whether she would get

College Student-Athletes: Challenges, Opportunities, and Policy Implications, pages 37–54
Copyright © 2009 by Information Age Publishing
37

a scholarship to play Division I softball, it was just a question of where she would choose to go.

There are many good athletes but there are those special athletes that have a unique quality that sets them apart. You cannot define this quality, but it's easy to spot it when you see it. Good coaches can spot this quality and when they do, they know they want those athletes on their teams and will do whatever it takes to recruit them. For Cyndi the whirlwind of the recruiting process began in her junior year and picked up to a feverish pitch in the summer between her junior and senior year following a strong performance at the ASA National Championships. Many major college coaches were in attendance and she captured the attention of everyone who saw her play. Soon she had two large boxes filled with materials from colleges all over the United States. She had phone calls, visits to her house, as well as alumni and friends of the coaches calling her. What started out as a glamorous process had suddenly become very stressful. One night her father found her sitting in her room engulfed in tears. Her father had been totally oblivious to the stress and pressure she had been feeling. "Dad, how do I decide? I have so many choices and opportunities. How do I pick one knowing that it will impact me for the rest of my life? I just don't know what to do!"

After much emotional strain she finally narrowed her choices to five colleges where she would make an official visit and one more school where she could make an "unofficial" visit. During each visit she was escorted by players and coaches and generally given a royal tour. At each stop she met wonderful people and had the opportunity to establish strong personal relationships with the best coaches and players in the country. They all wanted her to come to their school and each school tried to convince her that they were the very best place. It was an experience of a lifetime for a young 17-year-old girl. However, the experience changed when it came time to make the final choice. Again, her father found her in tears. She had developed such strong feelings for the coaches and the schools were so wonderful, how could she choose just one? How could she disappoint coaches and players that she felt such a strong bond with?

Many years later she was asked to reflect on her experience with the recruiting process. Without hesitation she began to talk about it as if it had happened yesterday.

> I'll never forget how difficult it was for me. I had developed a relationship with so many great coaches and players and now I had to tell them, no. I was 17 years old and I had never been equipped to tell highly successful and respected adults no. I just wasn't prepared to do that. It was an awful experience. I spent more time crying about this than anyone ever knew.

Cyndi's story is not unique, as it represents just how difficult the athletic recruitment process is for thousands of young high school athletes. The press portrays a highly glamorous view of the athlete recruiting process, with living room visits by highly visible coaches and lavish attention placed on the athlete. The process involves numerous colleges aggressively court-ing a young high school athlete who then will move on to fame and stardom portrayed with an air of drama and excitement. What young person does not want to have people begging to play sports at the highest level, get a high-quality education, and have all expenses covered by a scholarship? For many young athletes, especially those from impoverished areas, this is truly the "American Dream." Although a few athletes may truly relish the atten-tion and thrive on it, for most student-athletes it is one of the most difficult times of their lives. It is this difficulty, stress, and pressure that are rarely reported in the popular media. This chapter looks at what the literature revealed about the recruiting experience and then explores the experience of highly recruited athletes as they share their experiences through inter-views and focus groups.

HIGH STAKES AND PRESSURE IN ATHLETIC RECRUITMENT

According to the NCAA Guide for College-Bound Athletes (2007) there are over 380,000 student-athletes competing in 23 sports at over 1,000 mem-ber institutions. Not all of these student-athletes receive full or even partial athletic scholarships, but the number of students who do and the value of those scholarships is staggering. According to *www.scholarshiphelp.org*, there are 126,000 student-athletes receiving full or partial scholarships with a value of over $1 billion. As reported by the US Fed News Service (2008) the average annual cost of tuition and fees for 2007–08 at a four-year public university is $6,185 while the average annual tuition and fees at a four-year private university averages $23,717. When room, board, books, and miscel-laneous costs are added, the value of an athletic scholarship can range from $60,000 to over a quarter of a million dollars at exclusive private universi-ties. The cost value of an athletic scholarship makes it a very high-stakes game for the student-athlete.

For the college and university there is a significant financial investment in each student-athlete awarded a scholarship. The university often expects to receive a benefit from the student-athlete that transcends the academic mission of the college or university and results in tangible benefits returned to the college or university in the form of increased gate receipts for a win-ning team and possibly increased alumni giving. The value of a winning athletic team may go beyond publicity, increased gate receipts, and alumni satisfaction. Toma and Cross (1998) found that applications for under-graduate admissions increased when a school won the Division I National Championship in either football or basketball. In 1990 after winning the national championship in football, the admissions applications at Georgia Tech increased by 21%. After winning the national championship in football in 1987 the University of Miami saw an increase of 34% in undergraduate applications. The rewards of having winning teams will provide numerous benefits to the college or university, which makes the recruitment of top-quality student-athletes and the development of a winning program a high priority.

The pressure to win has placed tremendous pressure on the coaches and their staff who are responsible for recruiting. This pressure leads to aggressive action and often the rules may be bent. According to Wilson and Wolverton (2008), college coaches look to foreign athletes to fill their rosters with high-quality athletes. Feeling that the talent pool in the United States lacks the needed depth, coaches can recruit high-quality foreign athletes who can turn a losing program into an instant winner. In 2005–06, 30% of male tennis players, 23% of male ice hockey players, 14% of female golfers, and 10% of male soccer players were from foreign countries. Although not as high, the numbers are growing quickly in basketball, gymnastics, swimming, and track. Much of the pressure to win relates to money that can be generated by a winning team, especially at the Division I level. In Testimony before the Knight Commission (2006b), Peter Roby, the Director of Northeastern University's Center for the Study of Sport in Society, noted that the major athletic conferences generate a great deal of money from bowl games, post-season championships, and television contracts, while athletes miss more classes and can spend less time on their academic work. The sense of pressure that coaches feel will impact their approach to the process and will motivate them to look for every advantage possible. Sometimes this quest for a winning advantage may involve bending or even breaking the rules. This clearly defines the way many coaches feel about the recruiting process and how they feel compelled to seek every competitive advantage possible.

THE PRESSURES THAT IMPACT THE STUDENT-ATHLETE

The pressures and stress of the recruiting process on a student-athlete can be intense. Although student-athletes are often physically gifted and highly talented, they are still young 16- to 17-year-olds with limited exposure to the type of attention and hard-sell they will encounter throughout the recruiting process. One such stressor for the high school student has been the use of text messaging by coaches to maintain almost constant contact with the student-athlete. Under past NCAA regulations the coaches could send unlimited text messages to an athlete without regard to the time of day, or even night. Lipka (2006) reported that text messaging has gotten totally out of control. She tells of coaches who agree with her but are clear that they must exploit every competitive advantage they can get, even stating that they would do it to the extreme. Lipka describes the recruiting of basketball player and eventual All-American from UCLA, Kevin Love. Love was so inundated with text messages that he changed his cell phone number and only gave it out to a select group of coaches. The overuse and abuse of text messaging eventually resulted in a change to the NCAA Manual (2007) that governs the rules by which athletes may be recruited. The Manual now states in Bylaw 13.4.1.2 that:

> Electronically transmitted correspondence that may be sent to a prospective student-athlete is limited to electronic mail and facsimiles. (See Bylaw 13.1.7.2.) All other forms of electronically transmitted correspondence (e.g., Instant Messenger, text messaging) are prohibited. (p. 99)

The pressure that can be exerted upon a young and highly recruited student-athlete is often hard for anyone outside the major college recruiting realm to comprehend. The story of one athlete illustrates how colleges can pull out all the stops in their effort to land a top-level student-athlete. In testimony before the Knight Commission (2006), Myron Rolle, a highly recruited football player who eventually enrolled at Florida State, stated:

> I got to meet President T.K. Wetherell, I got a text message from Governor Jeb Bush on my visit to Florida State. I met the president of Florida, Mr. Machen; I met David Boren, the president of Oklahoma; Barry Switzer, Jimmy Johnson, I mean, Warren Sapp happened to be in the same room I was in when I walked into Miami. Emmitt Smith was around the corner when I walked through Florida. You know, just the amount of attention I got and the different things that happened to me on these recruiting visits just to pique my interest and get me to like this school even was just incredible.

In an effort to land the best athletes, coaches have implemented a tactic that requires the athlete to make a commitment to the college or university long before the official signing of a letter of intent. This technique is termed "early commitment." From a strictly legal perspective the athlete may not sign a National Letter of Intent, which then binds the college and the student-athlete to a contract, until their senior year of high school. In an effort to get the best athletes, however, many coaches will offer a scholarship to a high school athlete if they will commit to the college or university well before their senior year. Although these commitments are nonbinding among either party, they have a psychological effect of locking the student-athlete to the university, thus freeing the coach to focus on the recruitment of other student-athletes. According to Krome (2006):

The pressure for an early commitment also makes college coaches react with a hard sell consistent with a used car salesperson. It is not uncommon for a coach to tell an athlete that they must commit immediately or the scholarship offer will be withdrawn. The coaches will give the student an offer and tell them it is good for only a week. Mike Vorsang, a highly successful lacrosse coach at Niskayuna (NY) High School stated that "To decide on a college is hard on a family minus the athletic factor. With the added pressure to accept a scholarship now, when you're not sure—that's stressful."

Throughout the recruiting process, coaches will make every effort to develop a strong personal relationship with the young student-athlete. Student-athletes may make official, all-expense-paid trips to only five colleges or universities. Prior to but especially during the school visits, the coaches will attempt to form as strong a relationship as possible with the student-athlete. Regular education or nonathletes will choose the university they wish to attend using a variety of factors. According to Sax, Lindholm, Astin, Korn, and Mahoney (2001) in a national survey of college freshman, the number one factor in selecting which university to attend is the academic reputation of the university. The reputation of the university with regard to the quality of jobs obtained by its graduates ranks as number two. The size of the university ranks as the third most important factor, followed by the offer of any kind of financial aid. In making the final selection of which school to attend, the student-athlete will make his or her decision based on factors that differ from the regular education student. In a survey of 219 student-athletes from 39 schools, Cooper (1996) found that the most important factors in choosing a school were the coach's commitment to the program and the relationship that was developed between the athlete and the coach. Of the five most important factors, four were based on the coaching staff and the style of play that the coaches utilized. The fifth factor was the actual scholarship money that was available. Although the idea of a strong relationship between the coach and student-athlete may seem to be highly desirable, it creates a situation in which the athlete experiences extreme stress when they must select only one school from the five that were visited. In testimony before the Knight Commission (2006), former Notre Dame and WNBA basketball player Ruth Riley stated:

> But it's also hard for a high school student to tell a college no. You have these universities throwing a package at you and it's very difficult when you don't know exactly a lot about the university. So you want to make the right decision so telling the university no when they're throwing a sales pitch at you was probably the toughest thing that I had to face because some coaches don't accept no very well.

THE RECRUITING PROCESS FROM THE PERSPECTIVE OF THE STUDENT-ATHLETE

In an effort to study and give a voice to the experiences of student-athletes during the recruiting process, a study was conducted that involved student-athletes from three highly successful athletic programs in major athletic conferences. As a condition of the study the actual universities will not be identified to avoid any negative connotations being directed toward that university or its program. The athletes were directed not to focus on the tactics or experiences of the university they chose to attend, but rather to focus on their total recruiting experience with all colleges and universities. In total, 22 athletes were interviewed. Sixteen athletes were interviewed during three separate focus group meetings and the remainder were interviewed individually by telephone or in person. The sports represented in the interviews included women's gymnastics, swimming, softball, and volleyball as well as men's football, basketball, and baseball. Athletes were selected for the study based on their status as being *highly recruited* while in high school.

SUMMARY OF THE RESPONSES OF THE STUDENT-ATHLETES REGARDING THEIR RECRUITMENT EXPERIENCE

Each focus group and individual student-athlete was asked a standardized set of 13 questions. The questions are presented here followed by a summary of the comments. Following a summary of the comments there will be actual quotations, presented in italics, from the student-athletes to illuminate or illustrate the feelings that are representative of the group.

1. *How many schools contacted you? How many did you feel were seriously recruiting you?*

During the recruiting process, colleges and universities will make initial contact with a student-athlete by sending out general mailings to a large number of student-athletes. These general mailings are the college and university equivalent of bulk mailers. These mailings are sent to all potential recruits to gauge interest. This tactic is often done by Division I schools that are not in one of the major or Bowl Championship Series conferences. The mailings will be sent to top student-athletes who appear destined to play for major athletic powers in the hope that the student-athlete will show interest in a school playing at a slightly lower level in Division I.

Overall, the mean number of contacts for the student-athletes studied was 37 schools. The contacts for men in the revenue sports of football and basketball were much higher than the mean for all other student-athletes interviewed. The initial contacts ranged from 12 contacts to well over 100. The student-athletes were then asked to identify the number of serious contacts they had, with a serious contact being defined as a school that would actually offer a scholarship to the student-athlete and was aggressively recruiting them. The average number of serious contacts was 11 schools, with the student-athletes reporting a range of 4–25 schools. The purpose of this question was to gain a perspective on the nature of the student-athletes' experiences and to establish that they had experienced the recruiting process to a degree that would make them credible participants in the study.

2. *In what year of high school did you get your first recruiting contact?*

Three of the student-athletes reported having their first contact in the eighth grade, which supports reports in the literature about the practice of recruiting student-athletes at a young age. The other student-athletes reported a fairly even split between the freshman, sophomore, and junior years. There were no athletes in the group studied who had not been contacted prior to their senior year.

3. *How did you feel about this first contact?*

Excitement was the word that described every student-athlete in this study. There was an initial elation that their dreams had been realized. For the student-athletes it could best be described as a dream that had come true. They now knew that someone wanted them to play at the college level.

> I felt excited and confident. I realized for the first time that I would be able to play D-1 ball. I realized that I had a future beyond high school.
>
> A scholarship had been a long-term goal of mine and now I realized it would actually happen.
>
> Excited and confused. I didn't know how to approach it. (So) I talked to parents and friends.
>
> Excited because I knew that my work was paying off.

The football players in the study were all recruited by large schools at the highest level of competition. When asked a follow-up question about final aspirations, the football players all agreed that a student-athlete being recruited from high school by a high-level football program will have dreams about playing professional football. They also pointed out that this dream is often changed quickly after the first practice session when they see the level of play exhibited by all the other football players. Other student-athletes did not share this dream, particularly female student-athletes who pointed out that professional opportunities are very limited in their sports.

4. *As the process went on, how did you feel about it? Did your views about being recruited change?*

The student-athletes had an almost unanimous response to this question. They felt that the excitement of being recruited shifted into pressure and stress. When it came to defining the cause of stress, they were in strong agreement that the pressure and stress was caused by the coaches. The coaches were trying to maintain constant contact in an effort to build a strong personal relationship or bond with the student-athlete. Several student-athletes mentioned the pressure they felt to make an early commitment. One female athlete reported that a coach clearly told her that if she didn't make an early commitment, her scholarship might be taken by another student-athlete who was willing to make an early commitment. Although others said that this was not specifically stated to them with this degree of clarity, they knew very clearly that it was inferred from the coach's remarks.

> The excitement turned to stress.

> At the end of my junior year it got to a point where I just wanted to get it over with.

> The pressure was caused by the coaches.

> There was a lot of pressure to make a decision. There was pressure from the schools (coaches) to make a decision.

> I felt naive to the process and the politics.

> It got confusing about where I really wanted to go.

> After a while it just got annoying. There were persistent phone calls.

One student-athlete expressed a fairly cynical view of the process. Although other student-athletes did not specifically respond in this manner, there was little disagreement among the group being interviewed. This student-athlete commented:

> I had a reality check. . . . I realized that everyone was just lying to me to get me to come to their schools. The coaches would say something they thought was funny and laugh and I'd laugh too because it was so stupid.

5. *What was the most exciting aspect about being recruited?*

The excitement of making recruiting trips and visiting new places was almost a universal response to this question. A few athletes mentioned the attention they got from coaches or the excitement they felt in having the opportunity to play at the Division I level. But the universal response was still focused on making the recruiting trips to the colleges and universities. Many of the student-athletes had never experienced the level of travel that resulted from visiting five colleges or universities in a very short period of time. They commented that during the trips they felt extremely important as everything about the trip focused on them.

The visits. Everything is tailored to you. You get the best food and everything.

Seeing the really fantastic facilities. It was awesome.

Seeing the possibilities and trying to figure out which way I could go.

6. *What was the most difficult aspect of being recruited?*

Stress and pressure returned to the forefront in the student-athletes' response to this question. The most difficult thing that student-athletes had to do was to tell the coaches that they would not be attending their school. After making five official visits to the colleges or universities the student-athlete must tell four coaches that they will be attending another school.

Having to say no to coaches. Choosing schools.

Pressures. They needed you to commit and wanted you to make your decision.

Pressure from people on the street. They all wanted to know where you would commit to. Reporters would ask stupid questions and you'd find yourself quoted by people on websites.

The student-athletes also reported an abrupt change in their relationship with the coach when they told the coach they would be attending another school. The students-athletes reported a major shift by many coaches from warm and friendly to abrupt and in some cases, but not all, rude.

When I said no, one school just hung up on me.

The coaches made you feel guilty for saying no.

When you told them no, they would lay a big guilt trip on you. They would tell you that "I guess you don't want to be a part of a championship team," or that "You aren't committed to playing at this level."

I see some of these coaches at meets and they walk past me like they don't even know me and yet before they were my best friend.

About 50% of the students reported experiencing what they referred to as "The Room." The student-athletes reported that at the end of their school visit they would be placed alone in a room and would meet one-on-one with the head coach. The purpose of this meeting was to get the student-athlete to make a verbal commitment to the school. The first student-athlete who shared this experience reported that it made him feel very uncomfortable and was extremely awkward. One student-athlete reported that she was taken into the room and asked to make a verbal commitment when she visited her first of five schools. By making a commitment at that time she would have had to cancel her other four school visits without ever seeing what opportunities were available to her.

> I didn't like being put in a room and having them pressure me to commit.

> They wanted me to make a decision right now and one coach told me that if I couldn't commit they'd give my scholarship to someone else. I felt so stressed that I committed to three schools! I was only 17, just a kid. That was a lot of pressure.

7. *How did your friends view the recruiting process?*

The way student-athletes included or didn't include their friends was varied. In some instances the student-athletes didn't share with their friends what they were experiencing during the recruiting process. These student-athletes felt that they had been blessed with opportunities that their friends didn't have and to point this out would be very uncomfortable for them. Other student-athletes would share with teammates who they felt understood or even shared the recruiting experience. One student-athlete not only shared the experience verbally with his friends but he had them jump in the car and go with him on one trip.

> I didn't talk about it with my friends. They didn't have the opportunity that I had and I didn't want them to feel bad.

> You don't really have to even apply (for admission) and worry about being accepted so you didn't want to talk about that with friends because their experiences were so different.

> Some were jealous that the college coaches were seeing you and not them.

> I didn't share with my non-sports friends. With the athletes we talked about what we were seeing because they were being recruited too.

> I talked to my teammates but not the nonathletes. The nonathletes wouldn't understand. They think athletes have it easy.

8. *How did your family view the recruiting process? Did their views change as the process continued?*

The response given by the student-athletes regarding parental involvement and attitudes was extremely varied. Two of the athletes shared that they didn't have parents to assist them and that they were completely on their own. In one instance the student-athlete had a "mentor" who provided some help and support. About half of the student-athletes reported that their parents left it almost completely up to them. The other half reported varying degrees of parental support and assistance. However, in all but one instance the parents left the decision as to which college or university to attend up to the student-athlete. In one instance the student-athlete shared that he looked at the athletic side and his mother looked at the academic side of the decision. In a few instances the parents felt the stress and annoyance that the student-athlete felt over telephone calls and text-messaging.

> My mom got mad at all the text messages. Some coaches just didn't know when to stop.
>
> They felt the same pressures I did.
>
> My parents sat in the back. My parents didn't play sports.
>
> My sister played college ball and she gave me advice. My parents knew what was happening because of her.

9. *NCAA allows you to choose five schools for official visits. How did you decide on which ones to visit? Looking back, would you choose the same five schools again? Why?*

The response to this question was extremely interesting based on what was not said. None of the student-athletes narrowed their choice of schools based on the academic reputation of the school. The focus of the student-athletes was on the quality of the athletic program based on won–loss records, opportunities for television exposure, their relationship with the coaches, and their opportunity to play. When asked if they would choose to visit the same five schools again the athletes reported almost universally they would visit the same five schools again.

> I chose the five schools to visit based on playing time. I looked at who was leaving and what kind of opportunity I would have.
>
> I wanted to go to a school with a winning program.
>
> I looked for the best relationship with the coaches.
>
> As a little kid I saw the schools on TV and felt I had to give them a try.
>
> I looked at the coaches and tried to talk to seniors on the team about the quality of the coaching.
>
> I used a process of elimination and just tried to get the group down to a smaller and smaller size. (How did you eliminate?) I looked at their style of play. Who the teammates would be. The coaching staff. Whether I would be able to get playing time right away.

10. *Was the recruitment process what you had pictured or was it different? If different, how was it different?*

A couple of the student-athletes had older siblings who had gone through the recruiting process and this gave them a preview of what they could anticipate. The rest of the student-athletes universally agreed that they were not prepared for the stress and pressure of the recruiting process. The student-athletes had only viewed the recruiting process from the perspective of the media and were totally unaware of what they would be facing.

> On TV you see the fun stuff. In reality it is stressful.

> It was crazy and I just have to cringe when I think about those athletes who are rated in the top five (nationally) and what they must experience.

> It was the total opposite of what I had expected. The more letters I got the more I wanted it to stop.

> It was different because it sucked. The deeper you get into it the more heat and pressure you get.

> It was a lot more stress than I pictured it.

11. *What would you do differently now if you had to go through the entire process again?*

This question elicited one of the more enthusiastic responses of the survey. The student-athletes responded easily and quickly with a series of answers that focused on doing more research on the colleges and universities and being prepared. It appeared that this question was one that the student-athletes had given a lot of prior thought and reflection. Their answers were focused on ways to be more confident in their choice and to help reduce the stress that they experienced. In retrospect it seemed as if the student-athletes were voicing a desire to take greater control of the process rather than being a passive participant.

> I'd look more carefully at the academic status of the university and look carefully at the kind of academic support they gave to their players.

> I would start sooner and research the schools.

> I'd eliminate the schools earlier.

> I'd ask more questions about training.

> I'd work the system more like the coaches do. I was naive. I'd put more time into it and just generally take more time and not let them rush me.

> I would talk to players more. I'd ask the players if they were happy. What they liked and disliked about the program. I'd want to know what the coaches are really like after recruiting.

I'd ask more about the coaches.

I'd want to know more about how they get you prepared for university life.

I'd do more research on the coaches especially their backgrounds and history.

I'd do more research on the university ahead of time.

12. ***Knowing what you know now, what advice would you give to a young athlete who is just beginning to be recruited?***

The student-athletes provided a wide range of advice for young student-athletes who are about to begin the recruiting process. The advice they would give a prospective recruit is very similar to how they would approach the process if they were to do it again. Their responses covered a wide range of areas but focused on having the recruit research all aspects of the athletic program in depth. Only one student mentioned trying to share the pressures of the recruiting process. In a follow-up question they were asked why they failed to mention the most difficult thing they faced:

It's hard to explain the pressure and stress.

You can't really understand what it's like until you've gone through it yourself.

Take your time. Don't let them pressure you into committing while you are on a trip.

If the coach threatens to take away your offer if you don't commit right away then he really doesn't want you.

Make sure you like the coaches.

Know how the athletes are treated, really treated.

Don't just focus on the sports aspect alone. Look at what you are going to be doing after college.

Talk to the athletes. When they are hosting you there will usually be two or three around and they might not feel comfortable talking to you. Get their numbers and call them and talk one-on-one. Talk to the graduating seniors who have played there a long time and know the coaches.

Most athletes understand that it is a business, but few recruits really understand it. You need to know how you'll be treated if you are hurt.

I'd tell them to live their high school life because they only have one chance to do it.

I'd tell them to make sure they were making the right decision.

I would tell them to narrow it down earlier to the schools they were interested in.

Go to the schools and watch the actual workouts. See how the coaches actually work with the athletes. I also look at how many times they play on TV.

Get as much information as you can about the team and the school. Find out how they think and feel.

Look for happiness. Will you be happy there? Because if you are not happy it will take away your drive.

Ignore half of what they tell you because only a quarter of it is true.

13. *What changes would you make in the way recruiting is conducted to make it less stressful on the athlete?*

The student-athletes' responses to this question were very limited. One student talked about limiting telephone calls and another talked about a technical change regarding when student-athletes could begin their visitations in their senior year. The overall response of the student-athletes seemed to express that they knew how they would handle the process differently but they had either given little thought to the way the recruiting process could be changed or they had few ideas. It appeared that the student-athletes had reached a level of acceptance that the process is fairly engrained within the athletic culture and they couldn't envision a way in which meaningful change could occur.

CONCLUSIONS

The purpose of this chapter was to look at the recruiting process as seen through the experiences of highly recruited student-athletes. The popular media has written a great deal about the experiences of highly recruited student-athletes but in almost every case the focus has been on what appears to be a very glamorous process. The glamorous side to the recruiting process is the young student-athlete being pursued by major college athletic powers where the student-athlete will receive a free high-quality education and seek fame and notoriety on the playing field. The academic literature seems to focus on the mechanics of the recruiting process highlighting rules violations as well as other infractions or exploration of the role and place of athletics at an institution of higher education. There appears to be a void in the literature that gives a post-recruitment experience voice to the student-athlete.

In listening to student-athletes the following conclusions can be drawn. First, the recruiting process is extremely stressful for the young student-athlete. They enter the recruiting process with excitement and elation, recognizing a dream fulfilled, only to find they dread the experience and wish it would end. Second, the pressure and stress experienced by the student-athlete is one they don't feel can be shared with others. They felt that someone had to experience the pressures of the recruiting process before they would be able to truly understand it. Among highly recruited student-athletes there is what can only be described as a common bond that comes through common experience, an experience that is highly stressful and pressure-packed.

After the initial elation of recognizing that major colleges and universities want to offer them an athletic scholarship, the most exciting part of the recruiting process is the opportunity to make five official visits to colleges and universities. The chance to travel, see different universities, and be given the "royal treatment" is something that every student-athlete enjoyed.

All the student-athletes expressed the difficulty they had in choosing only one school to attend and then having to tell four other coaches that they would not be attending their schools. College coaches are extremely dynamic and powerful individuals who have made every effort to sell the student-athlete on attending their school. They possess powerful powers of persuasion and have sales skills that would make them highly successful in any other pure private enterprise sales position. As a tactic the coaches will attempt to build a very deep personal relationship with the athlete. Student-athletes choose the school they will attend based on the coach and primarily how they feel about that coach, which means that to tell a coach "no" is one of the most difficult things these young student-athletes have ever experienced and in some cases the coaches make it even more difficult.

The pressure to make an early commitment also placed a great deal of stress and pressure on the student-athlete. It is understandable why a coach would seek an early commitment from an athlete, even if that commitment is only morally binding. It allows the coach to tie up top recruits and then pursue other uncommitted student-athletes. The question that must be asked is, Does this need by the coach justify the threat to the student-athlete that they will lose their scholarship offer if the student-athlete doesn't commit immediately? Does this need by the coach justify a one-on-one meeting in a room between the coach and the young student-athlete to pressure them to make an immediate commitment? Although many young student-athletes have the physical appearance of much older and mature individuals, they are still young teenagers unprepared for the stress and pressure they are facing.

When it came to sharing the recruiting process with their friends, the student-athletes were divided. Some shared the experience with their friends while others felt uncomfortable about sharing their experience. Among those who felt uncomfortable, there was concern that the friends wouldn't understand or that there might be a problem with jealousy or envy.

Families, in most instances, played a major role for most of the student-athletes. Some gave support and advice, but in almost all cases the parents left the final decision totally up to the student-athlete.

Overall, the recurring theme from the student-athletes was one of excitement and elation followed by stress, pressure, and a desire to bring closure. The question that wasn't asked of the student-athletes was, would you like to do it over again?

RECOMMENDATIONS

The purpose of this chapter was to give a voice to the student-athlete about how they viewed the recruiting process. The final question of the interview process asked the student-athletes to give their opinions on how the process could be changed. In response to this question they were mostly silent. The NCAA (2007) has a manual of by-laws that govern the recruiting process. There are rules that specifically guide how the recruitment process shall be conducted, however, it is not the rules that create the most pressure and stress on the student-athlete. It is the personal dynamics between the coaches and the young student-athletes that are so problematic. This is not a situation that can be corrected by legalistic rules and regulations since it revolves around the values and ethics of the power players, the coaches, involved in the process. The pressure on major college coaches to win has created a level of pressure for them to win that requires that they get the very best athletes available.

There are things that can be done to train student-athletes on how to deal with the stress of the recruiting process. There can be seminars by student-athletes who have experienced the pressures of recruiting. High school athletic directors and coaches can take a bigger role in supporting and preparing their student-athletes for the rigors of the recruiting process and parents can be made more aware of the reality of recruiting and provide support for the student-athlete. All these actions will better prepare the young student-athlete, but it will not change the fundamental nature of the recruiting process. The recruiting process will not change as long as the goal of recruiting is to provide coaches and teams with the best possible athletes to ensure a winning record. As long as winning is the ultimate goal of many major college and university athletic programs, the recruiting process will fundamentally stay the same.

REFERENCES

District high school seniors earn increased number of athletic scholarships in 2007/08. (2008, June 19). *US Fed News Service, Including US State News.* Retrieved July 1, 2008, from Research Library database. (Document ID: 1502328311).
Knight Commission. (2006a, January 30). *A summit on the collegiate athletic experience.* Opening remarks by Dan Wetzel, sports journalist, Yahoo.com, and author,

Glory Road. Retrieved June 30, 2008, from http://www.knightcomission.org/about/summit_main/

Knight Commission. (2006b, January 30). *A summit on the collegiate athletic experience.* Opening remarks by Peter Roby, director of Northeastern University's Center for the Study of Sport in Society. Retrieved June 30, 2008, from http://www.knightcomission.org/about/summit_main/

Krome, P. (2006, April). Recruiting from the cradle. *Lacrosse.* Retrieved May 5, 2008, from http://www.uslacrosse.org/info/recruiting -LM.phtml

Lipka, S. (2006, October 10). Hot-button recruiting. *Chronicle of Higher Education.* p. A36.

NCAA. (2007, July). *2007–08 NCAA division I manual: Constitution, operating bylaws, administrative bylaws.* Indianapolis, IN: Author.

NCAA. (2007). *2007–08 Guide for college-bound student athletes.* Retrieved July 10, 2008, from http://www.ncaastudent.org/NCAA_Guide. pdf

Sax, L., Lindholm, J., Astin, A., Korn, W., & Mahoney, K. (2001). *The American college freshman: National norms for fall 2001.* Higher Education Research Institute. University of California, Los Angeles. Retrieved July 8, 2008, from http://www.scholarshiphelp.org/types_available.htm

Toma, J. D., & Cross, M. E. (1998). Intercollegiate athletics and student college choice: Exploring the impact of championship seasons on undergraduate applications. *Research in Higher Education, 30*(2), 633.

Wilson, R., & Wolverton, B. (2008, January 11). The new face of college sports. *Chronicle of Higher Education,* p. A27.

CHAPTER 5

HELPING STUDENT-ATHLETES ADAPT TO COLLEGE

The Role of an Academic Transition Course

Judy Stephen
Kristin Higgins
University of Arkansas

INSTRUCTOR'S INTRODUCTION

The challenges freshman student-athletes face as they enter and adjust to a university culture and academic experience are richly outlined in scholarly literature. Several researchers (Hyatt, 2003; Keim & Strickland, 2004) have detailed the time demands, fatigue, personal identity, and interpersonal conflicts inherent in the athlete's freshman year. The majority of these published studies include "implications for practice" intended to suggest institutional means of helping alleviate the adjustment burden freshman athletes bear. This chapter is written from the perspective of one educator's opportunity (JRS) to listen to student-athletes describe their turbulent first-year experiences in their own words. Since 1995 I have spent each fall semester teaching a life skills, transition to college class for freshman male athletes at a large Division I southeastern university. It is from the perspective of the podium in that classroom that I offer this chapter; the

---

College Student-Athletes: Challenges, Opportunities, and Policy Implications, pages 55–71 *story of the history and curriculum of a course that hopefully represents the accumulated expression of my students' themes of academic adjustment.*

RATIONALE: WHY TEACH A TRANSITION COURSE FOR NEW COLLEGE ATHLETES?

Transition courses for college freshmen have become "ubiquitous fixtures" (Porter & Swing, 2006, p. 89) on university campuses, with over 90% of colleges offering some type of first-year course. These first-year enhancement courses come in varied packages. Many are "orientation" courses intended to acquaint new students with the academic and social environment of higher education. Others are "study skills" courses intended to teach new students the adaptive study habits needed to succeed in college. Still others offer "diversity" courses intended to infuse new students with an appreciation and adaptability to living and studying on a multicultural campus (Porter & Swing, 2006). The tie that binds these courses is the classroom audience: students new to the campus or "first-timers."

Many transition classes are populated by homogeneous groups of new students who are expected to face similar types of adaptation concerns, such as freshmen, transfers, or nontraditional new students. However, one "nontraditional" freshman population "with their own culture and problems" (Sedlacek & Adams-Gaston, 1992, p. 726) that is surprisingly seldom grouped in a transition course is new college athletes. This particular group of new students has a substantially different educational experience than nonathletes, including challenges such as more severe and monitored competition for time and negative perceptions by teachers and fellow students (Ferrante, Etzel, & Lantz, 1996). It was in response to this unique set of concerns that a mid-sized university in the southeast created a transition course dedicated to address the expected issues that new college athletes face. This course was created in 1993 and has been offered through the same academic department and taught by the same university faculty member since 1995. The objective of this chapter is to outline the rationale, the implementation, the curriculum, and the administrative realities of Counselor Education (CNED) 1002, Life Skills Development, a transition course for freshman male athletes.

Over the 15-year span of both developing and teaching CNED 1002, the instructor has continued to focus on addressing the unique and changing concerns, issues, and challenges of freshman student-athletes. While this course was initially developed and continually revised and evaluated solely from the information gleaned from the student-athletes' classroom discussions, response assignments, issues, and insights, it was remarkable how the literature in this area has also teased out the same concerns, issues, and challenges, further validating the material covered in this course. In other words, this course has been able to bear witness to the foundational issues student-athletes are noting in class while keeping track of how these issues parallel the empirical literature on student-athletes. This complimentary parallel is highlighted through this chapter by providing supporting literature to this instructor's course development and changes throughout the years.

CNED 1002 came to life in a discussion between the first author, who is a faculty member in the university's counseling program, and a long-time administrator of the men's athletic academic support services. That frank discussion revolved around the mutually agreed-upon challenges that face new college athletes (Broughton & Neyer, 2001) and the types of programming typically offered to ameliorate those challenges. The idea for a dedicated transition course for incoming athletes arose from the discussants' agreement that in-house academic athletic programming, as is common on most university campuses, is not necessarily the most effective venue for freshmen to reflect upon their adjustment concerns (Valentine & Taub, 1999; Watt & Moore, 2001).

Although there are numerous benefits to student-athletes within this arrangement, such as proximity to other athletic services, conveniently scheduled services that conform to athletic practice times, and administrative control of programming, there are problematic concerns as well. For example, athletic support services housed within an athletic department can serve to further distance student-athletes from other nonathlete peers, as well as from the faculty relationships made possible by classroom experiences. In addition, the physical housing of freshman academic programming within athletic facilities can imply to student-athletes that their academic needs are substantially different from nonathletes whose academic services are typically housed on the academic campus. Furthermore, in-house athletic academic support services can limit student-athletes from willingly reflecting with candor about their adjustment concerns. They may fear that athletic coaching and advising staff are privy to those discussions and could therefore deem the student-athlete less athletically competitive. Also, in-house athletic academic advisors who often administer in-house academic programming may not be trained to effectively deal with the personal or "noncognitive" needs of student-athletes (Hyatt, 2003). Finally, in-house athletic support services can create the appearance to student-athletes that the on-campus academic cultural environment is less desirable and subtly encourage student-athletes to view themselves less as students and more as athletes (Killeya, 2001).

In light of these concerns, CNED 1002 was created as an attempt to provide an academically sound and protected forum for student-athletes to think, learn, and reflect upon their unique experiences as athletes who are attempting to adjust and succeed on a university campus. The benefits of such an academic departmental transition course versus in-house athletic departmental academic programming are clear. One benefit is the opportunity for students to experientially practice actual academic skills in the presence of an experienced faculty instructor who understands how first-year students are expected to perform in a university classroom. The small class size of an athlete academic transition course, with no more than 15 students per section, allows the instructor a "lens" into each student's strengths and challenges. It also allows the instructor to provide personal conferences with each student at least twice a semester to discuss these strengths and challenges and prepare a plan of action for remediating problems. The "lab" experience offered in the course also provides each student with a clear understanding of normative classroom university expectations, such as classroom behavior, note-taking, academic honesty practices, and peer and instructor interactions. The instructor can point out through the semester that all grading, lecturing, and class activities are designed to offer students a window into the expectations they will normally find as they progress through their first- and second-year college courses.

Another benefit of an academically housed transition course for athletes is the opportunity to create a faculty mentor relationship. Many freshman athletes are enrolled for their first semester in large lecture classes where interaction with faculty can seem particularly daunting. Howard-Hamilton and Sina (2001) suggest that "there is no doubt that faculty encouragement and support is instrumental in elevating the self-esteem and efficacy of college students" (p. 42). This mentoring relationship can help to alleviate any feeling of "lack of belonging" athletes may experience in the college classroom (Valentine & Taub, 1999, p. 167). It is with these suggestions in mind that CNED 1002 was conceptualized, constructed, implemented, and adapted. By and large, this format has facilitated positive pedagogical and personal relationships between student-athletes and faculty, helping to create a learning environment where critical thinking is encouraged and individual mentoring relationships are fostered.

HISTORY: HOW DID CNED 1002 COME TO LIFE AND GROW?

The administrative implementation of this freshman student-athlete transition course followed the standard academic procedure for creating new university courses. The counseling faculty submitted a course title, description, and syllabus to departmental college and university committees with a suggested title of CNED 1002 Life Skills Development. The course was designed to be used primarily with student-athletes, but was structured so as to be conducive to a variety of new student populations. The official course description as stated in the university's catalog is "... the study and practice of problem-solving, decision-making, goals and values clarification, and other developmental skills affecting personal issues and academic success." The course purpose as stated on the syllabus is "... to provide an opportunity for students to gain the knowledge and skills necessary for improving their personal effectiveness. Skills appropriate to the common life situations of college students will be examined and applied, as well as those skills necessary for adapting to the specific needs of living/working/study groups with which students may be affiliated." These descriptors allow for the possibility that sections of CNED 1002 could be created for other unique, nonathlete student groups.

CNED 1002 Life Skills Development was first taught in the fall semester of 1995 with a "first-year experience" curriculum focusing on the attainment of study skills and academic success. Since that time the curriculum has expanded, in response to the instructor's observation of students' changing needs and the available literature on college student-athletes and non-student-athletes, to include such psychoeducational "life skills" (Broughton & Neyer, 2001, p. 49), wellness issues (Watson & Kissinger, 2007), personal choice, self-responsibility, time management, stress management, emotional intelligence, and ethical decision making. Although the curricular focus has evolved, the instructor has maintained a strong and continuous commitment to the rigor of a highly structured, credit-bearing course by requiring weekly formal writing assignments, seminar discussions, and a final examination covering course topics. All course assignments and classroom activities are exercises that require critical thinking and a self-reflective component. Students earn 2 hours of academic elective credit for CNED 1002 with the course grade figured into the semester and overall grade point average.

For the first 3 years of the course, it was offered as a coeducational experience for male and female freshman athletes. Due to an administrative change within the university's athletic department, the course was later offered for males only. The benefits of this change were unexpected. The male student-athletes have often commented that they initially are disappointed to find only other males on the course roster. However, as the semester unfolds, the students typically suggest that having a same-sex classroom population ultimately allows for more candid discussion and reflection, as well as the formation of cross-sport friendships. For example, when discussing and responding to the literature (Murray & Karkatzke, 2007) related to dating violence and sexual assault among college students, an all-male environment allows for more open and candid discussions about this topic. More specifically, an all-male environment allows the opportunity for students to discuss whether sexual assault and dating violence in fact occur more often among student-athletes or whether they simply are more often caught in headlined sexual assault events.

In response to the NCAA eligibility requirements concerning degree progress, a career exploration seminar was added in 1999 to the freshman athlete first-year course sequence. This seminar has been offered each spring since that date as a means of systematically helping student-athletes choose an academic major. The course follows a traditional college career counseling group format, with a combination of career and personality assessment with exploration of the majors and courses available on campus. While many student-athletes focus on future careers solely within the sports arena, Lally and Kerr (2005) demonstrate that when student-athletes allow their student role and identities to help shape their career paths, they benefit by further exploration of diverse careers and fields. This course is an opportunity for student-athletes to focus more on the student role and thus become fully engaged in the various assignments and activities geared toward major and career exploration. Although a discussion of the curriculum of that course is beyond the scope of this chapter, anecdotal evidence suggests the course has added immeasurably to the students' perceptions of the practicality of freshman athlete course programming.

A significant factor in the history of CNED 1002 is the continuity of its academic reputation. Feedback from students, university faculty, and athletic counselors and administrators has been universally positive, further validating the success of this type of freshman athlete course. In addition, positive comments from students, student-athlete academic advisors, and university athletic administration, as well as consistent course evaluation ratings above 4.5 on a 5.0 scale, support the notion that this course is a success and meets the needs of the students. The instructor is a faculty member and licensed professional counselor in a graduate counseling program who has demonstrated to all constituents a balanced priority between helping student-athletes learn to succeed while maintaining academic rigor and integrity within the course. Another reason that academic credibility is essential for the success of a freshman male athlete first-year course is that a softly graded course could serve to compound one of the unique stressors that athletes face, the belief that they are treated preferentially (Hyatt, 2003). Student-athletes too often are less than confident of their academic potential and control. Therefore, any belief among student-athletes themselves that the course is an "easy A" would undermine the instructor's emphasis that student-athletes are as capable of academically challenging thinking and writing as any other student on campus. In addition, there is also the need to have rigor to counter the bias of the "dumb jock" and the bias among faculty and students alike that student-athletes don't possess the academic drive and intellect to succeed in higher education.

CURRICULUM: WHAT DO STUDENTS LEARN IN CNED 1002 AND HOW DO THEY LEARN IT?

As noted, the curriculum for CNED 1002 has evolved from a first-year "orientation" or academic success course to a personal effectiveness or "life skills" course. This evolution was primarily driven by the instructor's observation of several significant threads emerging in students' classroom discussions and writings. These threads, while solely emerging from this instructor's and the students' experiences, are not unlike the scholarly studies of the freshman athlete experience. The following are the threads that emerged from this instructor's experience, as well as documented supportive literature that parallels these threads, including:

1. Student-athletes respond more positively to learning academic behavioral self-control techniques than to didactic instruction.
2. Student-athletes suffer from the burden of conflicting academic and athletic expectations. Parallel findings in the literature are numerous, with experts in the field identifying the student-athlete experience not only as being qualitatively different from that of nonathletes (Ferrante, Etzel, & Lantz, 1996; Parham, 1993), but also the student-athlete's educational experience being marked by stereotypes and competing expectations from faculty and athletic staff (Ferrante et al., 1996).
3. Many student-athletes have unrealistic expectations of their academic ability and, when faced with the harsher reality of college courses, can begin to lose self-confidence, self-efficacy, and academic motivation (Fletcher, Benshoff, & Richburg, 2003).
4. Student-athletes are concerned about the academic stereotype of the "dumb jock" and most state they want to overcome that descriptor.
5. Student-athletes are concerned that the media attention given to the unruly personal and sport-specific behaviors of high-profile athletes will reflect on their own reputations.
6. Student-athletes face significant moral dilemmas in college due to their high-profile existence and the impact of a "win at all costs" athletic attitude (Watt & Moore, 2001, p. 12).

As indicated, the expansive scholarly literature concerning the developmental, academic, and personal concerns of student-athletes correlates clearly to the thematic threads CNED 1002 students describe of their own academic adjustment. An effective and unique aspect of the CNED 1002 curriculum has been exposing students by lecture to the breadth of this scholarly writing. Informing students of the demands that "experts" expect athletes to face as they adjust to college generates lively class discussions, and helps students normalize their personal experiences. Discussions surrounding the student-athlete's responses to the scholarly literature highlight the fact that this type of class can provide a venue for student-athletes to articulate their thoughts and concerns while comparing their own experiences with the empirical evidence gathered by researchers studying the student-athlete experience. Examples include students sharing responses to the research linking procrastination, substance abuse, and health (Glenn, 2002). In addition, the experience of relating the scholarly literature to their own experiences may be particularly important in cases where student-athletes have internalized various stereotypes. Moreover, it offers an environment where students may first come to explore their identity outside that of an athlete. This may be particularly important in cases where student-athletes overidentify with their athletic persona, a position that correlates poorly with academic achievement among student-athletes.

As a result of these observational and scholarly threads, CNED 1002 is described to students as a double-barreled curriculum. The first half of the semester initially addresses the skills students will need to adjust successfully to a university's academic demands. The second half of the semester explores the behavioral self-management skills and decision-making abilities they need to personally overcome any stereotypical characteristics they perceive others hold of them as athletes and any moral choices they may face.

Although the instructor reviews the pertinent literature and, in turn, regularly updates course topics, the objectives of the course have remained consistent. These include promoting students' critical examination of their ability to succeed in college, emphasizing self-reflection of academic strengths; providing practice in the behavioral components of academic success, such as setting and achieving goals; and examining the effective methods of making decisions and solving problems, especially those involving the unique challenges of a student-athlete's life. Students who successfully complete CNED 1002 are expected to be able to articulate to the instructor and their classmates the social, academic, ethical, and athletic demands they face, both in writing and in directed class discussion. They must also be able to objectively observe and analyze their personal behavior in problem solving, goal setting, and decision making. They must read and analyze academic and ethical issues presented in fictional and case studies. They must demonstrate an ability to communicate effectively in a university culture with faculty and other students in both formal and informal settings. For example, one of their course assignments is to conduct an interview with one of their faculty members where the focus is on getting to know the faculty, and gaining an understanding of the job and role faculty serve. In addition, students participate in an individual conference session with the CNED 1002 instructor where they must demonstrate effective and professional communication skills. Finally, they must demonstrate in class the ability to understand and respectfully consider the perspectives of their peers by demonstrating active listening skills.

Academic requirements for CNED 1002 include the following:

1. Seminar participation as evaluated by students' thoughtful analysis of ideas in directed class discussions and the demonstration of the highest standards of classroom behavior and respect for the ideas of others.
2. Response papers as evaluated by students' thoughtful, documented, and thorough response to course topics (described below).
3. Midterm essays describing the students' detailed description of their previous academic strengths, weaknesses, and behaviors; a set of specific academic goals for the freshman year and a distinct plan for accomplishing those goals based on course lectures and readings.
4. Final essays synthesizing course topics, with the characters and plots outlined in a popular novel concerning a college athlete engaged in illegal and academically dishonest behaviors.
5. A required conference with the course instructor and/or with any other of the students' course faculty members.
6. A PowerPoint-generated poster presentation of the students' 2-week implementation of a chosen and academically researched study technique.

The twice-weekly meetings of CNED 1002 include lecture, directed class discussion, and drill sessions for implementing skills. Specific "personal academic effectiveness" topics for the first half of the semester as outlined in the course syllabus include:

1. **College versus high school:** a directed discussion on students' perceptions of the differing expectations of a high school academic experience and a university experience (Harris, Altekruse, & Engels, 2003; Howard-Hamilton & Sina, 2001).
2. **College wellness factors for the first year:** individual and ongoing assessment of the personal dimensions that create a life in balance, including physical, intellectual, emotional, social, environmental, spiritual, and occupational strengths and challenges (Gibson & Myers, 2006; Watson & Kissinger, 2007).
3. **University academic culture and rules:** an analysis of university norms of behavior.
4. **Personal choice:** a discussion of the developmental shift from external to internal locus of control necessary for academic success in college and a comparison of the emphasis of personal choice between collegiate culture and athletic culture (Fletcher et al., 2003).

5. **Goals and willpower:** instruction in a method for decreasing unwanted behaviors or increasing desired behaviors as applied to academic success.

6. **Procrastination:** a lecture outlining the research on the relationship among procrastination, health, and stress and a behavioral analysis of each students' procrastination patterns (Glenn, 2002; Perry, Hladkyj, Pekrun, Clifton, & Chipperfield, 2005).

7. **Academic planning and goal setting:** in-class application of a daily set of behavioral goals entered into a written planning calendar with distinct self-instructions for completing each task and the importance of self-monitoring and modifying goals for success (Covey, 1990).

8. **Analysis of time use:** a class discussion on each student's analysis of time, typical daily use of time, and the importance of planning (Covey, 1990).

9. **Application of study techniques:** a lecture on how to apply practical and time-efficient approaches to improving studying and memory.

10. **Stress:** an examination of each student's physical, emotional, and personal patterns of stress and the practice of various stress management tools, such as meditation and breathing techniques (Gibson & Myers, 2006; Watson & Kissinger, 2007).

At the second half of the semester, "personal and interpersonal effectiveness" topics are presented in lecture and guided discussions of case studies. In the guided discussions, students are expected to demonstrate active listening skills rather than debating techniques. The topics include:

1. **Emotional intelligence:** a lecture and discussion on the psychological abilities that relate to life success (Zizzi, Deaner, & Hirschhorn, 2003).

2. **Listening and responding with understanding:** lecture and practice in active listening techniques to create empathy and respect in classroom and interpersonal relationships.

3. **Moral choices:** a lecture on the research on moral development among athletes; a discussion of the moral challenges student-athletes face on and off the field; and case study discussions examining each student's personal moral developmental level based on Kohlberg's theories of moral development (Carodine, Almond, & Grattos, 2001; Howard-Hamilton & Sina, 2001; Lumpkin, Stoll, & Beller, 1994; Simon, 1991).

4. **Diversity, stereotyping, and self-identity:** a lecture and guided discussion on the benefits and challenges of living on a multicultural campus, stereotyping of athletes and other groups, identifying personal

stereotypes, and personal ethnic and gender identity (Engstrom & Sedlacek, 1991; Smallman & Sowa, 1991; Smith, 1992).

5. **Dating violence:** an examination of gender-related violence; violence in sports; and personal choices in responsible sexual behavior based on university rules, social climate, and moral convictions (Flezzani & Behshokk, 2003; Killeya, 2001; Murray & Karkatzke, 2007).

6. **Performance-enhancing drugs:** a lecture and discussion on legality, ethics, and sportsmanship of the use of performance enhancing drugs.

7. **Winning, cheating, gamesmanship, and sportsmanship:** an examination of the moral and ethical elements in winning and the development of the student's personal definitions of the ethics of competition (Lumpkin et al., 1994; Shulman & Bowen, 2001; Simon, 1991).

Course topics, assignments, and instructor interventions are grounded in a philosophy emphasizing students' personal choice, self-responsibility, and the possibility of change. This philosophy is best articulated in the instructor's counseling philosophy and practice, which is heavily influenced by Carl Rogers's (1961) person-centered counseling and William Glasser's (1965, 1986, 1993) reality and choice theories. Simply, these counseling theories suggest that all people can change and learn if they are treated with respect and are expected to be responsible for their own actions. In addition, it is critical that the instructor create a warm, supportive classroom environment where empathy, unconditional positive regard, and genuineness are not only taught but modeled by the instructor as well. It is the instructor's intent to always underscore the students' choice in their behaviors, the university environment's emphasis on individual academic freedom, and the instructor's faith that each student can create and meet their own academic/personal/athletic goals. This emphasis on personal choice translates into clear and consistent in-class responses from the instructor, such as "What do you know will happen if you choose to turn your paper in late?"; "How will it affect you to earn the identified consequences for turning your paper in late?"; as well as, "How is your comment a demonstration of respect to others in this classroom or others outside this classroom?"

Student comments through formal evaluation and informal conversations with the CNED 1002 instructor reveal that certain class topics are viewed as the most helpful and memorable. Topics related to stress and the identification and implementation of personal stress management techniques consistently are ranked the most helpful. This is not surprising given the copious amount of scholarly interest in the personal problems and conflicting demands student-athletes encounter in college (Krane & Greenleaf, 1999; Witmer, Bostic, Phillips, & Waters; 1981). Students report that the level of their stress declines as they critically examine the sources and symptoms of that stress in writing and in class discussion. Learning such simple stress-reduction techniques as deep breathing, self-massage, mental focusing, and meditation can greatly reduce the mental and physical impact of student stress. It is not uncommon for students who have learned to use these techniques to request a time before class lecture or discussion begins to allow a moment in quiet to regain their mental focus, which may have slipped away from a full morning's classes and activities. As a certified yoga instructor, the CNED 1002 instructor is often able to incorporate beneficial stress relief and mindfulness techniques into the classroom.

The second most popular topic among students in CNED 1002 is the personal examination of their daily use of time. It is well recognized in the literature that juggling multiple time demands is one of the most challenging aspects student-athletes encounter when adapting to college (Howard-Hamilton & Sina, 2001; Perry et al., 2005). Traditional didactic methods of learning time management often neglect the important first step of asking students to "take a baseline" of their current use of time. This course takes a different strategy by assigning student-athletes to track and chart how they use time within a 48-hour span in order to identify and monitor issues that may be helping or hurting their academic performance. From that examination it is easy for students to see for themselves the value in a planned approach to their use of time rather than simply having the instructor point out the benefits of scheduling.

The course topic former students report as the most memorable is the discussion of "choice." The concept behind this topic is that college students are no longer controlled by others; the academic environment assumes that they recognize the implications of their own choices in all behaviors. Although it is often a shock to students, the instructor emphasizes that a personal shift from external to internal locus of control is the primary marker of a successful college student. Students are instructed to use language in class that reflects internal control, always saying "I *chose* to . . ." rather than "I *have* to . . ." (Covey, 1990, pp. 78–79). For many student-athletes, this language shift is a startling but empowering tool. Lively class discussions often ensue when student-athletes discuss their awakening awareness that success in their academic life requires an inner locus of control, yet success in their athletic life may involve following the control of others on their team or coaching staff.

INSTRUCTOR PERSPECTIVES: WHAT HAVE I LEARNED FROM CNED 1002 STUDENTS?

During the 15-year span of teaching CNED 1002 I have observed a surprisingly consistent set of concerns, perceptions, and behaviors among freshman male student-athletes. In both class discussions and the privacy of personal conferences with student-athletes, 15 years of CNED 1002 students have returned time and again to the following core issues:

- **"I'm stressed out!":** Stress is an overwhelming and surprising burden for first-year athletes. The liveliest discussions in class each year revolve around the negative impact of stress in an already challenging freshman experience. Students often report that their beginning semester in college is the first time they have suffered from persistent and excessive amounts of stress. Although many students describe extremely stressful life situations from their life prior to college, they often report that the existing social and familial support at home prevented them from the need to develop personal coping methods for dealing with stress. It is my perception that learning individualized, portable stress-reduction techniques has been the most useful tool I have offered students in CNED 1002. Many former students confess that simply learning deep breathing or mind focusing techniques tipped the balance of their freshman year from overwhelming to manageable stress. Learning these techniques in a classroom setting allows each student to "normalize" the worry often associated with uncontrolled stress.

- **"Reality bites":** Most freshman athletes arrive on campus with copious amounts of advice on what to expect in relation to the new athletic, academic, and social challenges and opportunities they find once they arrive on campus. Students can quote very distinct instructions from parents, friends, coaches, and high school teachers on how to successfully manage coursework, athletic demands, fatigue, and social obligations. However, it is my perception that it is not until these actual demands become a reality that students become truly interested in "success advice." For that reason I do not teach time management or study skills techniques until the first round of campus exams have occurred. Students are, by that time, very clear about their needs and rapt in their attention to improving their next round of exam grades.

- **"No one understands":** A common thread of discussion in CNED 1002 centers on the new student-athletes' disillusionment with their campus image. It is this author's perception that student-athletes can become surprised and hurt when they realize that many non-athlete students see them as privileged and pampered, rather than as the campus heroes they may have been seen as in high school (Harris et al., 2003). A productive discussion on this topic can be centered less on the speculation of the opinions of others not present in the classroom and more on the responsible and responsive means for athletes to create their own desired image. I often ask students to write and discuss, "How do I want others on campus to perceive me?" and "What am I now doing to create that perception?". I believe it is important for student-athletes to create a personal, practiced, and reasoned articulation about the realities of their day-to-day life.

ADMINISTRATIVE REALITIES: WHAT DOES IT TAKE TO MAINTAIN CNED 1002 WITHIN AN ACADEMIC DEPARTMENT?

Implementing an academic course to aid student-athletes in their successful transition to college can create administrative problems. However, several factors can assist in the successful creation and longitudinal success of such a course. The first factor is working with an athletic administrator who understands the importance of the teaching faculty's academic freedom regarding course topics, requirements, and grading. It is vital that the instructor have full independence from the athletic staff in regard to all instructional concerns. The instructor should be free of any inquiry from coaches, athletic advisors, and trainers regarding the content and functioning of the transition course. The simplest means to achieve this independence is for the teaching faculty member to hold a regular academic appointment within a university department and not be beholden to or associated with the athletic department. It can be tempting to employ teaching assistants for a course like CNED 1002 by utilizing graduate student instruction that is so often found in many first-year courses. However, for a dedicated student-athlete course, the continuity and experience of a fully appointed faculty instructor who functions independently of the athletic department and who teaches other nonathlete courses is essential. It is crucial that faculty instructor focus on the entire college experience and not just that of freshmen, freshman athletes, or the experiences of their freshman advisees.

A second factor in the success of a transition course for student-athletes is designing an administrative procedure for enrolling only student-athletes into the course. For starters, it is essential that equal and available transition courses for nonathlete freshmen exist so that there is no continuation of the concern that athletes have privileged academic services. A method for establishing this "athletes'-only" procedure is to create an administrative enrollment allowing the athletic department to submit the roster of new students and allowing the academic department to register them. The course can be advertised, but only as "by instructor consent."

A final factor in the success of a course like CNED 1002 is not only a clear understanding by traditional academic and athletic academic advisors that the course, while rigorous, is particularly beneficial for student-athletes. It is vital that students enter the course with an official communication of the expectations of course objectives and requirements. It may be tempting to athletic department staff to "sell" the transition course to new recruits as an institutionally-offered means to gain credit hours and a good letter grade to buffer eligibility and grade point averages. However, the recruitment value of the promise of a course respectful of athletes' challenges, but also of their academic prowess, is much more empowering to new students and their families.

INSTRUCTOR'S CONCLUSION

The view from the podium in a freshman transition course provides a unique window into the adjustments and challenges student-athletes face as they begin their new lives in college. As an instructor who has occupied that position for the past 15 years, I am certain that no other venue can better ensure student-athletes the privacy, structure, and training that an academic classroom and its inherent academic freedom can provide. The classroom setting provides a forum where student-athletes can gather twice weekly to think about, write about, and confront the unique issues they face, while practicing the very skills they will need for academic success. The classroom setting further provides the faculty member an opportunity to create respectful, active, and potentially longitudinal mentoring relationships with student-athletes founded on academic rather than athletic concerns. The classroom setting can also provide the instructor with an honest understanding of the challenging experiences student-athletes face as they adjust to college, an understanding based on the students' clear expressions of their journey. It has been so for me.

REFERENCES

Broughton, E., & Neyer, M. (2001). Advising and counseling student athletes. *New Directions for Student Services, 93*, 47–53. San Francisco: Jossey-Bass.

Carodine, K., Almond, K. F., & Grattos, K. K. (2001). College student athlete success in and out of the classroom. *New Directions for Student Services, 93*, 19–33. San Francisco: Jossey-Bass.

Covey, S. (1990). *The seven habits of highly effective people: Powerful lessons in personal change.* New York: Fireside.

Engstrom, C. H., & Sedlacek, W. E. (1991). A study of prejudice toward university student-athletes. *Journal of Counseling and Development, 70*, 189–193.

Ferrante, A. P., Etzel, E. F., & Lantz, C. (1996). Counseling college student-athletes: The problem, the need 1996. In E. F. Etzel, A. P. Ferrante, & J. W. Pinkney (Eds.), *Counseling college student-athletes: Issues and interventions* (2nd ed., pp. 3–26). Morgantown, WV: Fitness Information Technology.

Fletcher, T. B., Benshoff, J. M., & Richburg, M. J. (2003). A systems approach to understanding and counseling college student-athletes. *Journal of College Counseling, 6*, 35–45.

Flezzani, J. D., & Benshoff, J.M. (2003). Understanding sexual aggression in male college students: The role of self-monitoring and pluralistic ignorance. *Journal of College Counseling, 6,* 69–79.

Gibson, D. M., & Myers, J. E. (2006). Perceived stress, wellness, and mattering: A profile of first-year citadel cadets. *Journal of College Student Development, 47,* 647–660.

Glasser, W. (1965). *Reality Therapy: A new approach to psychiatry.* New York: Harper & Row.

Glasser, W. (1986). *Control theory in the classroom.* New York: Perennial Library.

Glasser. W. (1993). *The quality school teacher.* New York: HarperPerennial.

Glenn, D. (2002). *Procrastination in college students is a marker for unhealthy behaviors, study indicates.* Retrieved August 26, 2002, from http://chronicle.com/daily/2002/08/2002082602n.htm

Harris, H. L., Altekruse, M. K., & Engels, D. W. (2003). Helping freshmen student athletes adjust to college life using psychoeducational groups. *Journal for Specialists In Group Work, 28,* 64–81.

Howard-Hamilton, M. F., & Sina, J. A. (2001). How college affects student athletes. *New Directions for Student Services, 93,* 35–43.

Hyatt, R. (2003). Barriers to persistence among African-American intercollegiate athletes: A literature review of non-cognitive variables. *College Student Journal, 37,* 260–276.

Keim, M. C., & Strickland, J. M. (2004). Support services for two-year college student-athletes. *College Student Journal, 38,* 36–43.

Killeya, L. A. (2001). Idiosyncratic role-elaboration, academic performance, and adjustment among African-American and European-American male college student-athletes. *College Student Journal, 35,* 87–96.

Lally, P. S., & Kerr, G. A. (2005). The career planning, athletic identity, and student role identity of intercollegiate student athletes. *Research Quarterly for Exercise and Sport, 76*(3), 275–285.

Lumpkin, A., Stoll, S. K., & Beller, J. M. (1994). *Sports ethics: Ethics in college sport.* New York: Oryx.

Murray, C. E., & Karkatzke, K. N. (2007). Dating violence among college students: Key issues for college counselors. *Journal of College Counseling, 10,* 79–89.

Parham, W. (1993). The intercollegiate athlete: A 1990s profile. *The Counseling Psychologist, 21,* 411–429.

Perry, R. P., Hladkyj, S., Pekrun, R. H., Clifton, R. A., & Chipperfield, J. G. (2005). Perceived academic control and failure in college students: A three-year study of scholastic attainment. *Research in Higher Education, 46,* 535–569.

Porter, S. R., & Swing, R. L. (2006). Understanding how first-year seminars affect persistence. *Research in Higher Education, 47,* 89–109.

Rogers, C. (1961). *Becoming a person: A therapist's view of psychotherapy.* Boston: Houghton Mifflin.

Sedlacek, W. E., & Adams-Gaston, J. (1992). Predicting the academic success of student-athletes using SAT and noncognitive variables. *Journal of Counseling and Development, 70,* 724–727.

Shulman, J. L., & Bowen, W. G. (2001). *The game of life: College sports and educational values.* Princeton, NJ: Princeton University Press.

Simon, R. L. (1991). *Fair play: Sports, values, and society.* Boulder, CO: Westview Press.

Smallman, E., & Sowa, C. J. (1991). Ethnic and gender differences in student-athletes' responses to stressful life events. *Journal of College Student Development, 32*, 230–235.

Smith, C. F. (1992). *Lenny, lefty, and the chancellor: The Len Bias tragedy and the search for reform in big-time college basketball.* Baltimore: Bancroft.

Valentine, J. J., & Taub, D. J. (1999). Responding to the developmental needs of student athletes. *Journal of College Counseling, 2*, 164–179.

Watson, J. C., & Kissinger, D. B. (2007). Athletic participation and wellness: Implications for counseling college student-athletes. *Journal of College Counseling, 10*, 153–162.

Watt, S. K., & Moore, J. L. III. (2001). Who are student athletes? *New Directions for Student Services, 93*, 7–18.

Wittmer, J. Bostic, D., Phillips, T. D., & Waters, W. (1981). The personal, academic, and career problems of college student athletes: Some possible answers. *Personnel and Guidance Journal, 12*, 52–55.

Zizzi, S. J., Deaner, H. R., & Hirschhorn, D. K. (2003). The relationship between emotional intelligence and performance among college baseball players. *Journal of Applied Sport Psychology, 15*, 262–269.

CHAPTER 6

THE CYCLE OF TRANSITION FOR STUDENT-ATHLETES TO COLLEGE

Gregory V. Wolcott
Debbie Gore-Mann
University of San Francisco

The envelope looks like all the rest that have been sent the past several months, with one distinction. Printed at an angle across the front reads "Official Notice – Please Read Immediately." Would this be the one? The letter that alters my life forever? Did I get in? "Congratulations! You have been conditionally admitted to the University of San Francisco. *We are pleased to welcome you to our university community."*

Each spring, letters like these signify to students all across America that their lives will be changed forever. Hope springs eternal from the words "you have been accepted!" Hope has welled up over time, from the first presentation about college in middle school to the time when their path is finally set in motion. The future is bright and promises to be filled with energy, excitement, joy, and most certainly, transition.

Numerous researchers have studied the transition process that new college students experience. This process is usually defined as the pre-enrollment phase through the matriculation phase and concludes at the end of the freshman year (Perigo & Upcraft, 1989). This chapter attempts to quantify what that experience is like for an entering freshman. The life cycle of

College Student-Athletes: Challenges, Opportunities, and Policy Implications, pages 73–89

a college freshman is examined through five stages: Getting Started, Communications, Precollege Programs, Transition and Belonging, and Surviving the First Year. Through personal examples and theoretical support, the chapter aims to provide educators with a better understanding of this life cycle in order to help them develop approaches that support new student-athletes at various stages.

GETTING STARTED

The new student population has changed greatly over the past few decades. With the emergence of Generations X and Y, the surge of technology use among high school students, and the ever-changing global economy, today's students are different from those of previous decades. One thing that remains the same is that entering college implies a transition from being a dependent adolescent to becoming a mature young adult with new responsibilities.

High school students deal with many pressures when selecting a college. They must consider what their major will be, if a big or small school is right for them, and whether they want to stay close to home or go far away. Usually the most critical considerations are the *Big Three F's*: friends, family, and finances. Research has shown that students' peers are one of the greatest influences on them at this developmental stage in their lives. It can be comforting to know that friends will be attending the same college, or that they may have someone to room with once in school. Astin's (1993) study on student involvement found that a student's peer group is the most important influence on growth and development during college. It follows that experiencing the pre-enrollment process with friends can make it more manageable and enjoyable.

Each new generation of college students has unique experiences and events that shape the lives of its members. Howe and Strauss (2000) refered to the current group of traditional-aged college students as "Millennials" (p. 2). These are students who were born in or after 1982 and are described as idealistic, sheltered, committed to changing the world, and valuing relationships. They are culturally different from preceding generations of college students, with 35% being nonwhite or Latino. This generation is less ethnocentric, more social, more open to cultural differences, more tolerant of ambiguity, and more results-oriented with a focus on career and success (Cawthon & Miller, 2003).

This generation is also closer to their parents than any other generation to emerge. Therefore, college students tend to rely more on their parents for a wide variety of things, including academic and personal advice, and colleges will be forced to learn to deal with this by creating different responses (Jacobs & With, 2002). Because the decisions about attending college are laden with emotions, it follows that parental approval and support is critical to college freshmen (Austin, 2003). These familial relationships can make it challenging for university educators and administrators who have the students' best interest in mind, but are forced to deal with the often differing perspectives of parents and family members. Parents and students may view going to college in varying ways: an opportunity or an escape, a highly anxious time or complete freedom, the continuance of an old life or the forging of a new. It requires that university personnel are knowledgeable about who they are recruiting, and are intentional in the messages they convey.

COMMUNICATIONS WITH THE INSTITUTION

As evidenced in the opening passage of this chapter, applying and moving into the matriculation stage can be an overwhelming experience. Students range in their approach to applying to college from those who are fourth-generation students at a particular university to those who want to keep all their options open by applying to multiple schools. There is a popular approach to the application process that has emerged among recent generations: one "safety" school where admission is likely, one "dream" school such as an Ivy League, and one out-of-state school just to make parents feel uneasy. Once the application process is over, the waiting game begins. Typically the time from application to acceptance is several months, while families put life on hold until they can weigh their options.

After acceptance letters are received and decisions are made, families are able to better concentrate on their school of choice. Most families believe at first that the hard part is over, but actually it is about to begin. There are several steps to matriculating to any campus including financial aid applications, testing, and housing considerations. How will we pay for college? How much is needed beyond tuition, room, and board? What type of living environment would be best? Whether one is an only child or one of six, the leap to college housing can be a frightening prospect. Fortunately, universities have responded to families' needs at this stage by offering precollege programs that assists with the matriculation process and eases the transition to college.

PRECOLLEGE PROGRAMS

Research indicates that elements that students bring with them to college often dictate their level of satisfaction and success (Astin, 1993, 1997; Johnson, 2002; Ward-Roof, 2003). These elements include high school grades, admissions test scores, gender, and race, among others. However, precollege and orientation programs can do a great deal to level the playing field and greatly reduce the anxiety that is associated with the transition to college.

Precollege programs span the spectrum in terms of aims, format, and goals. Present-day programs include campus visits and tours, receptions for admitted students, and traditional orientation, advising, and registration programs. Orientation programs have been proven to help students with their adjustment to college and personal development (Devlin, 1996; Gardner & Hansen, 1993; Greenlaw, Anliker, & Barker, 1997; Perigo & Upcraft, 1989; Ward-Roof & Hatch, 2003). Adjustment and development are two of the major goals of orientation programs. Other goals include retaining students, promoting involvement, and providing academic and social integration (Council for the Advancement of Standards for Student Services/ Development Programs, 2001; Fox, Zakely, Morris, & Jundt, 1993; Tinto, 1993). Because today's college students are results- oriented and expect customer service (Howe & Strauss, 2000), activities at orientation should fit into an overarching theme and philosophy. Furthermore, the benefits for attending orientation should be articulated and orientation professionals should understand how their programs promote retention and persistence (Cawthon & Miller, 2003; Gardner & Hansen, 1993).

These programs can also help students and parents mitigate some of the inherent challenges and differences in perception they might have about the freshman year. Research suggests that institutions should develop orientation programs for parents, which indicate to them that they are a critical part of the student's transition process (Austin, 2003; Ward-Roof & Hatch, 2003). Parent orientation programs should be focused on "keeping family members attached in a renegotiated relationship" (Austin, 2003, p. 138) and illustrate how parents can serve as mentors to students. If parents become knowledgeable about the campus, they can serve as referral agents to the university. Parents need to understand, however, that students should take responsibility for interactions with the institution and parents should not do it for them.

TRANSITION AND BELONGING

A student's transition to college can be marked by experiences such as moving into the residence halls, making new friends, reconciling freedom with new responsibilities, and discovering a new lifestyle while maintaining former associations. It is a time of excitement and intrigue at every turn, and is accompanied by a roller coaster of emotions. Seminal research conducted on the first-year experience indicates that the first 2–6 weeks of college can be instrumental to student success, retention, and graduation (Levitz & Noel, 1989; Upcraft & Gardner, 1989). It is understandable then that educators and researchers alike have given considerable attention to this period in the lives of college students.

Tinto (1993) explained this transition as

> a period during which the person begins to interact in new ways with members of the new group into which membership is sought. Isolation, training, and sometimes ordeals are employed as mechanisms to insure the separation of the individual from past associations and the adoption of behaviors and norms appropriate to membership in the new group. (p. 93)

Incorporation, also called integration, is achieved when the individual takes on new patterns of interaction with the group and becomes a participant member.

Becoming integrated into the life of the new community can be multifaceted. This stage often begins with relationships with roommates. Housing officers are well aware of the stress that a new living environment can bring, causing them to develop policies such as not allowing any roommate switching until the fourth week of the semester. Usually students can work things out among themselves. As they are discovering their own patterns and schedules, they learn the tendencies of others and adapt accordingly. Issues at this stage also involve personal decisions such as how to schedule one's classes, methods and how often to study, and decisions about going home on the weekends. It is at this stage that the quality and responsiveness of faculty and staff can play a pivotal role in the ultimate integration into university life (Levitz & Noel, 1989).

Tinto (1993) viewed integration on both an academic and social level. The academic system is concerned with the formal education of students in the classroom and in interactions with faculty. The social system centers on daily life and interactions among students, faculty, and staff that take place outside the classroom. Tinto explained it is important to distinguish these two systems and the forms of "intellectual and social integration (membership)" that occurs in them (p. 107). For the first-year student, academic integration involves connecting with the material being learned and with the faculty who are responsible for their learning. Faculty can support students' integration by finding creative ways to present class material, gauging students' learning in a variety of ways, and making themselves available through office hours and study sessions. Tinto noted that some form of academic integration is required through the mandate of satisfactory grades, whereas social integration is not mandated. Social integration, however, can be viewed as equally critical to the success and retention of all students.

Social integration has also been described in the literature as involvement. Astin (1996) revisited his original study on student involvement and reviewed 20-year trends of longitudinal data on thousands of college students. He found that involvement continues to have a powerful impact on students. "[I]nvolvement with academics, faculty, and student peers are the most potent forms of positive involvement, while noninvolvement with campus life has a powerful negative impact on student outcomes" (as cited in Berger & Milem, 1999, p. 644). It follows, then, that much attention has been given in recent years to the critical role that student affairs programs play in the overall success of students. Students become socially integrated into university life by getting involved in clubs and organizations, attending a campus event, performing community service, or taking on a campus leadership role. These experiences help students feel more socially integrated and enhance their commitment to the institution.

FINISHING THE FIRST YEAR

As freshmen continue into their second semester, they take with them the positive experiences and challenges they have experienced early on. Students continue to develop their values, behaviors, and attitudes toward themselves and those around them. Terenzini, Springer, Yaeger, Pascarella, and Nora (1996) claimed the use of "validating experiences" too supports the success of college freshmen, particularly first-generation college students. The quantity and magnitude of these validating experiences ultimately determine how students move toward completing their freshman year.

Students also continue to refine what Astin (1997) referred to as student inputs, or the factors and experiences they brought with them to college. Students that come from backgrounds of privilege may find those privileges reinforced upon entering college. Conversely, depending on the college environment, these students may be challenged around issues of privilege, thereby causing them to behave in new ways. Similarly, students from disadvantaged backgrounds may struggle with the demands of their new environment because they may be experiencing things for the first time. However, renewed strength and confidence may be developed from overcoming the odds and achieving results in the new environment. Often these successes and challenges do not happen in a vacuum; most college freshmen have an ample supply of each, marking this one of the most unique times in their lives.

Another universal phenomenon that college freshmen deal with is responsibility for success. Many administrators and university personnel will put the onus of success directly on students. Others will claim that university personnel, programs, and services have the responsibility for student success. The fledgling philosophy major might attribute success to a higher power or force in the universe, while the business major may make reference to the popular slogan "only the strong survive." These concepts can be better understood through literature on internal locus of control, defined as "the extent to which an individual is self-directed or believes that one determines one's own fate" (Pascarella, Edison, Hagedorn, Nora, & Terenzini, 1996, p. 732). This approach can be juxtaposed with those more externally directed who believe outcomes are affected more by luck, fate, or other people. This concept is manifested in pop culture through statements such as "everything happens for a reason" or similar phrases that are uttered without much thought or consequence. Students would be wise to develop a philosophy that encompasses all of these viewpoints when considering their success.

Ultimately completion of the first year of college can be attributed to a variety of factors. Academic and social integration, validating experiences, student inputs, and continued personal development are all critical. Peers, faculty, and staff contribute in different ways to students' success, and play equal roles in the retention of college freshmen. University personnel must find ways to create seamless integration of all these facets to ensure the success of college freshmen at their respective institutions.

APPLYING THE FRESHMAN LIFE CYCLE
TO STUDENT-ATHLETES

The student-athlete freshman year cycle in many ways mirrors that of traditional freshmen. Those who influence their decision include family, peers, teachers, and counselors. Family resources, financial considerations, and the college size and location also play a role in deciding where to go to school. The key difference for student-athletes in this phase is that the process begins much earlier, usually in the ninth grade of high school. By the time students are 14 years old, the NCAA allows colleges to begin recruiting them. Students who are on a path to become college athletes become aware of NCAA eligibility and core classes required by the NCAA Clearinghouse. These guidelines determine the core courses they will take in high school to meet eligibility standards later on. This time is also marked by contact from college coaches who send letters and visit with families.

When potential college student-athletes enter high school, they eventually become encouraged to choose one sport if they have not already. This is partly out of necessity, as training and conditioning for each sport increases to year-round. Performance on high school teams becomes more closely evaluated and reported via the Amateur Athletics Union (AAU), while college recruiting intensifies by multiple colleges. By the senior year, most student-athletes have narrowed down the potential institutions at which they can play and receive a scholarship. However, the process is not over. There are still college entrance exams to take and final classes to complete, all of which have an impact on students' admission to the school of their choice. In addition to these standard procedures, potential college student-athletes must also sign a letter of intent (LOI), register with the NCAA Clearinghouse, and sometimes endure media coverage of their college admission process.

The application and commitment process usually ends by the middle of the student's senior year, if earlier commitments have not already been fortified. In this way, college student-athletes are more advanced than their traditional peers who often wait until the last minute to decide where to go to college. This advance decision is necessary given the additional steps and challenges that college student-athletes face as they begin their freshman year.

Much like in high school, college student-athletes share the same anxieties, fears, hopes, and dreams as their traditional peers regarding the freshman year, but have additional pressures placed upon them. They have the same responsibilities as other students to the university, but have other duties to their team and coaches. Many student-athletes arrive 2–4 weeks earlier than their peers. They begin to train and even compete before classes begin. Student-athletes receive training manuals from coaches and sports programs to help them get acquainted with their new role and responsibilities. This is all happening while student-athletes are trying to transcend their high school lives and integrate into a new environment.

Many college student-athletes perform below the academic metrics (graduation rates, grade point average, progress toward degree) of traditional students, and college leaders, administrators, and coaches are aware of the unique challenges that face incoming freshman student-athletes and some academic programs are put into place to help address the challenges of academics and athletic time management. The student-athlete is expected to manage: (1) academics (classes, tutoring, study hall), (2) athletics (practice, body/mind management, playing games), and (3) additional responsibilities such as incorporating travel and time away from campus.

First-year transition is vital since athletic eligibility hangs in the balance. A poor academic freshman year can result in NCAA ineligibility and/or loss of playing time. Therefore there is an increased focus on academics as seen in study hall hours, tutoring time, and extra coursework (such as special seminars for student-athletes and compliance courses). These are usually viewed by the general student population as "perks" to being a student-athlete. But ultimately it can result in less social time, and a less than enjoyable experience for freshmen student-athletes, sometimes resulting in their desire to leave the college.

First-year communications skills become crucial. There is a need to tell professors about travel schedules and missed class time. Coaches need to know when academic struggles surface due to impact on NCAA eligibility, and student-athletes must assist sports medicine staff in making the distinction between injuries and pain. Sometimes most important to success, there is the need for student-athletes to relate to teammates and create chemistry and cohesiveness within the team.

Unique challenges and opportunities exist for student-athletes. Some student-athletes are less academically prepared because they have spent a great deal of time focusing on their athletic performance rather than their academic performance. Some student-athletes may be the first in their family to attend college, while others may face tremendous challenges based on cultural, family, and social adjustments. Still others make decisions based on "athletic fit" and not "academic fit" or "social fit" and may become unhappy. Student-athletes face physical and mental fatigue in their freshman year. They must manage mental and physical challenges at a much higher level than high school. Time management for physical recovery and therapy create additional time demands. Pre/post-practice and pre/post-game sports medicine may be involved. These are things that add to an already demanding school, practice, and game schedule that students are trying to balance.

Teams and teammates provide an additional support system for student-athletes. Colleges have a dedicated athletics staff to assist with time management, tutoring, and academic advising. Social structure support with teammates who face similar academic and athletic challenges can also be helpful as students transition. Advice from teammates and upper classmen is also helpful regarding the best classes to take, the best professors, when to use tutoring, and how to negotiate shared living arrangements.

CONCLUSION

Students come to our campuses after a long process of preadmissions and communication with different entities. They are influenced by family and friends, and pay attention to the colleges that offer their major of choice. After researching fit, finances, location, and size, they finally decide to attend our institution. Regardless of students' identities they bring to campus—traditional student, athlete, student leader, honor student—there are common threads that run through their experiences in transition. Becoming knowledgeable about the cycle of college student transition can assist educators, administrators, and coaches alike in working with new students. This knowledge can then be translated into programs and services that ensure new students' successful transition to campus, and integration into the university community.

REFERENCES

Astin, A. W. (1993). *What matters in college: Four critical years revisited.* San Francisco: Jossey-Bass.

Astin, A. W. (1996). Involvement in learning revisited: Lessons we have learned. *Journal of College Student Development, 37*(2), 123–134.

Astin, A. W. (1997). How "good" is your institution's retention rate? *Research in Higher Education, 38*(6), 647–658.

Austin, D. (2003). The role of family influence on student success. In J. A. Ward-Roof & C. Hatch (Eds.), *Designing successful transitions: A guide for orientating students to college* (Monograph No. 13, 2nd ed., pp. 137–163). Columbia: University of South Carolina, National Resource Center for the Freshman Year Experience and Students in Transition.

Berger, J. B., & Milem, J. F. (1999). The role of student involvement and perceptions of integration in a causal model of student persistence. *Research in Higher Education, 40*(6), 641–664.

Cawthon, T. W., & Miller, M. (2003). Today's students an their impact on orientation and first-year programs. In J. A. Ward-Roof & C. Hatch (Eds.), *Designing successful transitions: A guide for orientating students to college* (Monograph No. 13, 2nd ed., pp. 1–13). Columbia: University of South Carolina. National Resource Center for the Freshman Year Experience and Students in Transition.

Council for the Advancement of Standards for Student Services/Development Programs. (2001). Student Orientation CAS Standards and Guidelines. In J. A. Ward-Roof & C. Hatch (Eds.), *Designing successful transitions: A guide for orientating students to college* (Monograph No. 13, 2nd ed., pp. 197–204). Columbia: National Resource Center for the Freshman Year Experience, University of South Carolina.

Devlin, A. S. (1996). Survival skills training during freshman orientation: Its role in college adjustment. *Journal of College Student Development, 37*(3), 324–334.

Fox, L., Zakely, J., Morris, R., & Jundt, M. (1993). Orientation as a catalyst: Effective retention through academic and social integration. In M. L. Upcraft (Ed.), *Designing successful transitions: A guide for orientating students to college* (Monograph No. 13, pp. 49–59). Columbia: National Resource Center for the Freshman Year Experience, University of South Carolina.

Gardener, J. N., & Hansen, D. A. (1993). Perspectives on the future of orientation. In M. L. Upcraft (Ed.), *Designing successful transitions: A guide for orientating students to college* (Monograph No. 13, pp. 183–194). Columbia: National Resource Center for the Freshman Year Experience, University of South Carolina.

Greenlaw, H. S., Anliker, M. E., & Barker, S. J. (1997). Orientation: A student affairs or academic affairs function? *NASPA Journal, 34*, 303–313.

Howe, N., & Strauss, W. (2000). *Millennials Rising.* New York: Random House.

Jacobs, B., & With, E. (2002). Orientation's role in addressing the developmental stages of parents. *Journal of College Orientation and Transition, 9*(2), 37–43.

Johnson, D. B. (2002). *Student persistence: A study of student pre-enrollment factors and freshman to sophomore student persistence at a public university.* Unpublished doctoral dissertation, University of Alabama.

Levitz, R., & Noel, L. (1989). Connecting students to institutions: Keys to retention and success. In M. L. Upcraft & J. N. Gardner (Eds.), *The freshman year experience: Helping students survive and succeed in college* (pp. 65–81). San Francisco: Jossey-Bass.

Pascarella, E. T., Edison, M., Hagedorn, L. S., Nora, A., & Terenzini, P. (1996). Influences on students' internal locus of attribution for academic success in the first year of college. *Research in Higher Education, 37*(6), 731–755.

Perigo, D. J., & Upcraft, M. L. (1989). Orientation programs. In M. L. Upcraft & J. N. Gardner (Eds.), *The freshman year experience: Helping students survive and succeed in college* (pp. 82–94). San Francisco: Jossey-Bass.

Terenzini, P. T., Springer, L., Yaeger, P. M., Pascarella, E. T., & Nora, A. (1996). First generation college students: Characteristics, experiences, and cognitive development. *Research in Higher Education, 37*(1), 1–21.

Tinto, V. (1993). *Leaving college: Rethinking the causes and cures of student attrition* (2nd ed.). Chicago: University of Chicago Press.

Upcraft, M. L., & Gardner, J. N. (Eds.). (1989). *The freshman year experience: Helping students survive and succeed in college.* San Francisco: Jossey-Bass.

Ward-Roof, J. A. (2003). *A study of transfer students' grade point ratio, gender, ethnicity, number of hours transferred/academic status, college enrolled, transfer institution, and age.* Unpublished doctoral dissertation, Clemson University.

Ward-Roof, J. A., & Hatch, C. (2003). *Designing successful transitions: A guide for orienting students to college* (Monograph No. 13, 2nd ed.). Columbia: National Resource Center for the Freshman Year Experience, University of South Carolina.

ATTACHMENT A

About The NCAA—The National Collegiate Athletic Association (NCAA) is a voluntary organization through which the nation's colleges and universities govern their athletics programs. It is comprised of institutions, conferences, organizations, and individuals committed to the best interests, education, and athletics participation of student-athletes. This section of the website contains more details about the Association, its goals and members, and corporate partnerships that help support programs for student-athletes.

ATTACHMENT B—NCAA CLEARINGHOUSE
https://web1.ncaa.org/eligibilitycenter/common/

All prospective student-athletes must complete the amateurism certification questionnaire. If you are looking to enroll fall 2008, you will need to login and sign the 10.1 statement now.

(If you enrolled full time in a Division I or II institution prior to 2007, you do not need to complete the amateurism questions.)

Student Release Form (U.S.)

In order to participate in athletics and receive athletically based financial aid, you must register with the NCAA Eligibility Center and meet academic and amateurism eligibility standards. In order to register with the eligibility center, you must have a valid U.S. Social Security number and a MasterCard, Visa, American Express, or Discover (debit or credit) card. If you do not have a credit or debit card, you may register using electronic check (eCheck). If you received a fee waiver for the ACT or SAT exam and are requesting a waiver of the eligibility center fee, you may indicate this in Section VII. NOTE that your registration will not be processed until the eligibility center receives a fee waiver confirmation from your high school counselor. If you are seeking a fee waiver, you should talk to your high school counselor to determine if you are eligible for the fee waiver. If so, your counselor will need to submit a fee waiver confirmation for you. High school counselors who have been issued a secure PIN may submit such confirmations through the High School Administrators section of the website.

Important Note:

Transcripts and test scores must be sent directly to the eligibility center. These documents cannot be faxed or submitted online. There are many reasons why a student's academic document could be determined to be "unofficial" and therefore unacceptable for eligibility center purposes. If a document is not received in an official high school envelope or is received with the student's return address, this document could be marked as "unofficial." "Official" high school documents must be received in an envelope easily determined to be from the school and on high school stationery. Test scores must come to the eligibility center directly from the testing agencies (selection of the eligibility center can be made using code "9999"). Please note that Student Score Reports and test scores taken from a Student Score Report cannot be used by the eligibility center.

Ethical Obligation

I understand it is my responsibility to be honest and provide accurate and complete personal, academic, and athletics participation information to the Eligibility Center, LLC ("NCAA Eligibility Center") and the National Collegiate Athletic Association ("NCAA") and to provide updated information through the date of my initial full-time enrollment at a college or university. I understand that knowingly furnishing the NCAA Eligibility Center, the NCAA, or any NCAA member institution with false or misleading information or omitting information concerning my athletics participation and/or academic credentials may result in a violation of the NCAA ethical conduct rules and could result in violations including my permanent ineligibility to participate in intercollegiate athletics at an NCAA member institution.

ATTACHMENT C

http://www.ncaa.org/wps/wcm/connect/resources/file/eb1afe0c529230b/
Quick_Reference_Sheet_for_IE_Standards-5-2-08.pdf?MOD=AJPERES

NCAA FRESHMAN-ELIGIBILITY STANDARDS QUICK REFERENCE SHEET

KNOW THE RULES:

Core Courses

- **NCAA Division I requires 16 core courses as of August 1, 2008.** This rule applies to any student first entering any Division I college or university on or after August 1, 2008. See the chart below for the breakdown of this 16 core-course requirement.
- **NCAA Division II requires 14 core courses.** See the breakdown of core-course requirements below. Please note, Division II will require 16 core courses beginning August 1, 2013.

Test Scores

- **Division I** has a sliding scale for test score and grade-point average. The sliding scale for those requirements is shown on page two of this sheet.
- **Division II** has a minimum SAT score requirement of 820 or an ACT sum score of 68.
- The SAT score used for NCAA purposes includes **only** the critical reading and math sections. The writing section of the SAT is not used.
- The ACT score used for NCAA purposes is a **sum** of the four sections on the ACT: English, mathematics, reading and science.
- **All SAT and ACT scores must be reported directly to the NCAA Eligibility Center by the testing agency. Test scores that appear on transcripts will not be used. When registering for the SAT or ACT, use the Eligibility Center code of 9999 to make sure the score is reported to the Eligibility Center.**

Grade-Point Average

- Only core courses are used in the calculation of the grade-point average.
- **Be sure** to look at your high school's list of NCAA-approved core courses on the Eligibility Center's Web site to make certain that courses being taken have been approved as core courses. The Web site is www.ncaaclearinghouse.net.
- **Division I** grade-point-average requirements are listed on page two of this sheet.
- **The Division II** grade-point-average requirement is a minimum of 2.000.

DIVISION I 16 Core-Course Rule	DIVISION II 14 Core-Course Rule
16 Core Courses:	**14 Core Courses:**
4 years of English.	3 years of English.
3 years of mathematics (Algebra I or higher).	2 years of mathematics (Algebra I or higher).
2 years of natural/physical science (1 year of lab if offered by high school).	2 years of natural/physical science (1 year of lab if offered by high school).
1 year of additional English, mathematics or natural/physical science.	2 years of additional English, mathematics or natural/physical science.
2 years of social science.	2 years of social science.
4 years of additional courses (from any area above, foreign language or nondoctrinal religion/philosophy).	3 years of additional courses (from any area above, foreign language or nondoctrinal religion/philosophy).

PLEASE NOTE: Beginning August 1, 2013, students planning to attend an NCAA Division II institution will be required to complete 16 core courses.

OTHER IMPORTANT INFORMATION

- Division II has no sliding scale. The minimum core grade-point average is 2.000. The minimum SAT score is 820 (verbal and math sections only) and the minimum ACT sum score is 68.

- 14 core courses are currently required for Division II. However, beginning 2013, students will be required to complete 16 core courses.

- 16 core courses are required for Division I.

- The SAT combined score is based on the verbal and math sections only. The writing section will not be used.

- SAT and ACT scores must be reported directly to the Eligibility Center from the testing agency. Scores on transcripts will not be used.

- Students enrolling at an NCAA Division I or II institution for the first time need to also complete the amateurism questionnaire through the Eligibility Center Web site. Students need to request final amateurism certification prior to enrollment.

ATTACHMENT D
STUDENT-ATHLETE, PERSONAL WELFARE

Athletes face even more personal and physical hazards than the average college student. Below are links to resources and programs that the NCAA conducts to help student-athletes stay healthy and make the proper choices about nutrition and drugs.

Health & Nutrition

- Health & Safety
- Nutrition & Performance
- Drug Testing
- Injury Surveillance System

Programs

- Student-Athlete Insurance Programs
- CHAMPS/Life Skills Program

PART II

TYPES OF STUDENT-ATHLETES AND THEIR IDENTITIES

CHAPTER 7

PROMOTING STUDENT-ATHLETE MENTAL HEALTH

The Role of Campus Counseling Services

Daniel B. Kissinger
University of Arkansas

Joshua C. Watson
Mississippi State University–Meridian

Intercollegiate athletics have long played an important role in defining the campus culture at many colleges and universities. In addition to providing students with the opportunity to further develop their athletic skills, they also help foster school pride among the student body and aid in recruiting efforts with prospective students. According to the National Collegiate Athletic Association (NCAA; 2008), over 360,000 student-athletes participate in 23 sanctioned sports at 1,033 member schools. For the men and women who compete in these athletic programs, their participation can simultaneously be a most rewarding and most stressful endeavor. As a result, college counselors and mental health professionals should be cognizant of the

College Student-Athletes: Challenges, Opportunities, and Policy Implications, pages 93–108
Copyright © 2009 by Information Age Publishing

potential effects athletic participation may have on the mental health of student-athletes.

In addition to managing many of the same academic, emotional, and personal goals and challenges as other college students, student-athletes also must manage several unique challenges associated with their athletic participation (Broughton & Neyer, 2001). Among these challenges, the most taxing may be balancing the dual roles of student and athlete. Discussing the specific challenges that student-athletes face, William Parham (1993) noted that the time and effort needed to be successful in both athletics and academics tests the mental and physical stamina of even the most well-balanced and committed student-athlete. While striving to meet such academic demands as attending class, completing homework assignments, meeting with tutors, and attending study halls, it is not uncommon for student-athletes to spend an additional 20 or more hours per week practicing and competing in their chosen sport. For some student-athletes, the successful balancing of these multiple responsibilities proves to be too much to handle, often leaving them more susceptible to mental and physical distress (Etzel, 1989). In fact, research suggests that the percentage of student-athletes who experience psychological issues that might warrant a need for professional counseling are actually greater than most campuswide averages (Watson & Kissinger, 2007).

STUDENT-ATHLETES AND COUNSELING SERVICES

Despite the apparent need for counseling services, campus counseling services are often underutilized by the student-athlete population. Historically, student-athletes have been hesitant to seek help from traditional campus sources such as counselors and support services personnel (Brewer, Van Raalte, Petipas, Bachman, & Weinhold, 1998). Instead of seeking professional help, student-athletes are more apt to turn to coaches, teammates, family, and friends for solace and advice (Selby, Weinstein, & Bird, 1990). Both anecdotal and research evidence suggest that a number of factors may play a role in determining whether or not a student-athlete will seek the services of a counseling professional.

Win-at-All Costs Philosophy

Many student-athletes have functioned throughout their athletic careers under the assumption that winning and peak performance are the ultimate goals of athletic competition. This notion is reinforced by the fact that student-athletes are rewarded for their accomplishments on the playing field.

To keep success at the forefront, student-athletes often condition themselves with such axioms as "no pain, no gain," and "there is no *I* in team" throughout their athletic careers. Given these attitudes, it is not hard to see how many might be compelled to view help-seeking as a sign of weakness. For student-athletes who are rewarded for their accomplishments on the playing field, admitting personal needs or issues could conceivably damage their chances to succeed by weakening their self-efficacy in their ability to perform, diminishing the level of trust established with their teammates, reducing playing time, or weakening their coach's confidence in their ability to perform (Etzel, Pinkney, & Hinkle, 1994). As a result, many will develop a sense of rugged individuality and persevere in striving for team goals rather than addressing individual problems and issues. As long as the personal problems do not impact their athletic performance, they are content to ignore their existence.

Social Stigma

For most students, seeking help is largely an anonymous act. This may not be so simple, however, for the highly recognized student-athlete (Etzel, Ferrante, & Pinkney, 1991). On many college campuses, particularly those where athletic programs are a major part of the campus culture, student-athletes enjoy a sense of "celebrity status" and may not want to be seen at a counseling center for fear it may jeopardize their image by revealing a perceived need for help (Etzel et al., 1991). In a study of students' attitudes and expectations about sport psychology (Linder, Pillow, & Reno, 1989), male and female undergraduate students rated case study athletes lower in terms of prestige if they were said to be seeking counseling services. When elite athletes were surveyed, they reported a reluctance to seek help because they perceived it as an act only for individuals with severe psychological disturbances (Martin, 1998). Therefore, student-athletes may rationalize that potential benefits of seeking help are less than negative consequences of a tarnished image and, subsequently, do not seek counseling services.

Counseling Misconceptions

A significant factor in student-athletes' hesitancy to seek counseling services may be their misconceptions of what exactly counseling services entail. In many accounts, student-athletes often report being unfamiliar with counseling and find it difficult to conceptualize what their participation in a counseling relationship might involve. Their perceptions of professional counseling services are often formed based on information from friends, teammates, and the popular media. In a 2001 study, Maniar, Curry, Sommers-Flanagan, and Walsh concluded that student-athletes generally expect counseling to be focused mainly on pathological issues. In other words, they see counseling as being reserved solely for the psychologically disturbed (Ravizza, 1988) and are afraid that they will simply be labeled and medicated.

One of the best ways to counteract these potential barriers to help-seeking behavior is education. College counselors and mental health professionals can take a proactive approach and help athletic departments, coaches, team officials, and the student-athletes themselves gain a better understanding of what counseling is and how it can be personally useful. By seeing how counseling could potentially help them achieve greater success both on the court/field and in the classroom, student-athletes may become more receptive to the idea of accessing available campus counseling services.

In addition, college counselors and mental health professionals also should seek to educate themselves on the specific challenges of student-athletes. As Greenspan and Anderson (1995) suggested, student-athletes may feel uncomfortable seeking help outside of the athletic department from service providers who may not understand special concerns, needs, and pressures faced by student-athletes. This assumption appears to be supported by Broughton and Neyer's (2001) study, which found that a counselor having knowledge of sports enhanced the relationship between counselor and student-athlete. To this end, college counselors and mental health professionals who anticipate working with this population should make it a priority to become familiar with the specific challenges college student-athletes face, the demands and requirements associated with their sport participation, and the operating structure of the institution's athletic department. This knowledge of the athletic system will allow them to more comprehensively and accurately conceptualize student-athlete issues (Fletcher, Benshoff, & Richburg, 2003).

Substance Use and Abuse

Recent studies have suggested that a significant proportion of college students are regular consumers of alcohol. According to O'Malley and Johnson (2002), a review of several national data sets related to alcohol consumption on college campuses indicates that 70% of students reported using alcohol in the past month, with 40% reporting multiple episodes of binge drinking in the same period. While these statistics may seem staggering, additional research suggests that they may be even higher for college student-athletes

(Hildebrand, Johnson, Bogle, 2001; Wilson, Pritchard, & Schaffer, 2004). While a definitive causal relationship between alcohol consumption and athletic participation has not been made, several researchers have suggested two preliminary hypotheses regarding how participation in sports may place college student-athletes at a greater risk for developing alcohol-related problems (O'Brien & Lyons, 2000; Tricker, Cook, & McGuire, 1989).

One hypothesis is that college student-athletes find themselves in a pressure-packed situation (Damm, 1991). They are asked to maintain a high level of performance, both athletically and academically, all under the constant scrutiny of coaches, teammates, fans, and the media. In these situations, athletes are in a no-win position (Axthelm, 1988). The pressures they feel are typically more than they can developmentally handle, and as a result they turn to alcohol to ease the burden of stress. Another hypothesis highlights the fact that college student-athletes are overly exposed to social settings that promote alcohol use (Stainback, 1997). Athletes travel frequently and, through their status as athletes, may gain access to settings not available to typical college students. Regardless of the reason for alcohol consumption, college student-athletes continue to be at risk for developing alcohol-related problems (Stainback, 1997). Further, reports on the use and abuse of alcohol and drugs by student-athletes are becoming more abundant and are beginning to permeate the national media (Overman & Terry, 1991). As a result, counseling professionals must become aware of the warning signs of potential substance abuse issues in college-athletes.

Eating Disorders

Another issue that athletic participation might exacerbate for many college student-athletes is eating disorders. At one time or another, most athletes, male and female, have dealt with weight management concerns in their careers (Swoap & Murphy, 1995). With increasing pressure to make a specific weight class, appear attractive for judges, or to optimize performance, for some athletes, their focus on weight management becomes obsessive and eating-disordered behaviors develop. As a result, it has become increasingly important for college counselors to be cognizant of these issues when working with college student-athletes.

According to Petrie and Rogers (2001, cited in Sanford-Martens et al., 2005, p. 79), interest in both the incidence and prevention of eating disorders among both male and female college student-athletes has increased significantly during the past two decades. In this time, several empirical studies have been conducted to examine the occurrence of eating-disordered behaviors in student-athletes. To date, the results of these studies have been inconclusive. For every study reporting that student-athletes are at a greater risk for developing eating disorders (e.g., DiBartolo & Shaffer, 2002; Dick, 1991), another exists showing that student-athletes are at no greater risk for developing eating disorders than the general college population (e.g., Ashley, Smith, Robinson, & Richardson, 1996; Warren, Stanton, & Blessing, 1990). Although results have been mixed, assessing for the presence of these disorders when working with college student-athletes is still suggested.

While the traditional belief has been that athletes in nonelite, non-weight-dependent sports would be more likely to report healthier eating behaviors and attitudes toward eating than their peers in elite or weight-dependent sports, Dick (1991) cautions that this is not always the case. He suggests that no sport or individual should be considered "exempt" from developing an eating disorder. In fact, counselors should look more to the individual athlete's emotional and psychological stability than to the sport in which they participate. For example, a relationship has been found between perfectionism and personal need for high achievement and the development of eating-disordered behaviors (Johnson, 1994). Additionally, those athletes who reported feeling the most distress due to the increased pressures from their coaches to improve their performance were also more likely to develop eating-disordered behaviors (Petrie, 1996). To assess for these and other related issues, counselors should seek to identify what role athletic participation plays in the life of the athlete and how they deal with the inevitable stress it creates. They also should make a concerted effort to focus on deemphasizing body weight, increasing nutritional education, and developing a healthy weight management regimen for their athletic clients.

Anxiety and Stress-Related Disorders

Research illustrates a long list of sports-related stressors. Among them are heightened competition levels, physical conditioning and performance pressures such as fear of failure, feelings of inadequacy, relationships with athletic personnel and teammates, balancing academic and athletic demands, and burnout, time management, and depression (Broughton & Neyer, 2001; Buceta, 1985; Ferrante, Etzel, & Lantz, 1996; Gould, Horn, & Spreeman, 1983; Murray, 1997; Parham, 1993; Scanlan & Passer, 1978). Although less apparent to those outside the athletic realm, athletic injuries (Anshel et al., 1997) and transitioning away from competitive athletics are often sources of considerable distress (Richards & Aries, 1999; Stone & Strange, 1989). Conversely, high injury rates have also been linked to positive life events (Hanson, McCullagh, & Tonymon, 1992; Petrie, 1993). Sports medicine professionals have noted the following primary associations between stress, anxiety, and athletic injury: (1) injury as a source ⌐f stress; (2) stress as a precursor to injury; (3) the interrelationship among stress, anxiety, and injury; and (4) stress and anxiety management interventions. Whatever the context, college counselors must be sensitive to not only the symptoms of anxiety and stress among student-athletes, but also of the situational and contextual factors specific to their role as student-athlete that could lead to significant levels of anxiety.

Counselors working with student-athletes should also be particularly aware of and responsive to the potential effects of anxiety on sports performance. In the sports psychology literature, the effects of anxiety on sport performance is of particular interest (Hanin, 2000), especially as it relates to competitive anxiety. Competitive anxiety is seen as being grounded in the multidimensional anxiety theory (Martens, Burton, Vealey, Bump, & Smith, 1990). This theory holds that competitive anxiety consists of cognitive anxiety and somatic anxiety (Martens, Vealy, & Burton, 1990), both of which are thought to be influenced by prior experiences and impact performance differently. In the case of cognitive anxiety, evaluative cues and negative feedback (Davidson & Schwartz, 1976; Martens et al., 1990) can lead to "a person's negative thoughts, concerns about performance, disrupted attention, and inability to concentrate" (Krane & Greenleaf, 1999, p. 262) and imperil performance (Bird & Horn, 1990; Martens et al., 1990). Cognitive anxiety has also been associated with sport-specific variables such as weak performances, negative individual and team performance expectations, lack of perceived readiness for competition, and negative attitudes toward prior performances and negative verbal feedback (Alexander & Krane, 199; Caruso, Dzewaltowski, Gil, & McElroy, 1990; Jones, Swain, & Cale, 1990; Krane, Williams, & Feltz, 1992, as cited in Krane & Greenleaf, 1999).

Being uninformed or misinformed about the stressors inherent in the athletic realm could lead to ill-timed therapeutic interventions that, in some cases, could disrupt adaptive levels of anxiety or stress that could lead to better athletic performances. As an example, certain levels of distressed cognitive patterns may actually facilitate optimal athletic performances (McKay, Selig, Carlson, & Morris, 1997) among some elite college athletes. Thus, concerns about performance anxiety must consider both the potential negative and positive effects of anxiety in order to prevent implementing interventions that could diminish adaptive levels of cognitive dissonance.

Somatic anxiety, on the other hand, is marked by an unhealthy focus on physiological symptoms and an increased negative arousal state that may include symptoms such as increased heart rate, sweating, or stomach butterflies (Davidson & Schwartz, 1976; Martens et al., 1990). Like cognitive anxiety, optimal levels of somatic anxiety may enhance performance, while the inverse is true when levels of somatic anxiety become unpalatable (Krante, Joyce, & Rafeld, 1994). Because individualized experiences of cognitive and somatic anxiety are the norm, consideration of the individual athlete's interpretation of the anxiety symptoms (Jones et al., 1993) is essential. For example, elite athletes may conceptualize cognitive and somatic anxiety as more facilitative than their less-competitive peers (Jones, Hanton, & Swain, 1994). As a result, constant reassessment of the levels of cognitive and somatic anxiety symptoms is needed in order to discern adaptive from maladaptive levels of anxiety for each college athlete.

Perfectionism, another correlate of competitive anxiety, is another common theme in therapeutic settings and certainly not an uncommon trait among elite college athletes. In the sports literature, perfectionism is characterized as a "... striving for flawlessness and setting excessively high standards for performance" (Stoeber, Otto, Pescheck, Becker, & Stoll, 2007, p. 959) accompanied by an overly critical self-definition. Researchers (Stoeber & Otto, 2006) contend that perfectionism should be further subdivided into positive and negative dimensions, with the positive dimension encompassing the healthy, adaptive (Gould, Dieffenbach, & Moffett, 2002) components of perfectionism while the negative dimension is a source of anxiety resulting from an unhealthy and maladaptive (Flett & Hewitt, 2005) focus on fears, doubts, and unhealthy expectations (Bieling, Israeli, & Antony, 2004; Hill et al., 2004; Suddarth & Slaney, 2001, as cited in Stoeber et al., 2007).

While college counselors are well acquainted with perfectionism among their clientele, perfectionism within elite athletic circles may constitute new ground for mental health professionals. What is perhaps of primary importance when working with a student-athlete with perfectionist traits is research that shows that these traits of perfectionism, when properly balanced, can enhance self-confidence and lead to improved athletic performances (DiBartolo, Frost, Change, LaSota, & Grills, 2004; Stoeber & Otto, 2006). Taken in combination with prior studies on perfectionism and competitive anxiety, these results illuminate the need to focus independently on each student-athlete's experience of anxiety. Ultimately, the ability to apply knowledge of these traits to the realm of competitive sport is crucial to understanding the student-athlete's subjective experience. Emphasizing an understanding of the unique traits of competitive anxiety, particularly at the outset of treatment, may also help diminish the belief among student-athletes that mental health professionals are unfamiliar with the unique blend of stressors they face (Greenspan & Anderson, 1995).

Targeted stress and anxiety management programs for student-athletes have also been developed that integrate psychological, philosophical, and vocational (Krace & Brown, 1989) dimensions. From the behavioral school, modeling (Flint, 1993) and behavioral rehearsal (Palmer & Dryden, 1995)

have been suggested for reducing a student-athlete's stress leve'
models and strategies shown to facilitate improved athletic peɪ ₁ᵤ
as well as diminish anxiety levels include thought stopping (Buceta, 1985),
positive self-talk (Williams & Leffingwell, 1996), and restructuring distorted
cognitions (Williams & Leffingwell, 1996). Sports medicine scholars have
also shown that stress management programs can help lower the stress levels
of athletes (Mace & Caroll, 1985), improve athletic performance (Crocker,
Alderman, & Smith, 1988), increase pain tolerance among athletes (Pen
& Fisher, 1994), and decrease levels of cognitive and somatic anxiety while
raising self-confidence (Maynard & Cotton, 1993; Maynard, Hemmings, &
Warwick-Evans, 1995; Maynard, Smith, & Warwick-Evans, 1995). Suggestions for reducing somatic anxiety, on the other hand, are geared toward
relaxation techniques such as deep breathing and progressive relaxation.

Sports Injuries

The intensity of competitive college athletics can leave student-athletes
vulnerable to a range of illnesses and injuries (Yukelson & Murphy, 1993)
involving cognitive, affective, and behavioral dimensions (Ray & Wiese-
Bjornstal, 1999, p. 276). It should be noted, however, that the degree of
the impact of a sports injury remains entirely subjective. For example, in
the case of a catastrophic sports injury, it is imperative that mental health
professionals recognize the potential for student-athletes to experience the
full range of the grief response cycle (Ray & Wiese-Bjornstal, 1999). A clear
example of the need to monitor the psychological recovery process of an
injury is perhaps best illustrated by Price's (1995) statement referring to
the recovery status of former tennis great Monica Seles, who was attacked
by a knife-wielding spectator as she competed in a tournament. According
to Price, "Her body came back first. It was the easiest part to rebuild" (p. 24,
as cited in Asken, 1999). However, injuries or illnesses as seemingly mun-
dane as sprained ankles or a case of the flu may be considered by student-
athletes as a serious blow to their ability to maintain their conditioning and
maintain their desired position on the team. Similar to that experienced
by one who has suffered a season- or career-ending injury, others may feel
that they have let their teammates down by not being able to perform. The
repercussions of a sports injury may also extend well beyond the afflict-
ed student-athlete and impact teammates, coaches, advisors, faculty, and
friends and family (Ray & Wiese-Bjornstal, 1999) directly and indirectly. In
addition to treating physical and emotional dimensions of the injury, one
factor that may be of considerable benefit when seeking to understand a
student-athlete's subjective response to an injury or illness is the construct
of athletic identity.

Athletic Identity

The notion that college athletes experience identity problems is not new to the sports literature (Nelson, 1983; Parham, 1993; Petipas & Champagne, 1988). However, the concept and implications of athletic identity specifically may be unknown or rarely considered to many mental health professionals. Athletic identity, or the degree to which identity is tied to the athletic persona (Brewer, 1993), has been linked to several factors that could have considerable implications for the personal and athletic success of college athletes. High degrees of athletic identity have been associated with heightened athletic performances, positive training experiences, commitment to athletic performances, and broadened social networks (Horton & Mack, 2000) and relationships (Anderson, 2004). Conversely, high levels of athletic identity have been linked to diminished academic interest (Cornelius, 1995) and an increased susceptibility to depression (Brewer, 1993) and performance-enhancing drugs (Cornelius, 1995). These examples illustrate the importance of assessing for levels of athletic identity among student-athletes presenting for counseling services.

The inclusion of athletic identity into the clinical assessment of student-athletes adds to the importance of focusing interventions and treatment plans on the holistic wellness of the student-athlete. This allows for the development of an identity that honors, but does not foreclose around, one's identity as an athlete (Wiese-Bjornstal & Shaffer, 1999). Furthermore, because of the stigma of mental health in athletics, mental health professionals should also be sensitive to the notion that even among a group of students known to be suspicious of mental health practitioners, resistance to seeking out mental health services may be particularly pronounced among student-athletes with heightened levels of athletic identity. In such cases, demystifying the counseling process and showing sensitivity to student-athlete issues could help reduce their reluctance to engage in meaningful dialogue with a mental health professional. Furthermore, since athletes often look to others for affirmation of their athletic identity (Brewer, Van Raalte, & Linder, 1993), the nonjudgmental, trusting elements inherent in a strong therapeutic relationship could provide the emotional and psychological security necessary for an in-depth exploration of the parameters of one's identity and any relationship therein regarding their specific experiences as a student-athlete.

Sensitivity to the student-athlete's level of athletic identity should remain central to any case conceptualization involving a college athlete (and students heavily involved in recreational/intramural sports) given the centrality of sports to their lives and, in many cases, their core identity. For example, awareness of a student-athlete's overcommitment to an athletic identity could be particularly useful information in cases where perfectionist traits are trained predominantly on athletics (Dunn, Gotwals, & Dunn, 2005). In doing so, individualized treatment plans can be developed that address their perfectionism within the broader concept of their core identity as an athlete. Not addressing the student-athlete's core athletic identity would seem a recipe for therapeutic interventions that are less likely to facilitate self-understanding nor lead to a positive return of health.

Additional Factors for Consideration

The parameters of this chapter prohibit us from addressing the full continuum of factors that could impact the mental health concerns experienced by college athletes. Nevertheless, several additional factors that should be duly noted. For example, the (eventually) discredited rape allegations against members of Duke University's lacrosse team and radio personality Don Imus's racially charged description of Rutgers University's women's basketball team as "nappy-headed ho's" are recent examples of how quickly student-athletes can be thrust into the glare of the national media spotlight. In such circumstances, it is not hard to imagine why student-athletes might avoid more scrutiny by being seen entering the campus counseling center, particularly given the well-established stigma against mental illness in athletic circles (Linder, Brewer, Van Raalte, & Delange, 1991). Another example of media influence in athletics involves the use of feminine and heterosexual descriptors ahead of athleticism when addressing female athletes, while depictions of male athletes primarily center on their athletic credentials (Boutilier & SanGiovanni, 1983). These descriptions help perpetuate heterosexism and homophobia that remains embedded in American society. In the sports realm, these views manifest when female athletes continually battle the bias that their athletic participation predicts their sexual orientation (Griffin, 1994, 1998; Theberge & Birrell, 1994) or that homosexuality is incongruent with the ideal male athlete (Griffin, 1998).

While relational issues surface often in athletics, they are often conceptualized within the context of the potential harm/benefit to athletic success. In reality, interpersonal relationships are, to varying degrees, an important dimension of a student-athlete's total phenomenological experience. Moreover, attention to the notion of an athletic support system is particularly relevant when considering the physical and psychological health of student-athletes given that athletic teams, in many ways, are analogous in form and function to families (Ray & Wiese-Bjornstal, 1999). For instance, studies indicate that a coach's interpersonal style and behavior are linked to an athlete's psychological, emotional, and physical reaction to their overall athletic experience (Duda, 2001; Smoll & Smith, 2002). As such, establishing trusting relationships and maintaining open communication lines with sports medicine professionals should be a priority of all college counseling personnel given that, in particular, trainers are often "ideally situated to assist with the psychological as well as physical sequelae of injury" (Ford & Gordon, 1998, p. 80).

Sexual health issues have also been found to be a concern of student-athletes, despite their reluctance to address them overtly (Flint, 1999). In terms of sexually based offenses, for example, social taboos and athletic idioms may diminish the potential that student-athletes would disclose abusive behaviors perpetrated by individuals inside and outside their athletic spheres of influence (Brackenridge, 1997). There is also a need to address sexual health issues among college athletes, particularly given the estimates that 19 million people between the ages of 15 and 24 are infected annually with sexually transmitted diseases (STDs) and infections (STIs) (United States Center for Disease Control and Prevention, 2004; Weinstock & Cates, 2004). Unfamiliarity with STDs and STIs, and/or a personal reluctance to examine their clinical implications, could leave student-athletes vulnerable to a litany of psychological (Dwyer & Neimann, 2002; Masters, Johnson, & Kolodny, 1995) and physical troubles (Ross, 1999) associated with STDs and STIs, including, for those formally diagnosed with an STD or STI, an increased susceptibility to HIV, the virus that causes AIDS (Clark, 1997).

Spirituality and religious issues could also be of considerable importance to a student-athlete's personal (i.e., psychological/emotional) and athletic success (Storch, Storch, Kolsky, & Silvestri, 2001). A recent study by Ridnour and Hammermeister (2008), for instance, found a link between higher scores of spiritual well-being and better athletic coping skills for sport performance. This led them to posit that, arguably, athletes with a stronger sense of the more narrowly defined view of spirituality possessed a stronger psychological constitution than those with a weaker sense of spiritual wellness. Hawks, Hull, Thalman, and Richins (1995) also suggested that athletes with a strong spiritual base tend to possess highly desirable traits for athletes such as trust, honesty, integrity, altruism, compassion, and service. What is perhaps most important to take away from this admittedly restricted review of the role of a particular spiritual and/or religious ideology in sport, however, is the need to consider these tenets within the context of a holistic framework that necessitates the inclusion of physical, emotional/psychological, and spiritual/religious dimensions to any clinical encounter and treatment plan.

Finally, mental health professionals need to have an understanding of specific indicators that suggest a student-athlete may be experiencing psychological distress. To that end, Petipas and Danish's (1995) set of criteria that was described for helping sports medicine professionals recognize high-risk athletes based on their presentation styles. In particular, sports medicine professionals are urged to remain sensitive to athletes who display any of the following behaviors: (1) excessive preoccupation with a quick return to their sport post injury; (2) denial of the negative effects of an injury; (3) expressions of guilt concerning their failure to contribute to the team, express arrogance about previous athletic success; (4) isolating or withdrawing from previous social support systems. When referrals to mental health issues are deemed necessary, the returning party should consider a number of issues for inclusion, including the clinician's theoretical orientation and financial and insurance considerations. Additional referral strategies by Glick and Horsfall (2001) have been slightly amended to fit the profile of the college athlete:

1. Appeal to the student-athlete's competitive nature of the athlete by reframing counseling as a "performance enhancement" strategy for the mind.
2. Distinguish between the needs of the "person" (i.e., student) and the "athlete."
3. Appeal to the student-athlete's self-interest by reframing the rationale for the counseling referral as an opportunity to address skill enhancement, quality of life, or financial status from a different perspective.
4. Work in partnership with consumer organizations such as Alcoholics Anonymous and/or Narcotics Anonymous (AA/NA) when necessary.
5. Recognize the importance of the therapeutic alliance for increasing the chances of compliance with the counseling referral and counseling professional.
6. Monitor "athletic envy" or hero worship by the professionals working with student-athletes (athletic, academic, faculty, administrative) that could diminish treatment efficacy.
7. Monitor for coercion.
8. Uphold a multidisciplinary and multicultural perspective.

CONCLUSION

While this chapter provides an overview of many of the issues, readers are urged to delve further into the empirical sports and counseling literature in order to gain the knowledge base necessary for working with this unique and often misunderstood subset of the college student population. Whether presenting with subclinical issues such as career concerns (Baille, 1993), personal competence (Parham, 1993), interpersonal problems (Parham, 1993), or clinical levels depression and anxiety (Brewer, Petipas, & Van Raalte, 1999), campus mental health professionals must be aware of the distinct challenges encountered by college athletes. In sum, the mental health needs of college athletes must remain a foundational consideration to any professional charged with their overall care and development.

REFERENCES

Ashley, C. D., Smith, J. F., Robinson, J. N., & Richardson, M. T. (1996). Disordered eating in female collegiate athletes and collegiate females in an advanced program of study: A preliminary investigation. *International Journal of Sport Nutrition, 6,* 391–401.

Axthelm, P. (1988, October 10). The doped-up games. *Newsweek,* pp. 54–56.

Boutilier, M. A., & SanGiovanni, L. (1983). *The sporting women.* Champaign, IL; Human Kinetics.

Brewer, B. W., Van Raalte, J. L., Petitpas, A. J., Bachman, A. D., & Weinhold, R. A. (1998). Newspaper portrayals of sport psychology in the United States, 1985–1993. *The Sport Psychologist, 12,* 89–94.

Broughton, E., & Neyer, M. (2001). *Advising and counseling student athletes* (New Directions for Student Services No. 93, pp. 47–53). San Francisco: Jossey-Bass.

Clark, J. R. (1997). Sexually transmitted diseases: Detection, differentiation, and treatment. *The Physician and Sportsmedicine, 25*(1).

Damm, J. (1991). Drugs and the college student-athlete. In E. F. Etzel, A. P. Ferrante, & J. W. Pinkney (Eds.), *Counseling college student-athletes: Issues and Interventions* (pp. 151–174). Morgantown, WV: Fitness Information Technology.

DiBartolo, P. M., & Shaffer, C. (2002). A comparison of female college athletes and nonathletes: Eating disorder symptomology and psychological well-being. *Journal of Sport and Exercise Psychology, 24,* 33–41.

Dick, R. W. (1991). Eating disorders in the NCAA athletics programs: Replication of a 1990 study. *NCAA Sports Sciences Education Newsletter,* pp. 3–4.

Duda, J. L. (2001). Achievement goal research in sport: Pushing the boundaries and Clarifying some misunderstandings. In G.C. Roberts (Ed.), *Advances in motivation in sport and exercise.* Champaign, IL: Human Kinetics.

Dwyer, T. F., & Niemann, S. H. (2002). Counseling and sexually transmitted diseases. In L. D. Burlew & D. Capuzzi (Eds.), *Sexuality counseling* (pp. 373–394). New York: Nova Science.

Etzel. E. (1989). *Life stress, locus-of-control and sport competition anxiety patterns of college student-athletes.* Unpublished doctoral dissertation, West Virginia University, Morgantown.

Etzel, E. F., Pinkney, J. W., & Hinkle, J. S. (1994). College student-athletes and needs assessment. In C. C. Thomas (Ed.), *Multicultural needs assessment for college and university student populations.* Springfield, IL: C.C. Thomas.

Etzel, E. F., Ferrante, A. P., & Pinkney, J. W. (Eds.). (1991). *Counseling college student athletes: Issues and interventions.* Morgantown, WV: Fitness Information Technology.

Fletcher, T. B., Benshoff, J. M., & Richburg, M. J. (2003). A systems approach to understanding and counseling college student-athletes. *Journal of College Counseling, 6*(1), 35–45.

Glick, J., & Horsfall, J. (2001). Psychiatric conditions in sports: Diagnosis, treatment, and quality of life. *The Physician and Sportsmedicine, 29*(8).

Greenspan, M., & Anderson, M. B. (1995). Providing psychological services to student athletes: A developmental psychology model. In S.M. Murphy (Ed.), *Sports psychology interventions* (pp. 177–191). Champaign, IL: Human Kinetics.

Griffin, P. (1998). *Strong women, deep closets: lesbians and homophobia in sport.* Champaign, IL: Human Kinetics.

Hawks, S. R., Hull, M., Thalman, R. L., & Richins, P. M., (1995). Review of spiritual health: Definition, role, and intervention strategies in health promotion. *American Journal of Health Promotion, 9,* 371–378.

Hildebrand, K. M., Johnson, D. J., & Bogle, K. (2001). Comparison of patterns of alcohol use between high and college athletes and nonathletes. *College Student Journal, 35,* 358–365.

Johnson, M. D. (2004). Disordered eating in active and athletic women. *Clinics in Sports Medicine, 13,* 355–369.

Linder, D. E., Brewer, B. W. Van Raalte, J. L., & Delange, N. (1991). A negative halo for athletes who consult sport psychologists: Replication and extension. *Journal of Sport and Exercise Psychology, 13,* 133–148.

Linder, D. E., Pillow, D., & Reno, R. (1989). Shrinking jocks: Derogation of athletes who consult a sport psychologist. *Journal of Sport & Exercise Psychology, 11,* 270–280.

Maniar, S. D., Curry, L. A., Sommers-Flanagan, J., & Walsh, J. A. (2001). Student-athlete preferences in seeking help when confronted with sport performance problems. *The Sport Psychologist, 15,* 215–223.

Martin, S. B. (1998). High school athletes' attitudes toward sport psychology services. *Journal of Applied Sport Psychology, 10,* 80.

Masters, W. H., Johnson, V. E., & Kolodny, R. C. (1995). *Human sexuality* (5th ed.). New York: HarperCollins.

National Collegiate Athletic Association. (2008). *NCAA membership statistics.* Retrieved September 2, 2008, from http://www.ncaa.org/wps/ncaa?ContentID=811

O'Brien, C. P., & Lyons, F. (2000). Alcohol and the athlete. *Sports Medicine, 29,* 295–300.

O'Malley, P. M., & Johnston, L. D. (2002). Epidemiology of alcohol and other drug use among American college students. *Journal of Studies on Alcohol, 14,* 23–39.

Overman, S. J., & Terry, T. (1991). Alcohol use and attitudes: A comparison of college athletes and nonathletes. *Journal of Drug Education, 21,* 107–117.

Parham, W. (1993). The intercollegiate athlete: A 1990's profile. *The Counseling Psychologist, 21,* 411–429.

Petrie, T. A. (1996). Differences between male and female college lean sport athletes, nonlean sport athletes, and non-athletes on behavioral and psychological indices of eating disorders. *Journal of Applied Sport Psychology, 8,* 218–230.

Ravizza, K. (1988). Gaining entry with athletic personnel for season-long consulting. *The Sport Psychologist, 2,* 243–254.

Sanford-Martens, T. C., Davidson, M. M., Yakushko, O. F., Martens, M. P., Hinton, P., & Beck, N. (2005). Clinical and subclinical eating disorders: An examination of collegiate athletes. *Journal of Applied Sport Psychology, 17,* 79–86.

Selby, R., Weinstein, H. M., & Bird, T. S. (1990). The health of university athletes: Attitudes, behaviors, and stressors. *Journal of American College Health, 39,* 11–18.

Smoll, F. L., & Smith, R. E. (2002). Coaching behavior research and intervention in youth sports. In F. L. Smoll & R. E. Smith (Eds.), Children and youth in sport: A biopsychological perspective (2nd ed., pp. 211–234). Dubuque, IA: Kendall/Hunt.

Stainback, R. D. (1997). *Alcohol and sport.* Champaign, IL: Human Kinetics.

Storch, J. B., Storch, E. A., Kolsky, A. R., & Silvestri, S. M. (2001). Religiosity of elite college athletes. *The Sport Psychologist, 15,* 346–351.

Swoap, R. A., & Murphy, S. M. (1995). Eating disorders and weight management in athletes. *Sport Psychology Interventions,* pp. 307–329.

Tricker, R., Cook, D. L., & McGuire, R. (1989). Issues related to drug abuse in college athletics: Athletes at risk. *The Sport Psychologist, 3,* 155–165.

Warren, B. J., Stanton, A. L., & Blessing, D. L. (1990). Disordered eating patterns in competitive female athletes. *International Journal of Eating Disorders, 9,* 565–569.

Watson, J. C., & Kissinger, D. B. (2007). Athletic participation and wellness: Implications for counseling college student-athletes. *Journal of College Counseling, 10,* 153–162.

Wilson, G. S., Pritchard, M. E., & Schaffer, J. (2004). Athletic status and drinking behavior in college students: The influence of gender and coping styles. *Journal of American College Health, 52,* 269–273.

CHAPTER 8

ATHLETICS IN COMMUNITY COLLEGES

A Primer

V. Barbara Bush
University of North Texas

Cindy Castañeda
Richland College, Dallas Community College District

Stephen G. Katsinas
David E. Hardy
University of Alabama

Most of the ever-increasing attention to intercollegiate athletics on the part of scholars (Bailey & Littleton, 1991; Gerdy, 2000; Sack & Staurowsky, 1998; Thelin, 1994; Zimbalist, 1999), media (Telander, 1996), national organizations (American Association of University Professors, 1999, 2002), and the Congress (General Accounting Office, 1992, 1996a, 1996b, 2001) has not been positive. Key issues include student-athlete graduation rates, governance, oversight, inappropriate payments to student-athletes by overzeal-

College Student-Athletes: Challenges, Opportunities, and Policy Implications, pages 109–121
Copyright © 2009 by Information Age Publishing
109

ous boosters, and the overall balance of intercollegiate athletics and the academic mission. The vast majority of scholarly, media, organizational, and congressional attention, however, has focused on the elite sports teams operated by large four-year universities participating in Division I of the National College Athletic Association (NCAA) (Castañeda, 2004). Calls to reform NCAA Division I have come from internal and external constituencies including the AAUP (1999, 2002), the Knight Commission on Intercollegiate Athletics (Knight Foundation, 1993), and at times, the NCAA itself (Dempsey, 2002). So although athletics clearly play an important role in America's community colleges, these institutions are not immune to violating rules for success, win games, and recruit key athletes, although these pressures are substantially lower than in many Division I athletic programs (Greene, 1981; Thornton, 1972).

LITERATURE REVIEW

This chapter presents a statistical profile of a component that has received little attention in the book-length treatments of community colleges. In his 1925 work, *The Junior College Movement,* Leonard V. Koos (1925) found that the larger the college, the larger the number of athletic teams. While Leland Medsker's 1960 book, *The Junior College: Progress and Prospects,* did not reference athletics, Fields's *The Community College Movement* (1962) and Thornton's *The Junior College Movement* (1972) both referenced athletics as an important student activity for participants and spectators. However, in their fifth edition of *The American Community College,* Arthur M. Cohen and Florence B. Brawer (2008) offered no empirical data on community college participation in athletics. The sole paragraph on athletics in this 566-page book reads as follows:

> Athletic activities vary widely. Some colleges field intercollegiate teams but nearly all offer intramural sports for interested students and even courses on sports activities. Clubs and ad hoc groups organized to engage in hiking, cycling, scuba diving, backpacking, and jogging have become widespread. Exercise classes open to staff members as well as students have also sprung up as the concern for physical fitness has grown among people of all ages. Aerobic dancing, swimming, and weightlifting have gained in popularity. In general, though, small percentages of students participate. (pp. 235–236)

Despite the low attention in book-length studies and treatments of community colleges, it is clear that intercollegiate athletics represent a very important student activity for public community colleges in the United States. Castañeda, Katsinas, and Hardy (2006, 2008) note that 72,558 student-athletes participated in community college–sponsored intercollegiate athletics in 2002–2003, of whom 26,698, or 37%, were female and 45,860, or 63%, were male. They conclude, "Intercollegiate athletics are a very important student activity for public community colleges in the United States generally, and for rural-serving community colleges specifically" (p. 97), suggesting strong ties between the institutions that host them, the students who participate in them, and the communities that support them.

METHOD

This chapter addresses the deficiency of national data on athletics at community colleges, drawing from a number of key sources. One primary source is Castañeda's 2004 dissertation, which drew on data from the Equity and Athletic Disclosure Act (EADA) to examine the prevalence of intercollegiate athletics at community colleges in 2002 (U.S. Department of Education, 2003). To further refine Castañeda's results, we employed the new 2005 Basic Classification of Associates Colleges released in February 2006 by the Carnegie Foundation for the Advancement of Teaching (http://www.carnegiefoundation.org/classifications/) to examine how participation in athletics is distributed across the categories of rural-, suburban-, and urban-serving community colleges.

The scope, organization, breadth, and penetration of intercollegiate athletics at American community colleges can be empirically assessed through data gathered from the EADA, initially passed in 1994 and incorporated into the Higher Education Act in 1996 and its subsequent reauthorizations. Under EADA, institutions receiving federal student aid under Title IV must prepare an annual report on student-athlete participation, staffing, and revenues for athletic teams by gender (U.S. Department of Education, 2004). In 2001, EADA began collecting its surveys online, and they are available at the U.S. Department of Education's website. Just 18 community colleges with intercollegiate athletics failed to submit EADA surveys in 2002–2003. Institutions that reported to both the Institutional Postsecondary Educational Data System (IPEDS) database in 2001 and EADA in 2003 were included in the analysis presented here. The new the 2005 Carnegie Basic Classifications presents seven "geographic" and four nongeographically based groupings of public two-year colleges. Our analysis here excludes Two-Year Under Four-Year, Primarily Baccalaureate Colleges, Baccalaureate Associates Colleges, and Special Use Institutions, as well as privately controlled two-year colleges including proprietary institutions. We believe that the use of EADA and IPEDS, analyzed through deployment of the new Carnegie Basic Classifications, reveals a more accurate picture of institutional and student participation in intercollegiate athletics at community colleges, to which attention is now turned.

COMMUNITY COLLEGE PARTICIPATION IN
INTERCOLLEGIATE ATHLETICS: FOCUS ON INSTITUTIONS

Classification and Participation

Table 8.1 shows that there are 860 identifiable districts and single campuses, and 1,552 identifiable individual campuses using the 2005 Carnegie Basic Classifications (Castañeda et al., 2006). In the IPEDS universe, there are 1,016 identifiable campuses. Table 8.1 shows 508 districts and 585 campuses under the Carnegie universe reporting to EADA and IPEDS participate in intercollegiate athletics. Of these 585 campuses, 318, or 54%, with intercollegiate athletics are located in settings defined by the Carnegie Basic Classifications as rural-serving, 151, or 18%, are suburban, and 116, or 20%, are urban. These percentages largely mirror the overall percentages of institutions in the Carnegie universe: Of the 860 indentifiable rural, suburban, and urban "geographic" community college districts, 64% are rural, 23% are suburban, and 13% are urban (Hardy & Katsinas, 2006). Additional evidence strongly suggests that these 318 rural-serving colleges use

TABLE 8.1   Districts and Campuses in the Carnegie Basic Classifications with Intercollegiate Athletics

Carnegie Classification	Number in population			Districts with Intercollegiate Athletics	Campuses with Intercollegiate Athletics
	Districts/ Single Campuses	Individual Campuses	IPEDS Identifiable Campuses		
Rural					
Small	140	206	167	52	54
Medium	303	499	330	170	170
Large	110	217	116	87	94
Rural subtotal	553	922	613	309	318
Suburban					
Single campus	122	122	122	78	84
Multi-campus	73	206	94	51	67
Suburban subtotal	195	328	216	129	151
Urban					
Single campus	44	44	44	24	25
Multi-campus	68	258	143	46	91
Urban subtotal	112	302	187	70	116
Grand total	860	1,552	1,016	508	585

Source: Castañeda, Katsinas, & Hardy (2006).

student-athletes as a vehicle to attract and enroll students to increase their full-time student enrollments (Castañeda, 2004; Castañeda et. al., 2006).

Table 8.2 shows participation by Associates Colleges in intercollegiate athletic associations in 2002–2003. Three intercollegiate athletic associations for community colleges account for roughly 95% of memberships in athletic associations. The largest of the three is the National Junior College Athletic Association (NJCAA), with members in 43 states (NJCAA, 2002). The next largest is the California Organization of Athletics (COA), which is limited to public community colleges in California. The third and smallest is the Northwest Athletic Association of Community Colleges (NWAACC), which includes representation primarily from Oregon and Washington, with one member from Idaho and two from British Columbia, Canada (NWAACC, 2004a, 2004b). The remaining 5% of community colleges with intercollegiate athletics, particularly in the northeast United States, participate in small intercollegiate college conferences not limited to community colleges. It is important that none of the three larger membership intercollegiate athletic conferences for community colleges covers all 50 states, as Table 8.2 indicates.

Table 8.3 shows that the three community college athletic associations sponsor a total of 19 sports. The sports that are offered vary by association, with the NJCAA and COA offering the greatest variety. The NJCAA member institutions offer 14 different men's and 11 different women's sports, compared to the COA, which offers 12 men's and 11 women's sports, and the NWACC, which offers 8 men's and 8 women's sports. The sports offered vary across the three community college athletic associations. The NJCAA exclusively offers hockey, lacrosse, bowling, and indoor and outdoor track and field. The COA, operating only in California, exclusively offers water polo, swimming, and badminton for women. Football, which will be discussed further below, is offered in the NJCAA and the COA, but is not offered at the 37 NWACC-member institutions.

TABLE 8.2 **Participation by Associates Colleges in Athletic Associations, 2002–2003**

Association	Number of Institutional Members	States Represented	Number of Sports	
			Men's	Women's
National Junior College Athletic Association	502	43	14	11
Commission on Athletics (California)	107	1	12	11
Northwest Athletic Association for Community Colleges	37	3	8	8
Total	639	43	15	15

TABLE 8.3   Sports Offered by Community College Athletic Associations by Gender, 2002–2004

Sports	NJCAA	COA	NWAACC
Badminton (Women only)	X		
Baseball/Software (Men & Women)	X	X	X
Basketball (Men & Women)	X	X	X
Bowling (Men & Women)	X		
Cross-Country (Men & Women)	X	X	X
Football (Men only)	X	X	
Golf (Men & Women)	X	X	X
Ice Hockey (Men only)	X		
Lacrosse (Men only)	X		
Soccer[a]	X	X	X
Swimming (Men & Women)		X	
Swimming & Diving (Men & Women)	X		
Tennis (Men & Women)	X	X	X
Track & Field/Cross Country (Men & Women)		X	X
Track & Field, Indoor (Men & Women)		X	
Track & Field, Outdoor (Men & Women)	X		
Water Polo (Men & Women)		X	
Wrestling (Men only)	X	X	X
Volleyball[b] (Men & Women)	X	X	X

[a] NJCAA recognizes only men's soccer
[b] NJCAA recognizes only women's volleyball
Source: Publications of NJCAA, COA, and NWAACC, 2002–2003

Athletically Related Financial Aid

The awarding of athletically related aid varies greatly depending on the athletic association as well as the sport. Both the NJCAA and NWAACC have at least some sports that offer athletically related aid, while the COA has for decades disallowed its member colleges from granting athletic aid, a prohibition written into California's Education Code. Of course, student-athletes at COA member institutions in California benefit from the much lower tuition and fees charged to California public community college students. In comparison, California students pay about five times less in required tuition and fees than do students attending community colleges in Minnesota.

The largest community college athletic association, the NJCAA, deploys a three-tiered system for its members based on aided scholarships. Under NJCAA rules, institutions choosing to participate in Division I (in NJCAA) sports may offer up to full-tuition scholarships and institutions choosing to participate in Division II sports may offer only partial scholarships. The NJ-CAA's Division III sports offer no scholarship aid at all to student-athletes.

The 8 men's and 8 women's sports sponsored by NWAACC members are classified as equivalent of the NJCAA's Division II. Interestingly, the NWAACC does not offer competition linked to levels of athletically related aid, instead deferring the decision to award scholarships to each individual college. This arrangement is a result of the association's history as a merger between the Washington State Junior College Athletic Conference and the Oregon Community College Athletic Conference in 1983–1984 (NWAACC, 2004b).

Thus, the largest association, the NJCAA, offers three levels of scholarship competition: Division I, II, and III. Division III is the nonscholarship division, and in this way is equivalent to colleges that are members of COA in California. Colleges sponsoring Division I or II sports may offer athletically related aid, with Division II limited to offering a maximum of partial financial aid. Oregon and Washington member community colleges of the NWAACC offer partial scholarships, with totals varying by college, making them comparable to NJCAA's Division II colleges.

Gender Equity

The sport of football has significant impact on the gender equity at associate's-level colleges, as Table 8.4 shows. In its analysis of EADA data, Table 8.4 shows that at those colleges without football, the number of institutions by gender that offer athletics are virtually the same: 429 for men and 421 for women. In terms of the average number and percentage of athletes who are men and women, there are an average of 55 male athletes and 40 female athletes at those institutions without football, or 58% male and

TABLE 8.4 The Impact of Football on Athletics at Associates Colleges, 2002

| Associates Colleges | Number of colleges reporting athletes who are... | | Average number and percentage of athletes who are... | | | |
| | | | Male | | Female | |
	Male	Female	Number	Percent	Number	Percent
Without Football	429	421	55	58	40	42
With Football	136	136	165	70	72	30

Source: Equity in Athletic Disclosure Act (EADA) 2002 Survey

42% female. In contrast, at the 136 associates colleges that report offering football, there are an average of 165 male athletes and 72 female athletes, or 70% male and 30% female. Thus, the greatest disparity in athletic participation by gender occurs in colleges that sponsor football teams. Football teams, which may have rosters of nearly 60 men or higher, invariably skew the gender ratios.

COMMUNITY COLLEGE PARTICIPATION IN INTERCOLLEGIATE ATHLETICS: FOCUS ON STUDENTS

To determine the average scholarship amount awarded to student-athletes with any level of precision requires using results from two different surveys. The IPEDS Graduation Rate Survey reports the number of students receiving athletically related aid, while the EADA Survey details the amount of athletically related aid, number of athletes per team, and unduplicated athlete count. At the time these data were collected, two data years were combined to derive the information in tables presented in this chapter, the 2001–2002 IPEDS Graduation Rate and the 2002–2003 EADA Surveys.

A clear trend emerges from our analysis of available athletically related aid at public community colleges in the United States. First, women received a higher average amount of athletic aid than did men in six of the seven institutional "geographic" categories using the new 2005 Carnegie Basic Classifications. The only institutional type where men received higher average amounts of athletic aid was urban-serving single-campus colleges. On average, across all institutional types, the estimated average athletic award was $3,225 for women and $2,951 for men. Small rural colleges provided the highest average estimated athletic aid awards for women at $6,500.

Another noticeable trend is that women received a greater proportion of athletic aid in terms of both the number of aided recipients and the aggregate of athletic aid awarded than their participation in athletics would suggest. As Castañeda et al. (2008) note, while women account for 37% of all athletes, they receive more than 44% of all athletically related aid dollars. Furthermore, they note that women account for 9,605, or 42%, of the 22,868 athletes reported as receiving athletically related aid in the IPEDS Graduation Rate survey (2008).

In terms of comparing the institutional commitment, it is clear that all types of rural-serving community colleges are highly committed to intercollegiate athletics. Rural medium-sized colleges offer by far the largest average number of aided athletic scholarships—127 athletic scholarships for men and 127 for women, an average that is about double that of the second-ranked institutional category, rural large community colleges. Interestingly, as Table 8.5 shows, the third-ranked institutional category, rural small col-

TABLE 8.5 Athletic Scholarships Expressed in Mean Averages and Dollar Values, 2002–2003, and Percentage of all Full-Time Degree- and Certificate-Seeking Students, by Gender and by 2005 Carnegie Basic Institutional Classification

| Classification | Average Athletic Scholarships by | | | | Percentage of All Full-Time Degree- and Certificate-Seeking Students Who Are... | | |
| | Number | | Dollar Value | | | | |
	Men	Women	Men	Women	Male	Female	Total
Rural Small	35	33	5,471	6,500	22	11	16
Rural Medium	127	127	2,636	2,393	12	6	9
Rural Large	65	64	2,892	3,198	8	4	6
Suburban Single Campus	28	29	2,205	3,384	8	4	6
Suburban Multi-Campus	20	21	3,048	4,181	9	4	6
Urban Single Campus	14	14	3,236	2,838	6	3	4
Urban Multi-Campus	32	30	2,951	3,226	10	5	7

leges, with an average enrollment of 1,699 (Hardy & Katsinas, 2006), offer more aided athletic scholarships for men (35) and women (33) than do giant urban multicommunity college districts, whose mean annual undupli-cated student enrollment per district of 38,402 is 22 times larger, and who award an average of 32 athletic scholarships for men and 30 for women.

The importance of athletics at rural community colleges is also docu-mented in the larger average dollar value of the athletic scholarships smaller colleges provide compared to other types of community colleges. Table 8.5 shows that rural-serving small colleges spent the greatest amount on athletically related aid for both men and women, averaging awards of $5,471 for men and $6,500 for women. This compares to an average across all seven types of institutions of $2,951 for men and $3,225 for women. Put differently, the average dollar value of an athletic scholarship at a rural small college is roughly double the overall average. The lowest estimated average aid was $2,036 for men at multicampus urban colleges, and $2,393 for women by medium rural colleges. Suburban colleges had the greatest difference by gender in both multi- and single-campus categories. Female athletes at suburban colleges were awarded an average of $1,100 more than their male counterparts.

Castañeda et al. (2006) document that athletes accounted for 6.3%, or 72,558, of all public community college students reported as full-time undergraduates in the IPEDS Fall 2002 survey using the 2005 Carnegie Basic Classifications. The comparison here must be among students that are enrolled full time, since only those students are eligible to compete in intercollegiate athletics, provided they meet academic eligibility guidelines. However, the extent of individual student participation in intercollegiate athletics in community colleges varies dramatically from the overall pattern of enrollment in community colleges. It is well known that women now account for percentages that approach 60% of all full-time students enrolled in community colleges, while the 26,698 women involved in intercollegiate athletics account for just 37% of all athletes, or about 4.4% of full-time female students. Meanwhile, a total of 45,860 men participated in athletics, accounting for 8.8% of all full-time male students and 63% of all intercollegiate athletes (p. 97). Sadly, the ratio of male to female athletes has not changed much since from the 65% male and 35% female participation rates reported by Brown in 1988.

The final three columns of Table 8.5 show the total impact of the percentage of intercollegiate athletics on overall institutional enrollments by Carnegie Basic Classification. Not only does Table 8.5 show a higher percentage of students at rural community colleges are athletes than at all other institutional types, but it also shows that the percentages are even more pronounced when only full-time degree-/certificate-seeking students are held as the comparison group for athletes. The highest incidence of athletics for both males and females is at rural small community colleges in which 22% and 11% of men and women full-time degree- and certificate-seeking students, respectively, are athletes. Intercollegiate athletics comprise a much larger percentage of first-time, full-time degree-seeking students at rural small and rural medium institutions than at any other institutional type. Additionally, male athletes account for a larger percentage of first-time full-time degree- or certificate-seeking students at urban multicampus community colleges than at other types of institutions.

DISCUSSION

Despite the limited empirical attention paid to intercollegiate athletics at community and junior colleges, with more than 70,000 participants nationwide, they are clearly one of the most popular and important student activities on community college campuses. Several benefits are seen from this level of participation, as Castañeda (2004) described the internal and external benefits for both institutions and students. Internal benefits for participating institutions included improved school spirit, the development of "true college experience," the positive benefits that flow from enrollment growth and state reimbursement for enrolled students, and stronger community linkages that can include increased publicity and marketing. Internal benefits for student-athletes included participation in activities that tie them to the lives of their institutions, opportunities for personal development, and the access provided by institutional scholarships and grant aid. External benefits for students can include athletic scholarships that facilitate transfer, and the stronger ties to four-year institutions through their recruitment of community college student-athletes, thus fostering greater rates of transfer. In sum, the motivation for hosting intercollegiate athletics at community colleges includes benefits for the institution, the community, and the participating students. These benefits are very much interrelated—the internal and external benefits for students and the community colleges in turn benefit their communities by physical proximity, clearly fitting the concept of *community* college. On the other hand, this proximity could mean that the community is a key stakeholder in decisions as to whether or not a college will have intercollegiate athletics (Castañeda, 2004; Castañeda et al., 2008), a decision that community college leadership has seen as its prerogative.

REFERENCES

American Association of University Professors. (1999). *The faculty role in the reform of intercollegiate athletics. A report of the Special Committee on Athletics* (ED316155). Washington, DC: Author.

American Association of University Professors. (2002). *The faculty role in the reform of intercollegiate athletics: Principles and recommended practice* (ED474172). Washington, DC: Author.

Bailey, W. S., & Littleton, T. D. (1991). *Athletics and academe: An anatomy of abuses and a prescription for reform.* New York: American Council on Education/MacMillan.

Brown, R.G. (1988). Current status of two-year college athletic programs in non-gender specific and non-football playing schools of the NJCAA. *Dissertation Abstracts International,* 0(05), 1189A. (UMI No. 8914987).

Carnegie Foundation for the Advancement of Teaching. (2006, February). *2005 Basic Classification of Institutions of Higher Education.* Retrieved August 31, 2008, from http://www.carnegiefoundation.org/classifications.asp?key=791

Castañeda, C. (2004). A national overview of intercollegiate athletics in public community colleges (Doctoral dissertation, University of North Texas, 2004). *Dissertation Abstracts International,* 65(08), 2915A.

Castañeda, C., Katsinas, S. G., & Hardy, D. E. (2006). *The importance of intercollegiate athletics at rural-serving community colleges. A policy brief by the Education Policy Center at the University of Alabama for the MidSouth Partnership for Rural Community Colleges.* Retrieved August 14, 2008, from http://www.ruralcommunitycolleges.org/docs/MSPBRIEFATHLETICS.pdf

Castañeda, C., Katsinas, S. G., & Hardy, D. E. (2008). *Meeting the challenge of gender equity in community college athletics* (New Directions for Community Colleges, no. 142, pp. 93–105). San Francisco: Jossey-Bass.

Cohen, A. M., & Brawer, F. B. (2008). *The American community college* (5th ed.). San Francisco: Jossey-Bass.

Dempsey, C. W. (2002). *President to president: The Will to Act Project* (ED470688). Indianapolis, IN: National Collegiate Athletic Association.

Fields, R. R. (1962). *The community college movement.* New York: McGraw-Hill.

General Accounting Office. (1992). *Intercollegiate athletics: Compensation varies for selected personnel in athletic departments, August, 1992* (GAO/HRD-92-121). Washington, DC: Author.

General Accounting Office. (1996a). *Intercollegiate athletics: Compensation of selected characteristics of men's and women's program, October, 1996* (GAO/HEHS-91-10). Washington, DC: Author.

General Accounting Office. (1996b). *Intercollegiate athletics: Status of efforts to promote gender equity.* Washington, DC: Author.

General Accounting Office. (2007). *Intercollegiate athletics: Recent trends in teams and participants in National Collegiate Athletic Association sports.* Washington, DC: Author.

Gerdy, J. R. (1997). *The successful college athletic program: The new standard.* Phoenix, AZ: American Council on Education/Oryx Press.

Greene, J. B. (1981). *Blitzing athletic abuses.* Paper presented at the Association of California Community College Administrators (ACCCA) Annual Conference, San Diego, CA. (ERIC Document Reproduction Service No. ED203949)

Hardy, D. E., & Katsinas, S. G. (2006). Using community college classifications in research: From conceptual model to useful tool. *Community College Journal of Research and Practice, 30*(4), 339–358.

Knight Foundation Commission on Intercollegiate Athletics. (1993). *Reports of the Knight Foundation Commission on Intercollegiate Athletics: March 1991–March 1993.* Available at http://www.knightcommission.org

Koos, L. V. *The junior college movement.* (1925). Minneapolis: University of Minnesota Press.

Medsker, L. L. (1960). *The junior college: Progress and prospect.* New York: McGraw-Hill.

National Junior College Athletic Association. (2002). *NJCAA Handbook and Casebook 2002–2003.* Denver, CO: Author.

Northwest Athletic Association of Community Colleges. (2004a). *Member schools.* Retrieved February 7, 2004, from http://www.nwacc.org/memberschools.htm.

Northwest Athletic Association of Community Colleges. (2004b). *NWAACC History.* Retrieved January 27, 2004, from http://www.nwacc.org/history/htm.

Sack, A. L., & Staurowsky, E. J. (1988). *College athletes for hire: The evolution and legacy of the NCAA's amateur myth.* Westport, CT: Praeger.

Telander, R. (1996). *The hundred yard lie: The corruption of college football and what we can do to stop it.* Urbana and Chicago: University of Illinois Press.

Thelin, J. R. (1994). *Games colleges play.* Baltimore: Johns Hopkins University Press.

Thornton, J. W. (1972). *The community junior college* (3rd ed.). New York: Wiley.

U.S. Department of Education. (2003). *Equity in Athletic Disclosure Act survey 2003–2004* [Data file]. Washington, DC: Author.

U.S. Department of Education. (2004). Athletic disclosure. Retrieved February 29, 2004, from http://surveys. ope.ed.gov/athletics/

Zimbalist, A. S. (1999). *Unpaid professional: Commercialism and conflict in big-time college sports.* Princeton, NJ: Princeton University Press.

CHAPTER 9

PRIVATE COLLEGE STUDENT-ATHLETES

The World of D3 and NAIA

Adam Morris
Crowder College

Athletic programs are part of the institutional culture of American higher education, as they contribute to enhancing team spirit, serve as an extra-curricular activity to foster involvement, and help to build a sense of community in the surrounding area (Tobin, 2005). College athletics have not and are not exclusively part of the billion-dollar enterprise that provides entertainment on television every evening. College athletics in the late 1800s resembled intramural games rather than grand events with national media attention. Many of today's current collegiate athletics started in private colleges, and the most popular sport of football was initiated between two private institutions. The first intercollegiate football in America was between Tufts University and Harvard University on June 4, 1875, in Cambridge, Massachusetts, won by Tufts 1–0 (Smith, 1988). Also, baseball's first collegiate game was also between two private colleges. The Fordham Rose Hill Baseball Club of St. John's College in New York, which is now Fordham

College Student-Athletes: Challenges, Opportunities, and Policy Implications, pages 123–132
Copyright © 2009 by Information Age Publishing
All rights of reproduction in any form reserved.

University, played the first ever college baseball game in its current format on November 3, 1859, against St. Francis Xavier College. Private institutions have had a significant historical impact on the formation of collegiate athletics. In many aspects they laid the groundwork on college athletics.

In the United States private colleges have been in existence for about 400 years. The first private college was called Newborn, which was founded in 1636. Newborn later changed its name to Cambridge, then eventually to its current name of Harvard. According to Schuman (2005), including Harvard, there are nine institutions of higher learning founded before the Revolutionary War that still exist today. The institutions are as follows with the year they were founded: William and Mary (1693), Yale (1701), Princeton (1746), Columbia (1754), the University of Pennsylvania (1755), Brown (1765), Rutgers (1766), and Dartmouth (1769). These institutions were critical in the formation of today's private college. They defined a pattern for American higher education that was distinct from European institutions. These private institutions provided a foundation for many colleges and universities that were founded after them. After the Civil War, there was a tremendous growth in student enrollments and number of private institutions. Also, during this time period private institutions began forming for women and African Americans. Private institutions continued to rise in the number of institutions up until World War II. After the war, the growth in higher education was primarily in the two-year college as well as regional state colleges and universities. While the number of private colleges have dwindled it is still a viable option for many college students.

Initially, private institutions began to meet the needs of the church by training clergy and future leaders of their congregation. The church deemed it necessary to have an education system that provided literate and well-trained clergy teaching their congregation. However, in the 1700s colleges began expanding their course offerings to expand the knowledge of clergy and ordinary individuals. Courses such as mathematics, surveying, modern languages, geography, and other disciplines began to appear on the curriculum (Lucas, 1994). The addition of these new courses allowed a different kind of student to enter college for an education. The education incorporated training a student for a professional career rather than teaching solely for the church. Private college curriculum began to become more focused on career preparation for the common individual.

Birnbaum (1988) wrote about the private institution in his book *How Colleges Work*. He expounds on a fictitious institution named Heritage College, located in a picturesque setting with many older buildings, large trees, and manicured grounds. The students are between the ages of 18 and 21, and finished in the top percentage of their high school class. The enrollment of the college is about 2,000 undergraduate students and there is a family/collegial atmosphere within the institution. According to Birnbaum, the mission of most private colleges is to provide liberating education in the Judeo-Christian tradition as preparation for a life of individual meaning and social purpose. Private colleges incorporate many aspects of learning to provide a well-rounded liberal arts education.

Private liberal arts colleges have a unique place in the higher education industry. These institutions are often described as small, enrolling 2,000 undergraduate students or fewer, and are fully committed to the education of the whole person. This typically takes the form of small faculty–student ratios, a limited number of academic majors to choose from, and reliance on faculty who are willing to commit to the ideal of the liberal arts experience. Additionally, from a business perspective, they rely on a commitment to the liberal arts and a dedication to teaching to compensate for an inability to offer high salaries. Furthermore, these institutions utilize creative human resource packages, such as discounting or waiving tuition at similar institutions, as an incentive to lure talented faculty (Morris & Miller, 2008).

Students enrolled in these colleges expect and report a greater sense of community (Gaudiani, 1997); a stronger, often personal relationship between students and faculty members (Pascarella, Wolniak, Seifer, Cruce, & Blaich, 2005); faculty who emphasize teaching (Henderson & Buchanan, 2007); an easier access to responsible, senior administrators by faculty and students (Pascarella et al., 2005); and students find an ability to express their individuality and experience diversity in ways and to a level that is often not found in public institutions.

A private college promotes a sense of community, according to Birnbaum (1988). The culture allows a family-type atmosphere where faculty and staff are personally invested in one another. Many faculty and administrators stay in the same private institution for many years, and have no aspirations to move to other institutions (Morris, 2008). Staff and faculty have a say in college operations, letting them feel involved. Private colleges have unique attributes no other institution will have. They are typically smaller than the regional institutions in student enrollment and faculty and staff employed. Culture, leadership, and how the day-to-day operations perform are different at the private college.

Birnbaum (1988) characterized the stereotype of the private liberal arts college in his depiction of Heritage College. In this setting, the administrators are serving in managerial capacities for a limited time before retreating to their teaching duties, students are committed to learning in the liberal arts, and consensus is the hallmark of decision making. This idyllic portrayal largely lacks the realities associated with financially or legally managing an institution that is reliant on tuition and accurately predicting enrollment for survival.

Rising costs have drastically impacted the private college in recent years. These institutions have been forced to reduce their budget and increase tuition in order to meet the financial demand necessary to run a private college. The cost of energy, salaries, and benefits has increased exponentially, causing fiscal hardship on many institutions. Since 1997 aid to college students has increased by 82%; however, this has not covered the rapid increase of college tuition (Sander, 2007). Also, Sander (2007) wrote that two surveys from the College Board indicate the cost of higher education is outpacing inflation, family income, and sources of grant aid. According to Sander, private four-year institutions increased tuition and fees 6.3% in 2006, with the average cost of tuition and fees being $23,172. This was an average increase of $1,404. With this level of increases private institutions need to find unique ways to increase enrollment and retain their current student population.

Alden (2000) writes that student recruitment and retention are the two main issues with small private colleges and universities. With private institutions relying on tuition revenue to meet operating expenses the student-athlete is an important component to the revenue stream. Student-athletes have many small institutions to choose from regarding athletics; however, many athletes do not choose a private institution based on athletics. According to Goss, Jubenville, and Orejan's (2006) study of 229 freshman student-athletes from three institutions from the National Association of Intercollegiate Athletics (NAIA) and three institutions from Division III, academic degree programs is the number one factor for student-athletes in selecting a small/private institution. Student-athletes at smaller institutions generally place a stronger emphasis on environmental factors outside their competitive sport when choosing an institution (Gabert, Hale, & Montalvo, 1999). This makes recruiting student-athletes at private colleges a unique dichotomy. Academics and athletics are co-mingled in the recruitment process of these athletes (Gabert et al., 1999). According to Goss et al. (2006), in a private college setting having broad academic programs is beneficial in student-athlete recruitment. Athletes are in many instances focused more on academics than athletics.

Division I athletes cannot always choose their preferred academic major while competing (Wolverton, 2007a). According to Mike Ritchey, University of Arkansas athletic academic advisor, many athletes cannot choose particular majors that have labs and other meetings because of the time constraints (personal communication). University of Arkansas gymnastics coach Rene Cook said, "Many athletes have to choose between their sport or academic major" (personal communication). Scheduling classes between games, practices, and other athletic activities can pose a challenge to these athletes. In a 2006 National Collegiate Athletic Association (NCAA) survey over 60% of Division I athletes believed they would have a higher grade point average if they had not participated in competitive sports (Wolverton, 2007a). According to Wolverton (2007a), some Division I athletes reported an imbalance between athletics and academics. Some sports such as baseball require as much as three days a week away from campus in order to compete. With this type of time commitment it makes academics difficult for the Division I athlete.

Private institution student-athletes reported being influenced to a greater extent by a religious and moral atmosphere that a private institution will sometimes have as part of their mission and values (Tisdell, 2007). Private institutions with religious backing have a different mission and purpose than other institutions. Every institution of higher learning has content in their mission statement that includes educating people; however, a private religious institution has an additional mission and purpose for their students. Religion can play an important role for a student-athlete and some will choose an institution based on their religious values. Students want an outlet in which they can have an active role in developing their spirituality (Tisdell, 2007). Public institutions take an academic approach to religion and not a faith-based approach (Kaplan, 2006). This causes student-athletes to choose a private institution if their faith is a priority in their spiritual life.

NCAA DIVISION III

The majority of private college athletic programs belong to the NAIA or the NCAA Division III organization. Some private colleges are NCAA Division I and II; however, the vast majority of the smaller private colleges do belong in either of these divisions. According to the NCAA website (*www.ncaa.org*), Division III consists of colleges and universities that choose not to offer athletic-based scholarships to their student-athletes. There are over 420 member institutions with 44 conferences, making Division III the largest of the three divisions sanctioned by the NCAA. As compared to Division I athletics, Division III does not make a profit on their athletic sports. The division has a commitment to treat athletics as an extracurricular activity instead of a revenue generator for the institution (Bennett, 2007). The primary emphasis is on the academic and mental development of the student-athlete. It has been said by some athletic officials associated with this division that this method of athletic participation is a "purer" way to compete in athletics compared to the other divisions within the NCAA (Suggs, 2004).

According to the NCAA, Division III institutions must sponsor at least five sports for men and five for women. There must be two team sports for each gender, and each playing season must be represented by each gender. Also, there are contest and participant minimums for each competitive sport. Division III athletics feature student-athletes who receive no financial aid related to athletic ability, and athletic departments are staffed and are allocated funds the same as any other administrative department at the institution. The website also writes that Division III athletics departments place a special emphasis on the impact athletics has on the ones that participate rather than on the ones watching. This is a significant statement because the primary focus is on the student-athlete's experience in college not how many games are won. Division III institutions are competitive and teams strive to win, it is not the primary focus of the mission of Division III athletics. In other words, Division III encourages participation by maximizing the number and variety of athletic sports available to students having an emphasis on regional competition.

Division III institutions have a wide range of student enrollments ranging from less than 500 to over 10,000 students. These schools compete in athletics as a non-revenue-making enterprise. This gives students an opportunity to participate in a sport they may not have been able to at a more competitive Division I institution. Many student-athletes choose a private institution because they do have the chance to play in their competitive sport. Also, institutions cannot redshirt freshmen for any sport allowing a student-athlete the opportunity to play right away.

Student-athletes at Division III colleges and universities receive no financial incentives based on athletic merit. Also, private institutions may not use endowments or other types of funding for the sole purpose of benefiting an athletic program. The NCAA by-laws prohibit these institutions from offering any aid for athletic reasons; however, financial aid and academic scholarships are available to these student-athletes (Goss et al., 2006). These institutions place a high priority on the overall educational experience. Athletics are used to complement academics and other learning opportunities. Division III student-athletes are well rounded and take advantage of nonathletic extracurricular activities. They have opportunities to engage in any activities in college life outside their sport that many Division I and II student-athletes cannot.

NATIONAL ASSOCIATION OF INTERCOLLEGIATE ATHLETICS

According to the NAIA website (*http://naia.cstv.com*), the NAIA began as a result of a basketball tournament based in the Kansas City metro area. The tournament was designed by Emil S. Liston, Dr. James Naismith, Frank Cramer, and others who envisioned a national basketball championship for small colleges and universities. The tournament soon turned into a collegiate sports organization, and in 1952 they named the organization the National Association of Intercollegiate Athletics. The NAIA website states that they have 284 member institutions, 28 conferences, and nearly 50,000 student-athletes throughout the country. Their headquarters is located in Kansas City, Missouri, and it has been located there since its inception.

Financial aid is similar to Division III in which student-athletes cannot receive a full athletic scholarship to play a competitive sport; however, many of them do receive financial aid in many different forms. Since only partial aid is given for many student-athletes, they have to find alternative financial resources to help meet their tuition costs. This may entail working, nonathletic scholarships, and private resources at their disposal.

Private institutions affiliated with the NAIA will oftentimes recruit academically gifted athletes to offset their athletic scholarship budgets. Academic scholarships at a private institution can be as much or more than an athletic scholarship (Blum, 1996). When an NAIA college or university gives an academic scholarship rather than an athletic one, it allows the institution to use their athletic scholarships for another student-athlete. Reporting of how aid is used can be confusing at an NAIA institution. Institutional aid at these institutions is reported in one lump sum. While there are limits placed by the NAIA on the amount of athletic scholarships that can be given, many private institutions value student-athletes for their academic superiority rather than athletic prowess.

The NAIA limits the amount of time a student-athlete can participate in a competitive sport. This division states that they cannot participate for more than five years. The rationale behind this decision was that college leaders of these private institutions were concerned about the role of athletics in higher education (Monaghan, 1995). While athletics is an important part of the student-athlete's development, academics will have priority in the NAIA colleges and universities.

The NAIA was the first collegiate sports organization to make significant strides toward diversity. They were the first to include African Americans in a sanctioned collegiate national championship. Also, they were the first to do this for women. The NAIA was not only a place for small colleges and universities to belong to a national organization, they also were instrumental in promoting diversity through athletics.

NAIA was the first collegiate sports organization to develop a character-education-based program for their student-athletes. According to the NAIA website, the program is structured around five core values for student-athletes, and is named "Champions of Character." The primary purpose of the program is to teach student-athletes core values that will not assist them on the playing field, but will give them good social values that will help them when they enter the workplace. The core values the NAIA emphasizes are Respect, Responsibility, Integrity, Servant Leadership, and Sportsmanship. This training has not only benefitted the student-athletes of the NAIA. According to Wolverton (2007b), over 100 NAIA institutions hold character-based training seminars for noncollegiate coaches and athletes; these seminars are conducted in local middle and high schools, and teach people the importance of respect and competition.

According to Parish, Henke, and Dopp (2007), there are Ten Commandments that the student-athlete must follow in order to be successful in academics and athletics:

1. Class attendance is a must, unless you want everything to go "bust."
2. Proper nutrition is a key, for without it you'll likely lack energy.
3. An adequate night's sleep is often essential, especially if you want to reach your full potential.
4. A "to-do list" can put you on top of your game, and also help you to achieve great fame.
5. Be smart from the start, and always strive to do your part.
6. Be prompt all the time, for to do otherwise could be a real crime.
7. Time management is important too, for greatness only comes to those who follow through.
8. Commitment and dedication are both super great, but if you don't have them, the coach will probably be irate.
9. Possessing confidence can be great too, as it could keep you from feeling really blue.
10. Always work hard and never give in, for in so doing, you'll more likely win.

While this is intended for any athlete, it is especially pertinent to the private college student-athlete. With athletics not being the primary motivation for the private college student-athlete, these Ten Commandments are a good guide for students to follow while in college. This is not to argue, however, that private college athletes only attend college for academic reasons, as many will still primarily identify themselves with their sports and opportunities to participate in athletic programs.

Student-athletes in private colleges do not face the same pressures as their Division I counterparts. There are pressures on the private college athlete; however, they are different than athletes in high-profile Division I institutions. With little media exposure on athletics there is not the time demand and pressure involved in dealing with the media and fans of their sport. The exposure level for athletes in private colleges can be a challenge and an opportunity. The opportunities allow for more time to spend on academic endeavors. The challenge may be not as much time to spend on their competitive sport.

Private college student-athletes are competing in athletic events that are not widely publicized by the media. Rarely does a private college receive national attention for a sport, and student-athletes who compete do so in front of generally small crowds mainly consisting of parents and people from the community (Suggs, 2004). These athletes will not make the cover of *Sports Illustrated* or be interviewed on *ESPN*, but are playing for the love of their sport (note, this is not a comparative statement with other student-athletes, but rather a highlight that these student-athletes have a special affinity for their sports). Private colleges have limited athletic budgets and do not make a profit off their major sports such as football and basketball. Coaches do not have multimillion-dollar contacts with huge incentives for winning a conference or national championship. On the contrary, many coaches have regular full-time jobs or other jobs at the college to supplement their income (Naughton, 1997). Most of these coaches coach because they love the game and love being around college student-athletes.

CONCLUSION

Private liberal arts institutions have a unique role in college athletics. Most of the student-athletes at these institutions will never play their sport professionally. They will enter the workforce just the same as millions of other college graduates. Jim Carr, president of the NAIA, said, "Our primary mission and responsibility is to build people of character, to prepare young people for life as opposed to winning games. If you're not in it for that, you're not an NAIA school" (Wolverton, 2007b, p. A34). The student-athletes at private colleges have various reasons they attend a private institution. Religion, major, academics, and athletics all play a part in their decision-making process. The literature is clear that athletics is not the major reason for a student choosing a private college or university. This chapter was designed specifically to highlight the positive aspects and the challenges facing private college athletes; it was not intended to condemn one set of athletes or cheer another, but rather to begin a critical discussion of some of the areas that defy stereotyping student-athletes in higher education.

REFERENCES

Alden, E. (2000). Forecasting finances: When developing long-term strategies for your athletic department, don't forget the part about the money. *Athletic Management, 12*, 33–38.

Bennett, D. (2007). Division III: Too big for its own good. *Chronicle of Higher Education, 53*(40), B12–B12.

Birnbaum, R. (1988). *How colleges work: The cybernetics of academic organization and leadership.* San Francisco: Jossey-Bass.

Blum, D. (1996). NAIA adopts policy to encourage colleges to recruit smart athletes. *Chronicle of Higher Education, 42*(36), A42.

Gabert, T., Hale, J., & Montvalo, G. (1999). Differences in college choice factors. *College Admission, 16,* 20–29.

Gaudiani, C. (1997). Catalyzing community: The college as a model of civil society. *Educational Record, 78*(3–4), 80–87.

Goss, B., Jubenville, C., & Orejan, J. (2006). An examination of influences and factors on the institutional selection processes of freshmen student athletes at small colleges and universities. *Journal of Marketing for Higher Education, 16*(2), 105–134.

Henderson, B., & Buchanan, H. (2007). The scholarship of teaching and learning: A special niche for faculty at comprehensive universities? *Research in Higher Education, 48*(5), 523–543.

Kaplan, M. (2006). Getting religion in the public research university. *Academe, 92*(4), 41–45.

Lucas, C. J. (1994). *American higher education: A history.* New York: St. Martin's Press.

Monaghan, P. (1995). NAIA rejects fifth year of sports participation. *Chronicle of Higher Education, 42*(6), A46.

Morris, A. A. (2008). *Leadership role of the department chair in private colleges.* Unpublished doctoral dissertation, University of Arkansas, Fayetteville.

Morris, A., & Miller, M. T. (2008). Profile of online programs in private colleges: From college to university with a click. *Journal of Academic Leadership, 6*(1).

Naughton, J. (1997). In Division III, college sports thrive with few fans and even fewer scandals. *Chronicle of Higher Education, 44*(13), A41.

Pascarella, E. T., Wolniak, G. C., Seifer, T. A., Cruce, T. M., & Blaich, C. F. (2005). *Liberal arts colleges and liberal arts education: New evidence on impacts* (ASHE Higher Education Report No. 31). Hoboken, NJ: Wiley.

Parish, T., Henke, W., & Dopp, A. (2007). The ten commandments for college student athletes. *College Student Journal, 41*(4), 1045.

Sander, L. (2007). Student aid is up, but college costs have risen faster, surveys find. *Chronicle of Higher Education, 54*(10), 37.

Smith, R. A. (1988). *Sports and freedom: The rise of big-time college athletics.* New York: Oxford University Press.

Suggs, W. (2004). Small colleges spent 41% of sports budgets on women's teams. *Chronicle of Higher Education, 50*(41), A35–A36.

Tisdell, E. (2007). In the new millennium: The role of spirituality and the cultural imagination in dealing with diversity and equity in the higher education classroom. *Teachers College Record, 109*(3), 531–560.

Tobin, E. (2005). Athletics in Division III institutions: Trends and concerns. *Phi Kappa Phi Forum, 85*(3), 24–27.

Wolverton, B. (2007a). Athletics participation prevents many players from choosing majors they want. *Chronicle of Higher Education, 53*(20), A36–A37.

Wolverton, B. (2007b). A small athletics association tries to revamp its image. *Chronicle of Higher Education, 53*(29), A33–A35.

CHAPTER 10

FEMALE STUDENT-ATHLETES

Counseling Considerations
for a Unique Culture

Richard G. Deaner
Augusta State University

Forty years ago a chapter about female college athletes may not have been championed. Before 1972, college athletic programs were synonymous with male student-athletes, with limited attention paid to the needs of female athletes. However, the 1972 Education Amendments to the Civil Rights Act, or Title IX, fundamentally transformed the face of college athletics. More specifically, Title IX mandated that institutions provide equal opportunities, accommodations, and resources to athletes, regardless of sex. The results have been dramatic, particularly in the sense of equalizing participation opportunities and financial resources.

Since the enactment of Title IX , female participation rates have risen a remarkable 450% (Women's Sports Foundation, 2008), from 32,000 in 1972 to about 146,000 in 2008. Financially, less than 1% of college athletics funds were allocated to female athletics (Sklover, 1997) prior to 1972, whereas in 2007 female athletics received 38% of those funds (Women's Sports Foun-

College Student-Athletes: Challenges, Opportunities, and Policy Implications, pages 133–149
Copyright © 2009 by Information Age Publishing
All rights of reproduction in any form reserved.

dation, 2008). And according to the National Collegiate Athletic Association (NCAA; 2007), there were 105 men's teams versus 133 women's teams added to the NCAA registry in the 2006–2007 season, with the trend of more women's teams being likely to continue in the near future. Although these figures represent profound improvements in women's intercollegiate athletics programs, Title IX is not without its detractors, particularly among those who resent the benefits that Title IX has afforded them (Greenlee, 1997), often at the expense of men's programs.

While a discussion of Title IX is fundamental to any analysis of female student-athletes, gaining a true understanding of their experiences involves exploring a broad range of issues and concerns. In some cases, these factors parallel those of their male counterparts. However, it is crucial that stakeholders recognize the concerns faced by female student-athletes in order to understand how best to interact with them in order to facilitate positive academic, athletic, and social outcomes. Thus, this chapter conceptualizes female college athletes as part of a rich and multifaceted institutional and, increasingly, national culture. In doing so, it is possible to shed light on the issues that stakeholders in their development must understand as they seek to facilitate their well-being.

Awareness of cultural differences inside and outside the athletic realm are important when considering the female student-athlete experience. As noted, female student-athletes historically received fewer participation opportunities, fewer operating dollars, and fewer scholarship resources (i.e., scholarship money) (Women's Sports Foundation, 2008) than their male counterparts. What is less commonly known, however, is that female student-athletes remain more likely to have male coaches and trainers (American Association of University Women, 2008) and share athletic facilities with men. One clearly negative implication of this close proximity is the potential for female student-athletes to be the targets of sexual harassment (Nielson, 2001). One study suggests, for example, that between 27 and 79% of female athletes across various sports report having been sexually harassed (Fasting, Brackenridge, & Walseth, 2007). However, limiting the focus to sexual harassment would be shortsighted.

Athletic personnel (coaches, managers, sports medicine professionals) are often themselves under tremendous pressure to provide a winning program and, whether directly or indirectly, to attract more money for their schools and programs. However, the pressure and expectations some coaches impose on their athletes may constitute emotional abuse. To varying degrees, athletes hold themselves open to abuse because the coaches hold the key to their success and future (Tofler, Stryer, Micheli, & Herman, 1996). The consequences coaches impose for inadequate performance include yelling, swearing, belittling, humiliation, throwing and kicking objects, and the silent treatment—hence the intense pressure to train hard, to perform well during games, and to win. Ruggiero and Lattin (2008), for example, noted the potential hazards of verbally aggressive communication between the athletes and their coaches. In their sample of African American female student-athletes, verbally aggressive communication emanating from coaches was interpreted negatively by the players. What is of particular interest with this study, given the context of this chapter, is the notion that both female and male coaches need to remain sensitive to their communication styles and the power inherent in their positions—in this case to perpetuate racial stereotypes within the context of their communication. The consequences of this harassment vary, of course, but all stakeholders in the wellness of female student-athletes need to remain cognizant of such contributing factors as well as their responsibilities for connecting the student-athlete with all available resources that could help them deal effectively with any associated psychological, emotional, or physical problems. This is especially true when her coach or manager sexually harasses her, thereby shattering her trust, confidence, and sense of personal safety (Fasting et al., 2007) or utilize language that the student-athlete interprets as having negative racial implications (Ruggiero & Lattin, 2008).

Jessica, a collegiate softball player interviewed for this chapter, explained that sometimes coaches "expect you to be perfect every single day...and especially in games . . . God forbid you mess up." This illustrates the need for stakeholders to remain sensitive to gender effects regarding performance-related issues such as coping styles, injury appraisal, and competitive stress. For example, Hammermeister and Burton (2004), in a study of male and female endurance athletes, found female athletes tend to utilize more emotion-focused coping strategies, while the men were more apt to employ problem-focused coping strategies. In other words, female athletes tend to lean on positive reinterpretation of events, social support, and dissociation, whereas men would deemphasize the emotional component and focus on fixing the problem. As a result, female athletes, as opposed to male athletes, may be more susceptible to emotional abuse at the hands of their coaches (Stirling & Kerr, 2007) because females may be more confiding and emotionally expressive than males (Unger & Crawford, 1992).

Erica, a collegiate soccer player, explained that teammates are also a source of stress: ". . . you have to be careful who you tell and how and what to say when you have something going on because some girls might blow it out of proportion and before you know it, you are in trouble with the coach. . . . It's a pretty cut-throat world because some girls will use whatever they can get to get playing time." Lisa, another collegiate soccer player, added, "The bigger the team, the more competitive it can be, so you have to watch what you say to other girls."

Another issue confronting female athletes, particularly those involved in stereotypically masculine sports, is *gender role conflict,* the notion that at-

tempting to enact both feminine and masculine traits produces inner conflict that must be resolved (Allison, 1991; Sage & Loudermilk, 1979). Female athletes tend to identify more strongly with the masculine gender role
than nonathletes (Lantz & Schroeder, 1999) and to hold more liberal or
feminist gender role attitudes than nonathletes (Salisbury & Passer, 1982).
For instance, a female basketball player who displays athleticism, competitiveness, and grit on the court might feel unfeminine compared with other
women or torn between her court-related persona and the more feminine
persona she assumes off the court. Katie, a collegiate basketball player interviewed for this study, validates this notion. According to Katie, "...you
have to have a sense of your own identity because you are always getting
pulled one way or another—always...and you can't get hung up on trying
to appease everyone else because it will drag you down. That's what happened to me my freshman year."

Female student-athletes could also experience *stereotype threat*, or the fear
of behaving in a way that confirms the negative stereotypes of her group
(Steele & Aronson, 1995). On the soccer field, for example, she must dis-
confirm the stereotype that her gender is weak, acquiescent, and noncom-
petitive. She strives to disprove the notion that she is undeserving of equal
resources and attention. Another challenge encountered by female student-
athletes involves dealing with the still prevalent homophobia within the
sports realm. Thus, off the field, a heterosexual female athlete may struggle
with the perception that their athletic status equates with a homosexual
orientation (Blum, 1994; Disch & Kane, 2000). More specifically, lesbian
student-athletes are often faced with the stereotype that her sexual orientation is the primary source of her athleticism because it produces more aggressive, masculine performance. In the classroom, female student-athletes
may also encounter that they are the "dumb jock," and that their talents
and interests lay predominantly in the sports arena, and by no means in
academia. It is clear that the student-athlete wears a great many hats, and
is expected to switch seamlessly between them. Support for this claim is
voiced by Michelle, a collegiate basketball player. In referencing the numerous challenges she faces as a student-athlete, she noted, "It never stops, you
have to balance being a student, friend, family member, classmate, athlete,
and person who just wants to have fun. . . . I feel like I can't ever relax and I
always have to appease someone."

FEMALE ATHLETE TRIAD

Of particular interest to those seeking a deeper understanding of the experiences of female student-athletes is the notion of the *female athlete triad*. In
1997, the American College of Sports Medicine published a position state-

ment regarding the clinical syndrome known as the female athlete triad, which addressed three core issues affecting female athletes (Otis, Drinkwater, Johnson, Loucks, & Wilmore, 1997). According to the position statement, the female athlete triad consists of three interrelated components: disordered eating, amenorrhea, and premature osteoporosis. These conditions were reported to be more prevalent with females involved in highly competitive sports with an emphasis on thinness, although they do exist in other sports as well (Otis et al., 1997). Personality characteristics, pressures to appease coaches, ethnicity, and gender are also recognized as possible contributors to the development of disordered eating (Williams, Leidy, Flecker, & Galucci, 2006), which is often the first of the three triadic components to appear (Sherman & Thompson, 2006). All three components of the triad need not be present in order to necessitate evaluation and/or treatment. It is important to note that when any one component of the triad is evident, assessment in regards to the remaining two components is essential.

Disordered eating is characterized by attempts to control eating habits excessively, ineffectively, and/or harmfully in efforts to lose weight, gain speed and endurance, and/or develop a lean appearance. Common disordered eating patterns include anorexia, bulimia, restricted eating, fasting, and abuse of laxatives, diet pills, and diuretics. In a recent study of judo athletes, 60% of women reported fasting to lose weight, compared with only 8% of men (Rouveix, Bouget, Pannafleux, Champely, & Filaire, 2006). According to Sherman and Thompson (2006), "Disordered eating with athletes typically involves a willful attempt by the athlete to create a negative energy balance" (p. 194). *Amenorrhea* is considered to be a severe menstrual cycle dysfunction. For the post-menarchal female college athlete, this dysfunction occurs when there is an absence of at least three consecutive menstrual cycles. According to Sherman and Thompson (2006), amenorrhea is present in 2–5% of nonathletes, compared with rates as high as 65% for some athletes. Sherman and Thompson alarmingly report that "amenorrhea is so common in some groups of athletes that it is sometimes viewed as normal" and "some athletes have used amenorrhea as a sign that they are training at a desired intensity level" (p. 194). Williams et al. (2006) contend, "Coaches, athletes and sports medicine personnel ought to consider using menstrual cycle length as a potential biomarker of unhealthy attitudes towards food and one's body" (p. 984). *Osteoporosis* is described as a disease characterized by decreased bone mass and deteriorating bone tissue, which results in bone fragility and an elevated risk of fracture. Malnutrition combined with amenorrhea can result in osteoporosis, although this is not the only means by which female athletes can be diagnosed with osteoporosis (Sherman & Thompson, 2006). When viewed together, it is clear that individuals working with female student-athletes must remain cognizant of how their physical health could be impacting their ability to function athletically, academically, and perhaps most importantly, on a personal level. Given the ongoing tendency to stereotype female athletes, however, stakeholders must be particularly sensitive to internalizing such prejudices.

For example, in 2004, the president of the Fédération Internationale de Football Association, the international association governing the rules and regulations of professional and amateur soccer, suggested that "tighter shorts" for female soccer players would increase game attendance and sponsorship by promoting "a more female aesthetic" (Christensen & Kelso, 2004). While women everywhere feel pressure to conform to contemporary society's ideal female form—revealing clothing over a slender body—women in the public eye are the subjects of even higher scrutiny. It comes as no surprise that female athletes' appearance is held to higher standards than their male counterparts (Powe-Allred & Powe, 1997). In addition, female athletes involved in judged sports are more likely to strive for thinness than those in refereed sports (Schwarz, Gairrett, Aruguete, & Gold, 2005; Zucker, Womble, Williamson, & Perrin, 1999). For example, sports in which the body's appearance is scrutinized (e.g., gymnastics and diving) and sports in which lower body weight is beneficial (e.g., running and cycling) are more closely associated with increased risk of the triad (Hausenblas & Carron, 1999). Although there are a number of concerns, it seems unsurprising to note that female athletes have shown resiliency in the face of the general public's attempts to objectify them based on gender (Fallon & Jome, 2007).

Awareness of the triad, both on the part of the student-athlete and institutional stakeholders, is important because it could lead to the recognition that appropriate professional services, such as mental health and/or nutritional counseling, are indicated. Additionally, family, friends, and teammates with an awareness of the triad could lead to a proper referral or simply the need to provide a safe environment for the student-athlete to talk about her issues. Conversely, failure to understand the triad may result in stakeholders who inadvertently contribute to the development and maintenance of the triad by overcontrolling the athlete's eating and exercising, and insisting on frequent weigh-ins (Nattiv, Agostini, Drinkwater, & Yaeger, 1994). In some cases, this drive for thinness might bring about a premature end to her athletic career, resulting in the student-athlete experiencing a physical deterioration, such as an early fracture associated with the premature onset of osteoporosis.

FEMALE STUDENT-ATHLETES: A UNIQUE SUBCULTURE

Culture-related factors provide a foundation upon which individuals build identity, meaning, hope, and strength. The professional counseling literature provides a solid framework for helping stakeholders of all disciplines recognize the importance of exploring the cultural factors at play with female student-athletes. Issues such as gender disparities, sexual harassment, gender role conflict, relationships with coaches and teammates, striving for thinness, perfectionism, and the female athlete triad may all at times interact to produce a culture specific only to female athletes. In the 2005 American Counseling Association (ACA) *Code of Ethics*, for example, sensitivity to the cultural traditions of others is a founding principle. Specifically, *culture* refers to the "membership in a socially constructed way of living, which incorporates collective values, beliefs, norms, boundaries, and lifestyles that are cocreated with others who share similar worldviews comprising biological, psychosocial, historical, psychological, and other factors" (Glossary of Terms, p. 20). Similarly, the *Ethical Principles and Code of Conduct* set forth by the American Psychological Association (2002) stresses cultural consideration and respect, awareness of cultural biases, and awareness of whether one is in fact competent to provide services to individuals of a given culture. Not surprisingly, the nuances of sports and their impact on the student-athlete's well-being have been increasingly recognized in both professional counseling and psychology (Ward, Sandstedt, Cox, & Beck, 2005). Professionals of all kinds who work with female student-athletes in particular must consistently monitor cultural variables. Absent a cultural perspective, it seems reasonable to suggest that a full understanding of the variables impacting the student-athlete would occur, particularly when there is a failure to address the potential impact of the female student-athlete within the subtext of the sports culture.

Within the culture of female college athletics there are many ethnic, racial, familial, socioeconomic, and other differences between individual athletes. Certainly, it is important to honor the special circumstances of the individual who presents for treatment. Addressing any specific intragroup differences is beyond the scope of this chapter, and we therefore focus on exploring considerations common to female college student-athletes as a unique group within an equally distinctive cultural context. For many stakeholders, the *Multicultural Counseling Competencies* set forth by Sue, Arredondo, and McDavis (1992) provide a platform from which to work more efficiently, in the diversity sense, with female student-athletes. These competencies include three dimensions: awareness, knowledge, and skills. Stakeholders are thus urged to integrate the dimensions "by *first* increasing their awareness of culturally learned assumptions, *second* increasing their access to culturally relevant knowledge, and *third* increasing their appropriate use of culturally sensitive skills" (p. 31). This view is supported in the psychology literature, with Ward et al. (2005) contending that "there are special issues and cultural values of which psychologists should be aware when working with athletes in order to maximize the effectiveness of treatment" (p. 331). Ultimately, increasing one's awareness, knowledge, and skills concerning the culture of female student-athletes is an essential journey for professionals seeking cultural sensitivity and competency when working with this group.

AWARENESS

Concepts such as training, competition, motivation, teamwork, coaching, time management, nutrition, and balance are pervasive in sport culture. Additional constructs to consider when working with female student-athletes include thinness, the female athlete triad, gender role conflict, stereotype threat, sexual harassment, and academic concerns. As we have stressed, professionals working with female athletes should be aware of the common issues involved in the environment of the female student-athlete. In order to properly identify competencies related to effective treatment of athletes, Ward et al. (2005) systematically developed competencies based on ratings by numerous professionals working with athletes. Ward et al. delineated 17 essential athlete-counseling competency statements for psychologists working with athletes. They remarked that these competencies have "an underlying theme of counseling awareness and sensitivity within sport culture" (p. 329), and are consistent with popular and contemporary literature concerning athletes. These competencies can be considered a template by which mental health professionals in higher education can enhance and deliver effective services for the female student-athlete.

First, in order to properly and competently respond to the needs of female student-athletes, one must acknowledge learned assumptions regarding cultural differences. This process of self-inspection is the primary step in achieving awareness regarding cultural issues. In order to process cultural differences, one must understand one's own culture and how the development of culture affects the formation of values, attitudes, beliefs, and perceptions. In this manner, professionals working with athletes should be "aware of their values and biases as they relate to athletes and the sport environment" (Ward et al., 2005, p. 326). Honoring cultural differences involves acknowledging and accepting differences and similarities among cultures, without judgment.

In the mental health realm, there is the additional need to avoid false assumptions of female student-athletes that could lead to misdiagnoses (Ward et al., 2005). For example, in response to stress management, some athletes may have rituals or exhibit superstitious behaviors prior to games. These behaviors may be viewed as foreign, unrealistic, and/or problematic by the professional who is working with the female athlete. Michelle, a college basketball player interviewed for this study, stated "Some people think

I'm crazy for my pre-game rituals that can last for a whole week prior to the game...but I know that a lot of girls do the same thing.... It's just part of playing and I've done it for years." Aspects related to this sentiment regarding pre-game rituals was shared by 8 of our 11 female student-athlete interviewees and seemed to be a significant aspect of the sport culture of the female athletes in our sample. Therefore, for these female student-athletes, honoring their athletic identity is integral to facilitating effective services.

Another competency described by Ward et al. (2005) involves the notion of recognizing "that a client's athletic identity may be as important to the counseling process as is his/her race, gender, age, etc." (p. 326). Indeed, being an athlete may not merely be a means for entertainment, scholarship, and/or interaction. Many athletes have been involved in the sport culture for years and the act of engaging in the sport activity is not necessarily a secondary gain for the athlete. Choice of friends, social isolation, future goals, and/or life tasks may be directly related to being involved in sports. It may not even be considered a reward at all for the athlete who is experiencing burnout issues or who experiences a lack of "playing time." However, the identity of being an "athlete" is highly individualistic. However, it may be important to know that research suggests that female student-athletes tend to be more engaged in seeking out positive educational experiences than male student-athletes (Crawford, 2007).

Another variable specific to student-athletes involves the perception toward training. As such, it is important for professionals to "respect athlete clients' beliefs and values about physical and mental training" (Ward et al., 2005, p. 326). Next, professionals should respect and work within the supportive resources displayed by the coach and apparent within the institution. Some coaches may be more personable than others, some coaches may be stricter than others, and some coaches may be more prohibitive regarding what athletes are allowed to do in their spare time. According to Erica, a collegiate soccer player, the relationship with the coach "is almost parental because they have so much to say in what goes on." In this manner, it may be advisable to include the coach as collaboration is initiated.

KNOWLEDGE

As noted, female student-athletes are confronted with a variety of issues aside from *triad*. Indeed, as indicated in previous pages, there are a number of distinct issues related to the female student-athlete. As such, Ward et al. (2005) contend that sport psychologists working with female athletes "acknowledge the existence of a distinct sport/athlete culture" (p. 236). Furthermore, it is important to understand the environmental influence within this sport/athlete culture. For some scholars, athletics is regarded as a "culture of risk" since many athletes risk injury during practice and games (Roderick, 1998; Thing, 2006). Fear of injury, experiencing acute and/or chronic injury, and avoiding injury may extraordinarily impact the behavior and emotions of athletes. Meanwhile, it is important to understand and respect the regulations of the institution as they may strictly influence the behavior of college athletes. As stated earlier, difference in coaching styles or communication patterns may impact athletes and how they go about experiencing their lives on campus and beyond.

The remaining tenets included by Ward et al. (2005) regarding competency and athletes is related to competencies already depicted in the American Psychological Association (APA; 2002) and American Counseling Association (ACA; 2005). In order to effectively and appropriately engage and affect any client, it is crucial for the practitioner to "understand how race, culture, and ethnicity affect the appropriateness of counseling treatments for their athlete clients" (Ward et al., 2005, p. 326). Both of these associations emphasize the importance of culture when working with any client and this is generally understood among professionals. However, the sports culture includes additional notions of which an inexperienced professional may not be aware. Therefore, it is beneficial for professionals working with female athletes to link with other professionals who have experience. Ward et al. suggest that it is important for those who work with athletes to have supervision with someone who has experience working with female athletes. Due to proximity issues, it may not be realistic to have supervision with an individual in the same town or city. However, it may be practical to form a meaningful supervisory relationship with a willing experienced practitioner at another college, university, or organization. This collaborative supervision may increase the likelihood of applying culturally appropriate skills while working with the female athlete.

SKILLS

Being able to identify, acknowledge, and accept one's limitations is a skill in itself. This ability to understand limitations introduces a primary cultural competency introduced by Ward et al. (2005). According to Ward et al., it is important to refer athlete clients to more qualified professionals when necessary. This notion of working within the range of training and experience is widely accepted in the ethical codes of ACA (Section C.2) and APA (Ethical Standard 2) as with many of the competencies discussed in this chapter. Furthermore, it is imperative that the professional accept the notion that the female athlete exists within a culturally significant context. As such, it is advisable to select culturally responsive theories, techniques, and theoretical frameworks (Ward et al., 2005). This cultural responsiveness highlights the emphasis on the individual within a unique and intimate cultural environment. Generally, an athlete and a professional working with the athlete may be at the same higher education institution. At times, it may be unavoidable to have dual relationships. Therefore, it is important for the higher education professional to emphasize and maintain focus on the counseling relationship in order to effectively support female athlete clients. At times, the professional may need to "intervene with institutions and organizations on behalf of their athlete clients while appreciating the complexity of confidentiality issues in a sport environment" (Ward et al., 2005, p. 327). In this sense, the professional may need to become an active change agent or advocate for the athlete. Sherman, Thompson, Dehass, and Wilfert (2005) suggested that educating and training coaches and athletic trainers may result in a preventative stance, especially in terms of issues related to disordered eating habits of female athletes. At times, the professional may need to enlist expertise when seeking consultation with coaches and any other relevant personnel. At other times, the psychologist and/or counselor should consider when necessary educating coaches, organizations, and institutions, as well as athletes in regards to the counseling process (Ward et al., 2005). This educational process may alleviate concerns and/or stigma, and may influence the formation of realistic expectations regarding effective treatment, goals, and the counseling process. Meanwhile, collaboration among those who work with athletes may be an essential application within the female athlete cultural context. Developing mentoring teams, assigning leaders, forming mediation teams, and/or initiating any other collaborative efforts that will work well within the culture-specific environment may be fruitful.

INITIATING INTERVIEWS

The female student-athlete may seek supportive services while wondering whether you will be able to help her, or even to understand her. It is crucial to begin building a therapeutic alliance in the very first session. To this end, it is essential for professionals working with female athletes to have, at minimum, a rudimentary understanding of the interrelatedness of disordered eating, amenorrhea, and osteoporosis. Familiarity with the female athlete triad, and other culture-specific issues discussed in this chapter, will aid in the development of rapport and the deepening of the relationship, factors that are vital to therapy outcome.

Additionally, college athletes as a whole tend to underuse counseling services (Cogan & Petrie, 1996). They might present with resistance to the therapy process for various reasons as they are driven into therapy by coaches or parents. They may not believe they have a problem. They may believe seeking support reflects weakness. They fear being perceived as impaired and therefore believe their coaches will keep them out of games due to "mental health" problems. Trying to convince an athlete of her need for assistance might be construed as argumentative, and that you are "siding with the coach" or whoever urged the athlete into seeking support and/or treatment. For the professional who is providing supportive services, it is imperative for the practitioner to suspend judgment. Let her know that you understand her dilemmas: *get therapy or get off the team; eat healthy and risk losing speed and leanness; eat satisfying foods with intense guilt; endure emotional abuse for the sake of a scholarship, or just a place on the team.* Another option is to collaboratively explore the pros and cons of different interventions and treatment plans. Furthermore, take a less conspicuous position. In other words, lead from behind, reminding her of options but letting her make the ultimate decisions. Still another positive and empirically valid therapeutic intervention is the group therapy format, in which senior athletes relate their experiences to novice athletes, may augment individual counseling if deemed appropriate.

Keep in mind that athletes might not meet full criteria for the eating disorders described in the *Diagnostic and Statistical Manual of Mental Disorders* (DSM-IV-TR; American Psychiatric Association, 2000). However, their nutritional practices might still be unhealthy in that they are creating a caloric deficiency, thereby opening the door for the other two components of the triad. We recommend collaborating with a nutritionist and an eating disorder specialist, and ensuring that the athlete's coach agrees to the prescribed regimen and sends a positive, encouraging message to the athlete. This may reduce the dissonance the athlete suffers when she eats nourishing, satisfying foods. In any case, it is essential to regard the issues related to the female athlete within a cultural context relative to the sport culture existing in colleges and universities across the United States. Overall, attending to the unique needs and circumstances of the student-athlete should involve the application of awareness, knowledge, and skills that are appropriate to the sports culture.

INTERVIEWS YIELDING A GLIMPSE

Prior to investigating issues related to awareness, knowledge, and skills, the authors of this chapter endeavored to provide supporting anecdotes from the interviews of current female student-athletes. We recorded the personal stories of female athletes and their coaches in order to illuminate understanding. We hoped that these stories would reveal practical information regarding the contemporary culture of female athletes in terms of awareness, knowledge, and skills. It is doubtful that the following excerpts from the interviewees provide an undeniable complete representation of female athletes; however, these revelations may provide a helpful glimpse into the personal culture of female athletes. Informed of our intentions, 17 female athletes were willing to be interviewed and responded to our questions voluntarily. Many were excited to do so, as one athlete fittingly replied "It's about time we women got some attention!" They were enrolled in a large university (Division I-A), small university (Division II-A), and small college (Division III-A) in the Southeastern region of the United States. Seven softball student-athletes, six soccer student-athletes, four basketball student-athletes, and two coaches were interviewed. According to the NCAA (2007), soccer has the highest number of female athletes since the 1999–2000 year. Meanwhile, track and field, softball, and basketball players rank as the second, third, and fourth highest number of female athletes in the country, respectively (NCAA, 2007). Each volunteer interviewee was interviewed via phone and email, and all of the volunteers were given the opportunity to include additional information through email correspondence. In order to protect anonymity, the names of these athletes have been changed and any relative information has been concealed and/or altered. The group of volunteers included athletes who were adjusting to the first year of college athletics (6) to those who were veterans with at least two years of experience (11). In terms of ethnicity, the group consisted of six African American, one Hispanic, and 10 Caucasian females. Nevertheless, the interviews yielded an interesting glimpse into the realm of the female student-athlete culture.

Interviewing female athletes revealed many facets related to the cultural environment of the female student-athlete in our small sample. Of course, it may be unlikely that our findings can be generalized; however, the excerpts may provide possibilities of exploration for professionals working with female student-athletes. An overwhelmingly common theme revealed from our interviews of female athletes was the notion of balance. Apparently, exploring and understanding the dynamics related to balance may be an integral aspect when working with female athletes. Many athletes cited balance as a fundamental element of concern and struggle. As Tina (soccer player) stated, "I constantly have to find time to study when I'm not practicing but there are a million other things that I have to do when I get home . . . and things that I want to do like hang out with my friends."

This statement underscores the theme of balance as well as the idea that the student-athlete may have many roles through which she must navigate. Balancing emotions was another aspect that was evident with some athletes, as depicted in the statement by Stephanie (soccer), "I really don't like always being expected to act a certain way for people. . . . Sometimes I might be upset about something (regarding soccer), and my friends and family just don't get it and want me to act like it doesn't really matter . . ." Stephanie added, ". . . that's why I just don't talk about it with my friends much." Therefore, the receptivity and understanding received from nonathletes may affect the emotional balance of some athletes. As such, some athletes may choose to isolate themselves or merely interact with other athletes. In fact, 11 of our female athletes reported choosing and having friends who were on the same team the majority of the time. Thus, the issues of social interaction and support may be somewhat challenging for some female athletes and there may be adapting response to such issues. For a new student-athlete, Emily (softball), these issues seemed to be daunting as "a lot of girls expect you to do things outside of practice...it's almost like initiation...but some girls are more cooler than others and I can get away with some things but I still can't trust anybody to keep secrets." Overall, it seemed that these expectations were directly related to the notion of balance. Appeasing the coach, professor, teammates, family members, and nonathlete friends were consistent throughout the interviews. In fact, one veteran student-athlete suggested, "...you have to have friends outside your team because you have to have something that is different than what you do every single day, in and out, in and out...but it can be hard because some of these friends get frustrated when you can't do something with them because you have to practice or whatever.... I have lost a lot of friends that way...'cause they just don't get it." The idea that nonathletes are not able to "get it" seems to be indicative of many athletes who report not being understood by professors and other nonathletes.

Some athletes seem to place more pressure on themselves based on their level of acceptance on the team. One freshman basketball athlete, Anna, said, "I know that I have to prove myself because everyone looks at me like I don't belong or something...especially when I'm not playing so hot.... That's why I'm really trying to practice my butt off." Performance expectation is also indicative in the classroom as this same athlete cited having "to prove to everyone that I should've been accepted [into the institution]." Meanwhile, professors expect students to complete assignments in a timely manner. In some cases, according to Tina, the stress related to performance expectation can result in some athletes exchanging prescribed medication. In such cases, "Some girls will give other girls their meds that help them focus or give them energy so they can do better in class or whatever." In our sample, all of the athletes denied having or witnessing any substance abuse issues related to alcohol and drugs such as marijuana and cocaine. However, three athletes reported witnessing the exchange of prescribed medication. Interestingly, most of the athletes did not seem to relate the exchange of prescribed medication as a substance abuse issue and relinquished the information only after probing questions were conducted by the interviewer. Nonetheless, it seems that the notion of balance, perceived stress, and the related issues of roles, expectations, and performance were experienced in varied manners among the female student-athletes. Overall, these issues seemed to be evident for many of the athletes and the general theme of balance was incredibly pervasive in the cultural environment of the female student-athlete in our small sample.

CONCLUSION

Clearly, it is important for professionals working in higher education to understand and acknowledge the many unique experiences encountered by the female student-athlete. Culture, both inside and outside athletics, inherently influences and directs human development and social interaction, thereby influencing identity formation in individuals and groups. Therefore, awareness and sensitivity to the gender and the socially constructed collective identities of college student-athletes is imperative. As such, it is important to acknowledge and understand two cultural ramifications for this population—the female student-athlete and the distinctive cultural context in which she lives. Furthermore, scholars agree that promoting awareness, knowledge, and skills regarding the effective support and treatment of female student-athletes is necessary.

Examining the cultural context in which female student-athletes live is crucial for practitioners in order to appropriately measure and attend to the needs of these student-athletes. First, it is reasonable to presume that female college athletes will face similar yet uniquely different experiences when compared with their male counterparts. McFadden (1999, 2003) contends that it is crucial for interdisciplinary professionals to recognize cultural–historical facets of inequality, power differentials, stereotypes, and oppression in order to properly attend to the needs of individuals from diverse cultures. Certainly, understanding issues related to gender as well as gender stereotypes are equally integral to working with female student-athletes. A rudimentary understanding of the female athlete triad as well as issues related to training, competition, motivation, teamwork, coaching, time management, nutrition, and balance is important for those working with female student-athletes. Honoring and exploring the sport culture of the female athlete, through open, honest, and nonjudgmental interviewing, may lead to increased understanding for this prolific and historically overlooked population.

REFERENCES

Allison, M. T. (1991). Role conflict and the female athlete: Preoccupations with little grounding. *Journal of Applied Sport Psychology, 3*, 49–60.

American Association of University Women. (2008). Title IX athletic statistics. Retrieved July 24, 2008, from http://www.aauw.org

American Counseling Association. (2005). *Code of ethics.* Alexandria, VA: Author.

American Psychiatric Association. (2000). *Diagnostic and statistical manual of mental disorders* (4th ed., text revision) Washington, DC: Author.

American Psychological Association. (2002). *Ethical principles of psychologists and code of conduct*. Washington, DC: Author.

Blum, D. E. (1994). College sports' L-word: Lesbian labels damage careers of female athletes. *Chronicle of Higher Education, 40*, 35–37.

Christensen, M., & Kelso, P. (2004). Soccer chief's plan to boost women's game? Hotpants. Retrieved July 11, 2008, from http://www.guardian.co.uk/uk/2004/jan/16/football.gender

Cogan, D. K., & Petrie, T. (1996). Consultation with college student athletes. *College Student Journal, 30*, 9–16.

Disch, L., & Kane, M. J. (2000). When a looker is really a bitch: Lisa Olsen, sport and the heterosexual matrix. In S. Birrell & M. G. McDonald (Eds.), *Reading sport: Critical essays on power and representation* (pp. 108–143). Boston: Northeastern University Press.

Fallon, M. A., & Jome, L. M. (2007). An exploration of gender-role expectations and conflict among women rugby players. *Psychology of Women Quarterly, 31*, 311–321.

Fasting, K., Brackenridge, C., & Walseth, K. (2007). Women athletes' personal responses to sexual harassment in sport. *Journal of Applied Sport Psychology, 19*, 419–433.

Greenlee, C. T. (1997). Title IX: Does help for women come at the expense of African Americans? *Black Issues in Higher Education, 14*, 24–28.

Hausenblas, H. A., & Carron, A. V. (1999). Eating disorder indices and athletes: An integration. *Journal of Sport and Exercise Psychology, 21*, 230–258.

Lantz, C. D., & Schroeder, P. J. (1999). Endorsement of masculine and feminine gender roles: Differences between participation in and identification with the athlete role. *Journal of Sport Behavior, 22*, 545–557.

McFadden, J. (Ed.). (1999). *Transcultural counseling* (2nd ed.). Alexandria, VA: American Counseling Association.

McFadden, J. (2003). Stylistic model for counseling across cultures. In F. D. Harper & J. McFadden (Eds.), *Culture and counseling: New approaches* (pp. 209–232). Boston: Pearson Education.

National Collegiate Athletic Association. (2007). *1981–1982—2006-2007: NCAA sports sponsorship and participation rates*. Indianapolis, IN: Author.

Nattiv, A., Agostini, R., Drinkwater, B., & Yeager, K. K. (1994). The female athlete triad: The inter-relatedness of disordered eating, amenorrhea, and osteoporosis. *Clinical Sports Medicine, 13*,405–418.

Nielson, J. T. (2001). The forbidden zone: Intimacy, sexual relations and misconduct in the relationship between coaches and athletes. *International Review for the Sociology of Sport, 36*, 165–182.

Otis, C. L., Drinkwater, B. L., Johnson, M., Loucks, A. B., & Whilmore, J. H. (1997). American College of Sports Medicine position stand on the female athlete triad. *Medicine and Science in Sports and Exercise, 29*, i–ix.

Powe-Allred, A., & Powe, M. (1997). *The quiet storm*. Indianapolis, IN: Masters Press.

Roderick, M. (1998). The sociology of risk, pain and injury: A comment on the work of Howard L. Nixon II. *Social Sport Journal, 15*, 64–79.

Rouveix, M., Bouget, M., Pannafleux, C., Champely, S., & Filaire, E. (2006). Eating attitudes, body esteem, perfectionism and anxiety of judo athletes and non-athletes. *International Journal of Sports Medicine, 28,* 340–345.

Ruggiero, T. E., & Lattin, K. S. (2008) Intercollegiate female coaches' use of verbally aggressive communication toward African American female athletes. *Howard Journal of Communications, 19(2),* 105–124.

Sage, G. H., & Loudermilk, S. (1979). The female athlete and role conflict. *Research Quarterly, 50,* 88–96.

Salisbury, J., & Passer, M. W. (1982). Gender role attitudes and participation in competitive activities of varying stereotypic femininity. *Personality and Social Psychology Bulletin, 8,* 486–493.

Schwarz, H. C., Gairrett, R. L., Aruguete, M. S., & Gold, E. S. (2005). Eating attitudes, body dissatisfaction, and perfectionism in female college athletes. *North American Journal of Psychology, 7,* 345–352.

Sherman, R. T., & Thompson, R. A. (2006). Practical use of the International Olympic Committee Medical Commission position stand on the female athlete triad: A case example. *International Journal of Eating Disorders, 39,* 193–201.

Sherman, R. T., Thompson, R. A., Dehass, D., & Wilfert, M. (2005). NCAA coaches survey: The role of the coach in identifying and managing athletes with disordered eating. *Eating Disorders, 13,* 447–466.

Sklover, B. (1997, Winter). Women sports. *American Association of University Women Outlook,* pp. 12–17.

Steele, C. M., & Aronson, J. (1995). Stereotype threat and the intellectual test performance of African Americans. *Journal of Personality and Social Psychology, 69,* 797–811.

Stirling, A. E., & Kerr, G. A. (2007). Elite female swimmers' experiences of emotional abuse across time. *Journal of Emotional Abuse, 7,* 89–113.

Sue, D. W., Arredondo, P., & McDavis, R. J. (1992). Multicultural counseling competencies: A call to the profession. *Journal of Counseling and Development, 70,* 477–486.

Thing, L. F. (2006). Voices of the broken body. *Scandinavian Journal of Medicine and Science in Sports, 16,* 364–375.

Tofler, I. R., Stryer, B. K., Micheli, L. J., & Herman, L. R. (1996). Physical and emotional problems of elite female gymnasts. *New England Journal of Medicine, 335,* 281–283.

Unger, R., & Crawford, M. (1992). *Women and gender: A feminist psychology.* New York: McGraw-Hill.

Ward, D. G., Sandstedt, S. D., Cox, R. H., & Beck, N. C. (2005). Athlete-Counseling Competencies for U.S. psychologists working with athletes. *The Sport Psychologist, 19,* 318–334.

Women's Sports Foundation. (2008). *2007 Statistics – Gender equity in high school and college athletics: Most recent participation and budget statistics.* Retrieved July 24, 2008, from http://www.womessportsfoundation.org

Zucker, N. L., Womble, L. G., Williamson, D. A., & Perrin, L. A. (1999). Protective factors for eating Disorders in female college athletes. *Eating Disorders, 7,* 207–218.

CHAPTER 11

BODY IMAGE AND FEMALE STUDENT-ATHLETES

Jennifer M. Miles
University of Arkansas

Women enroll in college for a number of reasons. Initially, women may decide to pursue college degrees for career preparation and for the sake of learning. The years in college, however, also offer women opportunities for personal growth and development. Because women represent over half of the current student population, the experience of female college students is becoming increasingly significant. They arrive on campus seeking to identify who they are as individuals and as a group.

Student-athletes enter college for additional reasons. These reasons can vary based on a variety of factors, including the student's athletic ability, the athletic division of the institution, the student's reliance on scholarships, and the influence of family, friends, and coaches. At institutions with less competitive athletic programs, students may decide to participate on an athletic team after being accepted to the institution. In that instance, the student's college career is not dependent upon their success in the sport. In other cases, however, students are heavily recruited by many institutions. They may choose to attend an institution based on the team's national ranking or based on the experience of the coach. In those cases, the student's

College Student-Athletes: Challenges, Opportunities, and Policy Implications, pages 151–159
Copyright © 2009 by Information Age Publishing
All rights of reproduction in any form reserved.

academic experience is inextricably linked to their experience on the team. For student-athletes, maintaining a minimum grade point average may be linked to scholarships. Student-athletes are not only at college to prepare for career or graduate or professional school, they are at that institution as a way to pay for college and/or because of skill and desire to compete.

An alarming number of women engage in self-destructive, unhealthy behaviors to conform to broad and societal-driven concepts of beauty. This is particularly true on college campuses (Levitt, 2004). Extensive research has been conducted regarding traditional-aged college students and body dissatisfaction (e.g., Forrest & Stuhldrehrer, 2007). Body image can affect how women see themselves and how they experience college. The years in college can be challenging, including new stressors and responsibilities as well as learning to manage time. Student-athletes must learn to balance the transition issues faced by all students and must, at the same time, learn to function as an effective member of a team. They are susceptible to the same influences of all students in terms of body image and the physical ideal, but must also balance needs in terms of fitness, weight, and health in order to perform as an athlete.

BODY IMAGE AND EATING DISORDERS

Women change the way they see themselves throughout their college careers. The undergraduate experience includes learning both inside and outside of the classroom. When women enter college, they find themselves in a new culture. They need to adjust how they see themselves in relation to other students, faculty, and staff. They need to learn a new vocabulary and adjust to a new set of expectations. The students must learn to use technology, to study, and to make a place for themselves. These experiences and challenges can be an opportunity for women to reinvent themselves. Consistent with Rudd and Lennon (2000), Trautmann, Worthy, and Lokken (2007) found that individuals may attempt to conform to a culture's physical ideal through diet, exercise, clothing choices, and surgery.

Body image can be defined as how an individual perceives her body (Cash & Pruzinsky, 1990, 2002). Regardless of how the societal definition of physical beauty has been developed, many college women seek conformity with the pages of magazines (Hawkins, Richards, Granley, & Stein, 2004). Hawkins et al. (2004) found that viewing images of the thin-ideal in magazines caused an increase in body dissatisfaction, negative mood states, and eating disorder symptoms. They also determined that viewing the images was associated with a decreased sense of self-esteem.

In the quest for some vision of beauty, college women may exercise excessively, to almost unhealthy levels, and develop eating disorders. Other women may decide that the images they see are physical impossibilities. Instead of working to conform to what they see as unattainable, these women may choose to abandon healthy lifestyles completely. Without proper nutrition and exercise, women may develop lower self-esteem, be unsatisfied with their physical appearance, and may not have the energy needed to pursue their desired lifestyles. This lack of satisfaction could affect all of their roles, including those of students, campus, and community leaders, friends, daughters, sisters, mothers, wives, employees, mentors, and athletes.

College women are at risk of developing eating disorders because of a variety of factors, including excessive exercise, social isolation, body dissatisfaction, high levels of anxiety, and disturbed eating and dieting patterns (Levitt, 2004). Body image disturbance has been associated with developing eating disorders (Bergstrom & Neighbors, 2006). Risks associated with developing an eating disorder may arise from overestimation of personal size and dissatisfaction with weight (Striegel-Moore et al., 2004). Additional risk factors include fear of fat, fear of failure, and a poor body image (Beals & Manore, 1994; Leon, 1991; Williams, Sargent, & Durstine, 2003).

An eating disorder is diagnosed when specific criteria are present. Psychopathlogy and psychological distress are included. The terms "subclinical eating disorders," however, and "disordered eating" are used to describe various abnormal behaviors that do not fulfill that diagnosis. These women may share symptoms of an eating disorder, but do not meet all of the criteria (Williams et al., 2003). A poor body image may or may not lead to an eating disorder meeting a clinical diagnosis; disordered eating, however, can still be problematic.

BODY IMAGE AND FEMALE STUDENT-ATHLETES

Etzel, Watson, Visek, and Maniar (2006) defined college student-athletes as "predominantly undergraduate students enrolled in colleges and universities across the United States who participate in institutionally sponsored, competitive sporting activities, not including club or intramural sports" (p. 519). Student-athletes participate in athletics sponsored by organizations including the National Collegiate Athletic Association, the National Association of Intercollegiate Athletics, the National Junior College Association, and the National Christian College Association (Etzel et al., 2006).

The enactment of Title IX of the Education Amendments Act in 1972 increased opportunities for women in college and university sports. Title IX prohibits discrimination on the basis of sex in any education program or activity that receives federal funding. Increased opportunities and societal acceptance has resulted in more women participating in intercollegiate athletics (Malinauskas, Cucchiara, Aeby, & Bruening, 2007). In addition to increased participation from students and financial commitments from institutions, the enforcement of this act has also led to athletic departments reassessing their structure and purpose (Gerdy, 2006).

Student-athletes represent a diverse and visible student population with their own needs and expectations (Parham, 1996). They are faced with the same developmental challenges as nonathletes, but must also deal with challenges associated with athletics (Etzel et al., 2006). As they try to fulfill the requirements associated with the roles of student and athlete, they are faced with specific pressures. Some of these pressures include separation from family and friends, academic expectations, injuries, and career preparation (Pinkerton, Hinz, & Barrow, 1989; Selby, Weinstein, & Bird, 1990; Williams et al., 2003).

Although athletes are considered emotionally healthy (Powers & Johnson, 1996), the additional pressures they confront can make them susceptible to health problems, including both psychological and physical problems (Etzel et al., 2006). Major health problems of student-athletes include alcohol use, eating disorders and dysfunctional eating behaviors, and coping with injury or stress (Selby et al., 1990). Mood and self-esteem can be affected by the student's weight (Seime & Damer, 1991).

In a study of subclinical eating disorders in female student-athletes, students were asked to indicate reasons for dieting and controlling their weight. The study included 587 female student-athletes from nine institutions and represented 13 sports. All institutions were in the state of Virginia. The sports included cross-country, diving, basketball, crew, gymnastics, golf, field hockey, lacrosse, swimming, volleyball, soccer, softball, and tennis. The reasons reported included enhancing performance, enhancing appearance, improving health, and because someone recommended they diet. The students who gave improving appearance as a reason for dieting represented 12 sports including diving, basketball, crew, gymnastics, golf, field hockey, lacrosse, swimming, volleyball, soccer, softball, and tennis. All sports except for cross-country had over 50% of the student reporting dieting or other methods to control their weight (Williams et al., 2003).

The "female athlete triad" is a three-part syndrome found in female student-athletes (American College of Sports Medicine, 1997). The triad includes disordered eating, amenorrhea, and osteoporosis (Etzel et al., 2006). In the short term, disordered eating can lead to lower weight and improved performance, but long-term effects may include major complications such as organ failure (Seime & Damer, 1991).

Low body fat can enhance an athlete's performance. This can place pressure on the athlete to reduce fat, specifically in sports where a specific weight is deemed critical for performance or appearance (Williams et al., 2003). Weigh-ins are sometimes a requirement to being a member of an athletic team (Willams et al., 2003). Female athletes may become preoccupied with food and may develop eating disorders (Beals & Manore, 2002; Wichmann & Martin, 1993). At the same time, adequate nutrition is necessary for a student-athlete to perform at his or her best (Williams et al., 2003). In response to disordered eating and health problems in student-athletes, athletic departments have developed eating disorder policies and prevention programs (Thompson & Sherman, 1993). Coaches and family members have been found to play a role regarding whether or not a student-athlete develops an eating disorder (Beals & Manore, 1994).

IMPLICATIONS FOR STUDENT AFFAIRS

Divisions of student affairs are responsible for creating a safe environment in which students can learn. This learning occurs both inside and outside the classroom. Student affairs is also charged with providing resources for students to help them succeed. Functional area assignments vary from institution to institution, especially regarding size of the institution and institutional mission. Some of the functions of divisions of student affairs customarily include housing, health centers, counseling, wellness, residence life, fraternity and sorority affairs, and leadership development.

One of the themes seen in student affairs involves assisting students with transitions. New student orientation programs are in place to assist students with the transition to college. The students learn about residence life, tutoring, course registration, and social opportunities. Career development centers provide assistance regarding transitioning from the role of student to employee. Students can receive help with resumé writing, interview preparation, and salary negotiation.

Moving from a high school student-athlete to a college student-athlete is another transition. Student affairs professionals are uniquely qualified to assist students with this transition. They oversee areas designed to ease transitions, such as counseling and health centers. Student-athletes also represent a specific subpopulation. Student affairs is charged with serving all populations of students and creating environments designed for success. Body image can affect all students. While in college, students feel a need to conform and fit in with the community. Student affairs personnel are uniquely positioned to help all students through the transition.

In a study examining help-seeking preferences in college women, Prouty, Protinsky, and Canady (2002) found that college women prefer to seek help from friends instead of professionals. There is a need for programs in which student leaders can learn the symptoms of eating disorders. Training may be provided by college counselors. Counselors can also provide training to faculty, staff, and coaches. This training may fall under the purview of a division of student affairs. University physicians should be trained to screen students for disordered eating. Campus awareness is a vital component in helping women with eating disorders find appropriate treatment (Meyer, 2005).

Professionals in sports medicine look at more than just physical health, but also mental health issues, including anxiety, depression, substance abuse, and grief (Brown & Blanton, 2002; Hinkle, 1996). Student affairs can be instrumental in helping athletes with these problems (Etzel et al., 2006). The isolation of student-athlete departments from the rest of the student population may encourage coaches and athletic staff to handle problems within their program or off campus (Etzel et al., 2006). Given their in-depth knowledge regarding student development, student affairs professionals are in the unique position to collaborate effectively with coaches and trainers to provide appropriate and timely interventions and programs to the students.

Communication between student affairs and administrators and coaches, as well as regular confidential meetings between student-athletes and student affairs staff, may prevent serious health problems from occurring or escalating (Etzel et al., 2006). Student-athletes face additional and special stressors as they balance responsibilities of students and athletes. Student-athletes are exposed to different health risks than nonathletes (Etzel et al., 2006). Student affairs professionals would benefit from familiarizing themselves with the health issues of this student population (Etzel et al., 2006).

DISCUSSION

Women attend college to further themselves through education, but are confronted with traditional concepts of beauty and stereotypes regarding physical appearance. College and university women also receive mixed messages regarding their value as students and the importance of attractiveness. For many women, college is a paradox between the serious nature of intellectual curiosity and the pull to conform to societal expectations. These expectations can be powerful forces as they define themselves mentally and physically. This quest for recognition of a physical definition presents many problems, particularly as female students attempt to conform to often distorted views of beauty and self-image (Bergstrom & Neighbors, 2006).

Like all students, student-athletes must learn how to function as a member of a new community. In addition to the transitional issues experienced by all college students, student-athletes must also cope and adjust to the pressures of serving on an athletic team. Involvement in athletics may also involve increased expectations for successful academic performance. These increased expectations may come from coaches, academic advisors, teammates, and the students themselves. The success of a college or university's athletic program is tied to wins and losses, television appearances, championships, and revenue generated (Gerdy, 2006). Student-athletes may feel pressure to perform to contribute to the success of their institution.

Concern with body image starts well before the college years. In a study of middle school boys and girls, Wiseman, Peltzman, Halmi, and Sunday (2004) found that a relationship exists between a drive for thinness and self-esteem in girls. This relationship could put them at risk to develop eating disorders. The researchers have also examined body dissatisfaction, the drive for thinness, and self-esteem in middle school students. When children first begin to participate in athletics, measures can be taken to avoid negative consequences seen in older athletes. Coaches and parents can assist by becoming aware of the positive and negative psychological effects associated with athletics (Etzel et al., 2006).

Female athletes are subject to the pressures on all athletes to maintain a certain weight and fitness level. Student-athletes may diet to improve their performance, their appearance, or their overall health. Student-athletes who have heard others comment on their body weight were more likely to develop subclinical eating disorders (Williams et al., 2003). Preventive education is important for coaches and athletes (Williams et al., 2003).

Female student-athletes are faced with the pressures placed on all women to be thin. The ideal woman portrayed in the media is slim (Maliauskas et al., 2007), but that body type may not be ideal or healthy for a female athlete to excel at her particular sport. This pressure and mixed messages may lead female student-athletes to pursue an unrealistic body size (Beals & Manore, 1994). This preoccupation with an unattainable ideal may affect a student's athletic performance, academic performance, and overall success as a student.

REFERENCES

American College of Sports Medicine. (1997). ACSM position on female athlete triad. *Medicine and Science in Sports and Exercise, 29*(5), i–ix.

Beals, K. A., & Manore, M. M. (1994). The prevalence and consequences of subclinical eating disorders in female athletes. *International Journal of Sport Nutrition, 4*(2), 175–195.

Beals, K. A., & Manore, M. M. (2002). Disorders of the female athlete triad among collegiate athletes. *International Journal Sport Nutrition and Exercise Metabolism, 12*(3), 281–293.

Bergstrom, R. L., & Neighbors, C. (2006). Body image disturbance and the social norms approach: An integrative review of the literature. *Journal of Social and Clinical Psychology, 25*(9), 975–1000.

Brown, D., & Blanton, C. (2002). Physical activity, sports participation, and suicidal behavior among college students. *Medicine and Science in Sports and Exercise, 34*(7), 1087–1096.

Cash, T. F., & Pruzinsky, T. (Eds.). (1990). *Body images: Development , deviance, and change*. New York: Guilford Press.

Cash, T. F., & Pruzinsky, T. (Eds.). (2002). *Body image: A handbook of theory, research, and clinical practice*. New York: Guilford Press.

Etzel, E. F., Watson, J. C., Visek, A. J., & Maniar, S. D. (2006). Understanding and promoting college student-athlete health: Essential issues for student affairs professionals. *NASPA Journal, 43*(3), 518–546.

Forrest, K. Y. Z., & Stuhldreher, W. L. (2007). Patterns and correlates of body image dissatisfaction and distortion among college students. *American Journal of Health Studies, 22*(1), 18–25.

Gerdy, J. R. (2006). *Air ball: American education's failed experiment with elite athletics*. Jackson: University Press of Mississippi.

Hawkins, N., Richards, P. S., Granley, H. M., & Stein, D. M. (2004). The impact of exposure to the thin-ideal media image on women. *Eating Disorders, 12*, 35–50.

Hinkle, J. (1996). Depression, adjustment disorder, generalized anxiety, and substance abuse: An overview for sports professionals working with student athletes. In E. F. Etzel, A. P. Ferrante, & J. W. Pinkney (Eds.), *Counseling college student-athletes: Issues and interventions* (2nd ed., pp. 109–136). Morgantown, WV: Fitness Information Technology.

Leon, G. R. (1991). Eating disorders in female athletes. *Sports Medicine, 12*(4), 219–227.

Levitt, D. H. (2004). Drive for thinness and fear of fat among college women: Implications for practice and assessment. *Journal of College Counseling, 7*, 109–117.

Maliauskas, B. M., Cucchiara, A. J., Aeby, V. G., & Bruening, C. C. (2007). Physical activity, disordered eating risk, and anthropometric measurement: A comparison of college female athletes and non athletes. *College Student Journal, 41*(1), 217–222.

Meyer, D. F. (2005). Psychological correlates of help seeking for eating-disorder symptoms in female students, *Journal of College Counseling, 8*, 20–30.

Parham, W. (1996). Diversity within intercollegiate athletics: Current profile and welcomed opportunities. In E. F. Etzel, A. P. Ferrante, & J. W. Pinkney (Eds.), *Counseling college student-athletes: Issues and interventions* (2nd ed., pp. 26–49). Morgantown, WV: Fitness Information Technology.

Pinkerton, R. S., Hinz, L. D., & Barrow, J. C. (1989). The college student-athlete: Pschological considerations and interventions. *Journal of American College Health, 37*(5), 218–226.

Powers, P. S., & Johnson, C. (1996). Small victories: Prevention of eating disorders among athletes. *Eating Disorders, 4*(4), 364–377.

Prouty, A. M., Protinsky, H. O., & Canady, D. (2002). College women: Eating behaviors and help-seeking preferences. *Adolescence, 37*, 353–363.

Rudd, N. A., & Lennon, S. J. (2000). Body image and appearance-management behaviors in college women. *Clothing and Textiles Research Journal, 18*(3), 152–162.

Seime, R., & Damer, D. (1991). Identification and treatment of the athlete with an eating disorder. In E. F. Etzel, A. P. Ferrante, & J. W. Pinkney (Eds.), *Counseling college student-athletes: Issues and interventions* (pp. 175–198), Morgantown, WV: Fitness information Technology.

Selby, R., Weinstein, H. M., & Bird, T. S. (1990). The health of university athletes: Attitudes, behaviors, and stressors. *Journal of American College Health, 39*(1), 11–18.

Striegel-Moore, R. H., Franko, D. L., Thompson, D., Barton, B., Schreiber, G. G., & Daniels, S. R. (2004). Changes in weight and body image over time in women with eating disorders. *International Journal of Eating Disorders, 36*, 315–327.

Thompson, R., & Sherman, R. (1993). *Helping athletes with eating disorders.* Champaign, IL: Human Kinetics.

Trautmann, J., Worthy, S. L., & Lokken, K. L. (2007). Body dissatisfaction, bulimic symptoms, and clothing practices among college women. *Journal of Psychology, 141*(5), 485–498.

Wichmann, S., & Martin, D. R. (1993). Eating disoreders in athletes: Weighing the risks. *Physician and Sportsmedicine, 21*(5), 126–135.

Williams, P. L., Sargent, R. G., & Durstine, L. J. (2003). Prevalence of subclinical eating disorders in collegiate female athletes. *Women in Sport and Physical Activity Journal, 12*(2), 127–145.

Wiseman, C. V., Peltzman, B., Halmi, K. A., & Sunday, S. R. (2004). Risk factors for eating disorders: Surprising similarities between middle school boys and girls. *Eating Disorders, 12*, 315–320.

CHAPTER 12

INTERNATIONAL STUDENT-ATHLETES

Daniel B. Kissinger
University of Arkansas, Fayetteville

Athletic programs represent an increasingly influential dimension of life on American college and university campuses. Adorned in their team's colors, students, faculty, alumni, and fans, often with several generations in tow, converge on campuses nationwide to attend athletic events. The exploits of players and coaches, along with prominent institutional and athletic department personnel and boosters, generate narratives that can unite the school's constituents or cause deep fissures that resonate at all levels of the school's leadership and detract from the institution's core educational mission. What is often absent from both the general and empirical discourse regarding collegiate athletics, however, are discussions regarding the phenomenological experiences of college athletes and how their athletic participation impacts their overall development (Etzel, Pinkney, & Hinkle, 1994; Ferrante, Etzel, & Lantz, 1996).

Too often the primary value accorded a student-athlete correlates with the prestige their athletic performances bring to the institution. In reality, college athletes encounter a cross section of opportunities and challenges unique to their status as a student-athlete. Navigating these challenges

College Student-Athletes: Challenges, Opportunities, and Policy Implications, pages 161–180
Copyright © 2009 by Information Age Publishing
161

and opportunities can certainly tax the physical and emotional reserves of domestic (American) student-athletes. For international student-athletes, however, these challenges may be magnified given their exposure and need to adjust to the cultural milieu of a foreign country. Adding to the challenge is the need to acclimate to the distinctive American sports culture. Today, while international student-athletes are recognized as being important contributors to the athletic and cultural environment of the chosen institutions (Ridinger & Pastore, 2001), little empirical data exists to help us understand how foreign student-athletes experience their time at American colleges and universities. Therefore, the central premise of this chapter is to provide an overview of the current understanding of challenges and benefits encountered by, and derived from, international student-athletes at American colleges and universities.

HISTORY

Foreign students and scholars factor substantially into the social, economic, and intellectual fabric of U.S. colleges and universities. International students help diversify student populations, provide American students with their first sustained contact with foreigners, help fill classrooms, and often assume teaching and research responsibilities (Johnson, 2003). Geopolitical benefits may also occur as U.S.-educated international students and scholars rise to leadership positions after returning to their home countries (Altbach, 1998; Johnson, 2003). However, while international students and scholars have long inhabited the classrooms and strolled the campus greens of American colleges and universities, the prominence of foreign student-athletes on the athletic rosters of America's higher education institutions has only recently begun garnering the attention of those outside the athletic domain.

American colleges and universities have a long-standing affinity for utilizing talented foreign athletes to gain a competitive advantage. Canadian track and field athletes, for example, were first noted at American schools in the early 1900s. The vigorous pursuit of foreign athletes continued throughout the 1950s and 1960s, with intercollegiate track and field programs among the most active recruiters of foreign athletes (Ridinger & Pastore, 2001). Today, the athletic skill and solid academic preparation of international students continues to make them a valuable commodity for U.S. college athletic programs, particularly given the intense competition for elite American athletes. This is evidenced by the broader range of sports where their skills have added to the success and prestige of American college and university athletic programs (Hoffer, 1994; NCAA, 1996; Riley, 1997).

By the Numbers: International Students at American Colleges and Universities

After a lull of a few years, international student enrollments are again on the rise at American colleges and universities. According to the Open Doors report, an annual publication of the Institute of International Education, 582,984 international students were enrolled in American colleges and universities in 2006–07, a 3% increase and the first increase since 2001–02. This trend is also noted among international student-athletes. According to the National Collegiate Athletic Association's (NCAA) 2006 participation report, of the 380,000 students participating in NCAA affiliated programs, 12,356 (6.2%) were foreign nationals. These numbers reflect similar gender participation rates, with 3% of male and 3.2% of female student-athletes hailing from foreign lands. Distinctions in participation rates are perhaps most noticeable in terms of divisional affiliation.

At the Division I level, considered the pinnacle of intercollegiate athletics in the United States, participation rates were 4.6% for male and 5.6% for female international student-athletes. While male international student-athletes outnumbered their female counterparts in overall participation rates (6,922 to 5,434, respectively), the largest participation gaps outside of gender were found between Division I and Division III programs. Male participation rates, for example, declined from 4.6% at the Division I level to 3.5% and 1.2% at the Division II and III levels, respectively. A similar pattern was noted for women, with participation rates of 5.6%, 3.1%, and .6% for Divisions I, II, and III, respectively.

Also important to note is that the NCAA is not the sole source of athletic opportunities for international students at U.S. higher education institutions. In addition to the NCAA's better known triadic framework (i.e., Division I, II, III), the National Junior College Athletic Association (NJCAA) reported 32,920 men and 19,071 women participating in athletic programs during the 2007–08 season (W. Bodey, personal communication, July 3, 2008). Unfortunately, no data is yet available regarding the prevalence of foreign student-athletes at Junior and Community College institutions. Still, regardless of the institution's size, governing body, or divisional affiliation participation, participation rates alone offer little in the way of understanding the individual narratives of each international student-athlete.

CHALLENGES AND OPPORTUNITIES

Federal, State, and Institutional Policies

Well before participation benefits are realized, international students must navigate a number of U.S. legal and regulatory issues. For starters, international student-athletes, like all foreigners traveling to the United States, are subject to U.S. federal policies such as the Patriot Act and student visa requirements (Chandler, 2004) that directly affect immigration status. For example, Altbach (2004) found that immigration laws, especially the initial entrance interview, often were enough to discourage foreign student applications. Thus, it is particularly important to provide early insights into U.S. immigration policy to foreign students interested in competing in U.S. institutions, lest they become discouraged trying to navigate U.S. immigration and SEVIS policies.

Perhaps less obvious to potential international student-athletes, at least initially, are the barriers to enrollment and athletic participation that are not predicated on U.S. Federal law and national security issues. In the past, for example, U.S. coaches, athletic associations (Hoffer, 1994), and state lawmakers (Blum, 1996) have all at times worked to enact quotas and/or bans against foreign students (Maguire & Bale, 1994). Their actions were aimed at helping American athletes maintain their competitive edge and/or to ensure that funding for athletic scholarships remained the province of domestic athletes, especially when funding was to be drawn from state coffers (Blum, 1996). Asher (1994), for one, has criticized the view that these attempts is a form of athletic protectionism that contradicts the American higher education system's core philosophy of a diverse educational environment.

Another critical issue facing international student-athletes involves academic eligibility. At NCAA-affiliated schools all student-athletes must be approved by the NCAA's eligibility clearinghouse, which verifies that they have met the 14 core academic course requirements in high school and obtained a relevant score on the ACT or SAT. Another important central feature of this process is the need for international student-athletes to verify their amateur status. To clarify the procedures and legal policies inherent in this transition, several programs and policies have been developed, including the NCAA's creation of the NCAA Eligibility Center. The need to address the academic and amateur eligibility of foreign student-athletes led the NCAA to create the NCAA Eligibility Center. Specific features of the center include programs and guides dedicated to clarifying eligibility standards. In addition, the NCAA publishes the *NCAA Guide to International Academic Standards for Athletics Eligibility* (NCAA, 2008), which details the academic parameters required for entrance into U.S. colleges and universities.

Specifically, "the guide is to provide specific criteria to be used as a guide in reviewing the initial eligibility (graduation, core curriculum, grade-point average and ACT/SAT test scores) of students who have completed any portion of their secondary education in a non–United States educational system for intercollegiate athletics participation" (NCAA, 2008, p. 4). In short, parents, coaches, recruiters, and students should become well versed of the entrance requirements and eligibility requirements at the institutional level and appropriate athletic governing body (i.e., NCAA, NJCAA). It is important to remember, also, that at least one athletic governing body, the NCAA, requires that responsibility be shared between all constituents (including the prospective student-athlete) involved in bringing international student-athletes to American colleges and universities. Equally important is the fact that American colleges and universities, not athletic governing bodies, retain the right to refuse admission to any student not meeting their declared entrance requirements. Once cleared of all the necessary legal, immigration, and NCAA governance issues, however, international student-athletes are quickly introduced to the nuances of American culture.

Developmental and Adjustment Challenges

College student-athletes are expected to operate successfully in both the academic and athletic realm, each of which exposes them to any number of psychosocial stressors. Sports medicine professionals note that psychosocial stressors can impede athletic performance and increase injury potential (Wiese-Bjornstal & Shaffer, 1999). Other studies (Bergandi & Wittig, 1984; Etzel, 1989; Etzel et al., 1994; Ferrante et al., 1996) have shown the potential for student-athletes to experience higher levels of emotional and psychological distress and less overall sense of personal wellness (Watson & Kissinger, 2007). From this example, it seems reasonable to suggest that foreign student-athletes who are struggling with adjustment issues may experience higher anxiety levels associated with psychosocial stressors than those student-athletes (foreign and domestic) that have adapted well to their new environment.

Developmental challenges associated with the transition to college can tax the physical and emotional reserves (Richards & Aries, 1999) of even the most resilient college student. The array of challenges can be daunting, from career exploration, social adjustment, and intellectual growth to the more pragmatic tasks of navigating around campus, attending class, and developing social relationships (Watt & Moore, 2001). The literature on student-athletes at U.S. institutions suggests these concerns may be exacerbated by participating in college athletics. As noted, studies suggest that intense competition, coupled with the rigorous physical and emotional strain of intercollegiate athletics, could make student-athletes more susceptible to developmental crises and psychological duress than nonathletes (Bergandi & Wittig, 1984; Etzel, 1989; Etzel et al., 1994; Ferrante et al., 1996). It seems reasonable to suggest, then, that the transition and acculturation issues facing foreign student-athletes could compound normal developmental crises. Conversely, it should not be assumed that either normal or unanticipated developmental or cultural events would have a negative impact, as the very act of living and studying abroad indicates a desire for new experiences. What is particularly important is that personnel with oversight of international student-athletes consider the central importance of the holistic development of the student-athlete. This requires sensitivity not only to the myriad developmental changes they must navigate, but also that they are doing so in an unfamiliar setting far away from their primary support groups.

Adjustment Issues

Professionals working with international students (athletes) must recognize the primacy of adjustment issues as a potential barrier to a positive collegiate experience (Boyer & Dedlacek, 1988; Church, 1982; Kaczmarek, Matlock, Merta, Ames, & Ross, 1994). Predictably, this concern for the difficulties international students experience in developing rewarding personal and social relationships (Pritchard & Skinner, 2002) is consistently noted in the literature. Contributing to potential interpersonal problems may be their false or inaccurate preconceptions of American college life and culture (Klomegah, 2006). Another issue that could deter foreign students from engaging in social activities on campus could be perceived or real biases toward their native attire (Bevis, 2002; Cole & Ahmadi, 2003). Clearly, though, not all international student-athletes will experience the same degree of adjustment or perceived bias. For instance, an individual's country of origin appears to ease adjustment concerns (Marion, 1986), as evidenced by Western and European students experiencing fewer acculturation problems. These changes are credited in part to better language proficiencies and lesser degrees of cultural distance (Chapdellaine & Alexitch, 2004; Trice, 2004). Some foreign athletes may also be solicited by faculty and students, as well as campus and community multicultural offices or programs, to speak about their cultures and experiences. Nevertheless, any degree of perceived or real bias could have serious repercussions and deter international student-athletes from engaging in the very activities that have been found to facilitate positive adjustments to campus for international students.

Adjusting to new relationships naturally extends to the athletic realm. Even without the added dimension of cultural differences, one of the primary challenges student-athletes face is adapting to differing coaching styles. Thus, it is important to consider, for example, that coaching and leadership styles may differ between domestic and international coaches. Some of the more visible differences may lie in the leadership style and focus on personal relationships in the coach–student–athlete dyad (or team). One European student commented, for example, that "In America there's not really that much of a coach–player relationship. [In Europe the coaches] really talk to you and ask for your opinion, but in America it's the coach's way or the highway" (Watkins, 2004, p. 1). Of course, other foreign student-athletes may find the scrutiny of American coaches useful (Watkins, 2004). What is perhaps most important, then, is the need to anticipate that the worldview of international student-athletes could have significant bearing on how well they adjust to the coaching styles and other elements of their new athletic environment.

Dietary concerns represent another real issue for many foreign student-athletes. Some degree of struggle adjusting to the cuisine in a new country would seem normal, of course, and international students certainly fit this assumption. Given the intense training and competition schedules of international student-athletes, however, proper nutritional levels become especially critical. For many student-athletes, especially those on full or partial athletic scholarships, meal plans are provided. The problem often is one of choice, as the vast majority of their options are likely to be based on American cuisine. As such, athletic departments should monitor international student-athletes to ensure they are adjusting to their new American diet, including sensitivity to cultural and/or religious/spiritual traditions that may require special food accommodations or involve rituals that could affect performance (i.e., fasting or dietary controls). Foreign student-athletes without the benefit of a monitored meal plan may need extra scrutiny to ensure they are able to maintain the proper nutritional levels necessary to allow them to maintain their rigorous academic and athletic schedules.

Monitoring for isolating behaviors among foreign students and student-athletes is also a concern. Although feelings of isolation would seem a normal consequence of living and competing abroad, it is important to monitor those whose feelings of isolation may lead them to segregate themselves as a means of self-preservation. In some cases, this can further enflame their sense of marginalization and alienation (Benjamin, Van Tran, & Benjamin, 1983). Awareness of these behaviors is particularly important for international student-athletes given the existing research indicating that the student-athlete role can trigger a sense of isolation on campus even among domestic student-athletes (Lanning & Toye, 1993; Sparent, 1988).

It should also not be forgotten that despite varying degrees of discomfort, communication barriers may inhibit the ability of many international student-athletes to clearly articulate their concerns (Lee & Rice, 2007).

Thus, working with student-athletes requires sensitivity to statements or behaviors suggesting that foreign student-athletes feel isolated or disconnected from peers, coaches, or teammates. Specific indicators may include missing classes, practices, or other team-related activities (i.e., meals, mandatory study halls). Furthermore, the notoriety often accorded to student-athletes on American campuses pose additional problems for international student-athletes. For instance, foreign student-athletes hailing from collectivistic cultures where individual accolades are discouraged may find the notion of individualism espoused in American (sports) culture particularly disconcerting. In some cases, this unsolicited attention could add to their psychological duress as they struggle to understand and adapt to the social tenets of American society as well as the unique cultural milieu of their institution.

Ridinger and Pastore's (2000) conceptual model for examining the adjustment issues of international student-athletes provides a foundation for examining how best to facilitate their academic, athletic, and personal successes. Of particular significance is the dimension that recognizes the importance of athletic department personnel in aiding the positive adjustment of foreign student-athletes. Athletic departments could take several steps to counter negative adjustment issues, such as foreign student-athletes with other students from their country of origin (Hull, 1978; Lee & Rice, 2007). Coalitions could also be fostered with international student and multicultural offices within student affairs departments (Watt & Moore, 2001). Beneficial relationships also could be established with community liaisons and programs outside of the academic community (Owie, 1982), including host families and/or community-based secular and/or religious organizations that connect international student-athletes to persons and traditions from their native cultures. In such cases it is essential for collegiate athletic departments to ensure that all potential off-campus contacts remain in compliance with appropriate governing bodies (i.e., NCAA). Failure to do so could have serious repercussions, including eligibility problems for the student-athlete, negative athletic sanctions for the athletic departments (i.e., reduced number of scholarships), and, in some cases, bringing dishonor and negative publicity to the mission of the institution. Creating social opportunities outside their normal athletic cliques could be especially helpful given that student-athletes may find their social options restricted by the demands of their athletic and academic schedules. Such options could exist in campus activities or through athletic department programs that enlist student-athletes for community service activities such as reading mentors to elementary school children.

Overall, creating and developing opportunities for campus and community-oriented extracurricular activities may help ease an international student's transition to campus life (Klomegah, 2006).

ACADEMICS

Cultural diversity and sensitivity in classroom settings underlies the philosophy of American higher education. Predictably, though, disparities between domestic and foreign students in the classroom are found in the literature. Examples include learning style differences (Ladd & Ruby, 1999), language proficiency, and engagement styles in the classroom. American faculty members who encounter international student-athletes in the classroom or campus settings should also recognize that an international student's subjective experience of the classroom setting may not match their outward demeanor. In Hsieh's (2007) recent qualitative study, for example, one Chinese student revealed that her silent, deferential demeanor in the classroom hid an internal narrative where she perceived herself as "useless" to her classmates (p. 379). In short, foreign students who are normally bright and articulate when conversing in their native tongue may appear disengaged or confused as they struggle to adjust to the American classroom setting and teaching styles (Hsieh, 2007; Lee & Rice, 2007). Faculty members also need to monitor their biases toward students from all geographic regions. Thus, faculty members who already have a negative bias toward student-athletes will need to be especially mindful not to stigmatize international student-athletes when they perceive their actions in class to be inadequate. In certain cases, they may need to place foreign students in contact with classmates or tutors who are receptive to helping them acclimate to the classroom (and possibly institutional) environment. For example, international students hailing from Western and English-speaking locales have been found to experience significantly less, and in some cases, no discrimination due to better language proficiencies and understanding of American culture (Hsieh, 2007; Lee & Rice, 2007). Overall, creating positive learning environments for international student-athletes involves establishing a safe, stimulating educational environment founded on a solid faculty–student (athlete) working alliance (Bordin, 1979).

Institutional Role

Providing for the academic and social deficits that may accompany international student-athletes as they adjust to their new environment requires a concerted effort by the institution's athletic, academic, and administrative departments. For example, while athletic academic advisors and recruiters are likely to be familiar with NCAA guidelines for international student-athletes, their focus is on maintaining their athletic eligibility and thus they may be less cognizant of the abundance of adjustment issues facing foreign nationals. Regardless of one's vocational affiliation (i.e., athletic department personnel, faculty, administration), it is critical to resist conceptualizing international students within a "problem framework" (Lee & Rice, 2007) or to categorize all problems as adjustment issues. Lee and Rice (2007), in a study exploring international students' perceptions of discrimination at U.S. institutions, argue that "...not all of the issues international students face can be viewed as matters of adjustment, as much research does, but that some of the more serious challenges are due to inadequacies within the host society" (p. 381). In other words, American colleges and universities must be willing to explore their policies and take steps to eradicate programs and policies with real or perceived biases.

Failure to recognize and redress potential biases within programs, policies, or specific individuals or groups may increase the risk of further marginalizing international students (Beoku-Betts, 2004; Lee, 2005). Studies in the United States (Perucci & Hu, 1995; Schram & Lauver, 1988), the United Kingdom (Hsieh, 2007; Lee & Rice, 2007), and Australia (Lee & Rice, 2007) highlight the trend among higher education institutions to discount their responsibilities in facilitating the international student's adjustment to their campus (Bevis, 2002). These findings have led to calls for improved orientation, intervention, and assessment programs that can help international students better acclimate to their new surroundings (Schram & Lauver, 1988). There is also more recognition for the need to implement programming that is more attuned to helping student-athletes optimize their academic, personal, and social successes. To that end, Watt and Moore (2001) made several suggestions for student-affairs professionals that, in certain cases, have been amended for international student-athletes. Their suggestions include:

- Educate faculty and coaches about the unique and complex balance between the academic and athletic life of domestic and foreign student-athletes.
- Design courses and seminars to help student-athletes balance both academics and athletics.
- Be flexible and creative when offering programming, counseling, and advising sessions and recognize barriers to student-athletes seeking mental health services.
- Maintain a network of former student-athletes by working in partnerships with graduates who were student-athletes.
- Arrange opportunities for faculty, coaches, and athletic academic advisors to dialogue on the needs and experiences of international student-athletes.

ATHLETIC ISSUES

Recruiting

Successful collegiate athletic programs are fundamentally tied to effective recruiting. A large part of the challenge facing contemporary college athletic recruiters involves the task of convincing prospective student-athletes that "there are more people competing for fewer scholarships than at any time in the modern era…" (as cited in Sander, 2008, p. 3). Still, while recruiting is recognized as "the backbone of college athletics" (Sander, 2008, p. 1), importing talented international players continues to draw its share of supporters and detractors. Supporters argue that foreign student-athletes provide an array of benefits to players and institutions. Asher's (1994) research, for example, found that coaches perceived international student-athletes as more mature, possessed a better work ethic, and were more goal-oriented than their American peers. Coaches have also expressed their appreciation of the limited sense of entitlement found among foreign student-athletes, which often contrasts with that of their American counterparts (Hoffer, 1994). In short, the presence of international student-athletes may be the catalyst for an increase in cultural awareness and a reduction in cultural marginalization (Bevis, 2002; Harrison, 2002; Ridinger & Pastore, 2001) within both the academic and athletic domains. Data compiled by the NCAA suggests that many athletic programs see validity in these arguments, as the number of international student-athletes participating in NCAA-affiliated athletic programs has risen from 6,833 in 1991–92 to 12,356 in the most recent NCAA participation report in 2005–06.

Conversely, Ridinger and Pastore (2001) found that even within the coaching ranks, disagreements existed concerning international student-athlete recruitment. Their study, which focused on basketball, field hockey, ice hockey, soccer, swimming, tennis, and track coaches, as these sports have historically held higher percentages of international students (Hoffer, 1994; NCAA, 1996; Riley, 1997), found that track coaches were more likely to be concerned about recruiting foreign athletes than soccer or basketball coaches. The authors suggest this may be due partly to the prominence of international track and field athletes at American schools. From a divisional standpoint, Division I coaches were more likely than Division II and III coaches to observe that the recruitment of international student-athletes could be perceived negatively by critical stakeholders such as parents, opponents, teammates, and the institution's administration. The authors suggested a number of reasons that could help explain these findings. Outside of the coaching realm, for instance, this unease may be vested in concerns about the use of U.S. tax dollars for recruiting and sponsoring international student-athletes through athletic scholarships, thus allowing fewer scholarship opportunities for U.S. citizens. An additional concern was that the superior athletic skills of an international student-athlete could negatively impact collegiate competition in the United States (Ridinger & Pastore, 2001). In certain cases, athletic departments hesitant of attracting negative attention to their programs or universities may choose to discourage the recruitment of international student-athletes in favor of domestic talent. Today, however, the win-at-all-costs philosophy of contemporary American sports culture may serve as the guiding force in decision making given the fiscal and status incentives associated with successful college athletic programs.

Coaches from NCAA programs also perceived international student-athletes as benefitting their teams more so than their National Junior College Athletic Association (NJCAA) counterparts. This supports previous studies indicating that NCAA coaches felt that international student-athletes possessed a better academic and athletic work ethic, increased levels of personal maturity, and a refined focus on goal setting more than their American peers (Asher, 1994; Hoffer, 1994). Additionally, more NCAA coaches than NJCAA coaches and more public school coaches than private school coaches held this opinion. In other words, NCAA coaches and coaches from public institutions held more positive attitudes toward the inclusion of international student-athletes on their teams. Ultimately, they concluded that NCAA coaches are likely to hold a recruiting edge both domestically and abroad over their NJCAA competitors, supporting the view that international student-athletes will gravitate toward the top-tier American athletic programs (Ridinger & Pastore, 2001). Overall, their findings provide a revealing glimpse into the myriad considerations affecting a coach's perception of international student-athletes and, by extension, how these perceptions could materialize during the recruitment phase and impact the international student-athlete's relationship with their coaches and teammates.

Athletic Environment

Even at institutions with historically less successful athletic programs, the dawning of each new athletic season brings the possibility of athletic glory and a renewed sense of team and institutional pride. New seasons invite endless comparisons and speculation between past and present teams and individual players. Although common to the average college sports fan, international students who are unaware of some of the undercurrents of American sports culture may find these behaviors disquieting, particularly if they play Fall semester sports and have had limited time to adjust to their new environment. The breadth and depth of the literature on the culture of American sports is beyond the scope of this volume, but it is important to highlight some key variables that could impact the experiences of international student-athletes.

For starters, American sports are increasingly characterized by a hypercompetitive, success-oriented culture. International student-athletes may find this competitive mentality particularly challenging if it clashes with their cultural upbringing or worldview. For example, a Hispanic student-athlete could struggle adhering to a win-at-all-costs attitude given that Hispanic culture generally downplays competition and behaviors that distinguish one from peers (Baruth & Maning, 2007). Support for the notion of competitive differences among cultures is found in Popp's (2007) recent study of NCAA Division I student-athletes. Using a sample of 174 international student-athletes and 114 domestic student-athletes, Popp found that international student-athletes ranked competitiveness lower than domestic student-athletes. Ultimately, consideration of both intercultural and intracultural factors is a necessary component of any conceptualization of the cultural factors impacting the international student-athlete's experience.

Symptoms of the American sports culture's win-at-all-costs philosophy (Ridinger & Pastore, 2001) may be embedded within coaching philosophies, relationships with teammates, sports marketing campaigns, training schedules, and academics. For example, international student-athletes competing at the Division I level, particularly in popular American sports like basketball, football, and baseball, are likely to have American teammates who view their athletic scholarship as a springboard to athletic success and financial security. From an academic standpoint, they may be advised to take courses with faculty members known to be less rigid with attendance or course workloads (Bale, 1991) in order to help ensure future eligibility.

Perhaps one of the most deeply embedded athletic stereotypes in the United States is the notion of student-athletes as "dumb jocks." Despite the acclaim and privilege they may encounter on campus and in the community by virtue of being an athlete, research reveals that students and faculty (Simon, Bosworth, Fujita, & Jensen, 2007) alike often view student-athletes as dumb jocks (Engstrom & Sedlacek, 1989; Knapp, Rasmussen, & Barnhart, 2001) who do not possess the intellectual acumen or academic motivation to succeed in higher education institutions (Leach & Conners, 1984; Zingg, 1982). As noted, this stereotype may seem especially unwarranted when applied to international student-athletes given they are often better prepared academically than their American counterparts (Asher, 1994; Hoffer, 1994) and view their degree as the primary objective of their presence on American campuses (Bale, 1991). As a result, they may be less prepared to deal with stigmas that diminish their intellect, particularly when the voice of discrimination is spoken by those showering praise on athletic talents. Lee and Rice (2007) suggested ways to accommodate international students in academic settings:

1. Create classroom and campus environments that ban discriminatory dialogue and behaviors. This extends to all university faculty, staff, and students.
2. Create institutional accountability for alleviating on-campus discrimination through effective programming and monitoring.
3. Set guidelines for teaching and working with international students so that administrators and faculty are aware of their responsibility in providing a safe and welcoming environment for international student-athletes.

There are several additional elements of American sports culture that could affect international student-athletes. These include, but are certainly not limited to, the "sport ethic endemic" (Wiese-Bjornstal & Shaffer, 1999), overidentification with the masculine identity, the aforementioned win-at-all-costs philosophy, and the stigmatization of mental illness. In many cases, elements of each could combine to cause significant levels of distress for domestic and international student-athletes alike.

According to Hughes and Coakley (1991), the sport ethic endemic is the "system of principles and beliefs, held predominantly by athletes, that advocates personal sacrifice, risk taking, and playing with pain to promote conformity and adherence to sport norms" and is viewed as the central feature that predisposes athletes to injury (Wiese-Bjornstal & Shaffer, 1999). Among American student-athletes, masking or denying pain and/or non-compliance with medical treatment to avoid being viewed as weak are possible manifestations of the sport ethic endemic (Wiese-Bjornstal & Shaffer, 1999). Given the competitive nature of elite college athletes, it is certainly possible that international student-athletes could adopt such unhealthy behaviors, especially once they are modeled consistently by their American counterparts.

A specific aspect of the sport ethic thought to increase an athlete's susceptibility to injury is the internalization of the masculine identity, which could lead to athletes who "risk becoming disconnected from their emotions, which could lead them to the literal view of their body as a weapon" (Young, White, & McTeer, 1994, as cited in Weise-Bjornstal & Shaffer, 1999, p. 25). Such philosophies may be subtle or overt, but surface primarily among male college athletes where physical dominance of their opponent is increasingly synonymous with personal and athletic excellence. These edicts of American sports may be especially uncomfortable for international student-athletes who view competition as less important (Potts, 2007) than obtaining a college degree (Bale, 1991).

Negative undercurrents also exist within the American sports culture regarding mental illness. Thus, university personnel (faculty, athletic administrators, mental health and wellness professionals, sports medicine professionals) need to understand the issues that could impede international student-athletes from seeking professional help for their problems. For starters, awareness of the stigma of mental illness in athletics is particularly important given that student-athletes experience problems requiring professional help at rates that are parallel to, and at times eclipse, the rates of nonathletes (Brewer & Petrie, 1996). Equally important is to not assume that foreign or domestic student-athletes will follow any specific response pattern in times of personal crises. For example, foreign students and domestic student-athletes often turn first to families and friends (Zahi, 2002) along with teammates, coaches, and athletic trainers for support. However, in some cases, such as the death of a family member, cultural norms may require distinct responses and behaviors from foreign student-athletes that may seem atypical to Americans. As such, school personnel must remain sensitive to the cultural needs of international student-athletes to ensure they are allowed to respond to personal crises in ways that are congruent with their cultural norms. This sensitivity should also extend to non–crisis situations where cultural incongruencies surface.

Student-athletes often carry a distorted view of mental health that limits their willingness to engage with mental health professionals. Studies have documented a number of reasons for their reluctance, including their sense that counseling is futile (Martin, Wrisberg, Beitel, & Lounsbury, 1997), or that it signifies personal weakness (Linder, Brewer, Van Raalte, & DeLange, 1991) or a psychological defect (Ravizza, 1988). One way to address some of these potential barriers with international student-athletes is to recognize that mental illness is conceptualized (and stigmatized) differently and are of varying degrees throughout the world. For example, what is labeled as mental illness by an American mental health professional may be viewed as "bad blood" (Rita, 1996, p. 327, as cited in Baruth & Manning, 2007) in some Asian cultures.

Procedurally, mental health professionals must also consider the inherent biases of Western counseling and psychotherapy paradigms that favor individualism over collectivism (Sadeghi, Fischer, & House, 2003, as cited in Olivas & Li, 2006). For example, treatment plans emphasizing individual achievement may be embraced by American student-athletes. However, the same treatment plan for a Hispanic or Asian student-athlete may warrant immediate suspicion and resistance given their culture's collectivistic ideology where success is defined within a group or family context. Careful forethought is thus required given that cultures often have their own unique biases and treatment regimens for what Americans may label mental health–related concerns. Unfortunately, the current evidence suggests that counseling services are often offered belatedly to international student-athletes, thereby diminishing the potential to facilitate a positive resolution to their problems.

Alternatively, an international student-athlete's immersion in American sports culture may be an asset in reducing the degree of bias they experience on American campuses. Several studies lend credence to this suggestion. First, prior studies have found that student-athletes identify chiefly with their teammates (Carron, 1982; Widmeyer, Carron, & Brawley, 1993). As a result, teammates that are accepting and nurturing of individual and cultural differences can be an invaluable resource for international student-athletes. Ford and Gordon's (1988) notion of a "raceless" elite athlete whom, by virtue of their athlete status, is shielded from racial bias both inside and outside the sports environment also seems applicable to international student-athletes. Others suggest that athletic environments can diminish racial biases between (Hoberman, 1984, 1997; Jefferson, 1998) and among (Ford & Gordon, 1988) athletes. Brown and his colleagues (2003), for example, proposed that inherent within the competitive sports culture is the notion that racial status is unimportant. In essence, focusing on competition-based norms such as fair play, meritocracy, teamwork, and cooperation (Coakely, 1990, 1993; Lapchick, 1996; MacClancy, 1996) could result in an athletic environment where racial discord is incongruent with the true spirit of athletic competition. Given the elite status of college athletes, it would seem especially likely that most would have been exposed to such highly competitive sports environments. Ultimately, while racial bias is the common denominator of these studies, they suggest that Americans raised in competitive sports environments may be more inclined to accept the unique characteristics and experiences of international student-athletes.

CONCLUSION

International student-athletes provide tremendous opportunities for American higher education institutions and their constituents to broaden their worldview while strengthening their athletic and academic reputations. To optimize their success potential, however, those involved in the care and development of foreign student-athletes need to sensitize themselves to the range of issues and challenges that could affect their ability to adapt to the challenges and opportunities inherent in the student-athlete role at many American colleges and universities. More specifically, possessing accurate knowledge about the core issues facing domestic student-athletes (and nonathletes) at American institutions is necessary but not sufficient when attempting to understand the experiences of international student-athletes. What is perhaps most readily apparent, however, is the fact that optimizing an international student-athlete's academic, athletic, and personal potential requires sensitivity to the interplay of unique cultural norms and worldviews that could impact their willingness or ability to maximize their academic and athletic potential. With this holistic view in mind, this chapter outlines many of the factors that could influence an international student-athlete's adjustment and ability to thrive within the unique academic, athletic, and sociocultural boundaries of American culture and, more specifically, within their host institution and athletic program. In doing so, university and athletic department personnel can become more adept at developing relationships that help ensure that international students are able to live, study, and compete in environments that care as much about their personal and vocational successes as their athletic accomplishments.

REFERENCES

Altbach, P. (1998). *Comparative higher education: Knowledge, the university, and development.* Greenwich, CT: Ablex.

Altbach, P. (2004). Higher education crosses borders. *Change, 36*(2), 18–25.

Asher, K. (1994, June/July). Multi-cultural cultivation. *Coaching Volleyball,* 18–23.

Bale, J. (1991). *The brawn drain: Foreign student-athletes in American universities.* Urbana: University of Illinois Press.

Baruth, L. G., & Manning, M. L. (2003). *Multicultural counseling and psychotherapy: A lifespan perspective.* Upper Saddle River, NJ: Merrill Prentice Hall.

Benjamin, R., Van Tran, T., & Benjamin, M. E. (1983). Alienation among Vietnamese students in the United States. *Creative Sociology, 11*(1), 33–34.

Beoku-Betts, J. (2004). African women pursuing graduate studies in the sciences: Racism, gender bias, and Third World marginality. *NWSA Journal, 16*(1), 116–135.

Bergandi, T., & Wittig, A. (1984). Availability of attitudes towards counseling services for the collegiate athlete. *Journal of College Student Personnel, 25,* 557–558.

Bevis, T. B. (2002). At a glance: International students in the United States. *International Educator, 11*(3), 12–17.

Blum, D. E. (1996, January 12). Alabama 2-year colleges ban state aid for foreign athletes. *The Chronicle of Higher Education.*

Bordin, H. (1979). The generalizability of the psychoanalytic concept of the working alliance. *Psychotherapy: Theory, Research, and Practice, 16,* 252–260.

Boyer, S. P., & Sedlacek, W. E. (1998). Noncognitive prediction of academic success for international students: A longitudinal study. *Journal of College Student Development, 29,* 218–223.

Brewer, B. W., & Petrie, T. A. (1996). Psychopathology in sport and exercise. In J. L. Van Raalte & B. Brewer (Eds.), *Exploring sport and exercise psychopathology* (pp. 257–274). Washington, DC: American Psychological Association.

Brown, T., Jackson, J., Brown, K., Sellers, R., Keiper, S., & Manual, W. (2003). There's no race on the playing field: Perceptions of racial discrimination among white and black athletes. *Journal of Sport and Social Issues, 27*(2), 162–183.

Carron, A. V. (1982). Cohesiveness in sport groups: Interpretations and considerations. *Journal of Sport Psychology, 4,* 123–138.

Chandler, D. (2004). Reversing the tide: A complex visa process has contributed to a decline in the number of international students coming to the country since 9/11. *Black Issues in Higher Education, 21*(19), 20–24.

Chapdelaine, R. F., & Alexitch, L. R. (2004). Social skills difficulty: Model of culture shock for international graduate students. *Journal of College Student Development, 45*(2), 167–184.

Church, A. T. (1982). Sojourner adjustment. *Psychological Bulletin, 91,* 540–572.

Coakley, J. J. (1990). *Sport in society: Issues and controversies.* St. Louis, MO: Mosby.

Coakley, J. J. (1993). Socialization and sport. In R. N. Singer, M. Murphy, & L. K. Tennant (Eds.), *Handbook of research on sport psychology* (pp. 571–586). Boston: McGraw-Hill.

Cole, D., & Ahmadi, S. (2003). Perspectives and experiences of Muslim women who veil on campuses. *Journal of College Student Development, 44*(1), 47–66.

Engstrom, C. M., & Sedlacek, W. E. (1989). *Attitude of residence hall students toward student-athletes: Implications for advising, training and programming* (Research Report # 19-89, 143 Reports: Research, 160 Tests/Questionnaires). College Park: University of Maryland.

Etzel. E. (1989). *Life stress, locus-of-control and sport competition anxiety patterns of college student-athletes. Unpublished doctoral dissertation.* West Virginia University, Morgantown.

Etzel, E. F., Pinkney, J. W., & Hinkle, J. S. (1994). College student- athletes and needs assessment. In C.C. Thomas (Ed.), *Multicultural needs assessment for college and university student populations.* Springfield, IL: C.C. Thomas.

Ferrante, A. P., & Etzel, E., & Lantz, C. (1996). Counseling college student-athletes: The problem, the need. In E. Etzel, A. P. Ferrante, & J. W. Pinkney (Eds.), *Counseling college student-athletes: Issues and interventions.* Morgantown, WV: Fitness Information Technology.

Ford, I., & Gordon, S. (1998). Perspectives of sport trainers and athletic therapists on the psychological content of their practice and training. *Journal of Sport Rehabilitation, 7,* 79–94.

Harrison, P. (2002). Educational exchange for international understanding. *International Educator, 11*(4), 2–4.

Hoberman, J. M. (1984). *Sport and political ideology.* Austin: University of Texas Press.

Hoberman, J. M. (1997). *Darwin's athletes: How sport has damaged Black America and preserved the myth of race.* Boston: Mariner.

Hoffer, R. (1994). Foreign legions. *Sports Illustrated, 80*(22), 46–49.

Hsieh, M. (2007). Challenges for international students in higher education: One student's narrated story of invisibility and struggle. *College Student Journal, 41*(2), 379–391.

Hughes, R., & Coakley, J. (1991) Positive Deviance among athletes: The implications of Over Conformity to the Sport Ethic. *Sociology of Sport Journal, 8*(4), 307–325.

Hull, W. F. (1978). *Foreign students in the United States of America: Coping behavior within the educational environment.* New York: Praeger.

Jefferson, S. (1998). *Pro bound: Do you have what it takes to become a professional athlete?* Queens Village, NY: Author.

Johnson, V. (2003). When we hinder foreign students and scholars, we endanger our national security. *Chronicle of Higher Education, 49*(31), B7.

Kaczmarek, P. G., Matlock, G., Merta, R. Ames, M. H., & Ross, M. (1995). An assessment of international college student adjustment. *International Journal for the Advancement of Counseling, 17*, 241–247.

Klomegah, R. Y. (2006). Social factors relating to alienation experienced by international students in the United States. *College Student Journal, 40*(2), 303–315.

Knapp, T. J., Rasmussen, C., & Barnhart, R. K. (2001). What college students say about intercollegiate athletics: A survey of attitudes and beliefs. *College Student Journal, 35*, 96–100.

Lanning, W., & Toye, P. (1993). Counseling athletes in higher education. In W. D. Kirk & S. V. Kirk (Eds.), *Student athletes: Shattering the myths and sharing the realities.* Alexandria, VA: American Counseling Association.

Lapchick, R. E. (1996). Race and college sports: A long way to go. In R. E. Lapchick (Ed.), *Sport and society: Equal opportunity or business as usual* (pp. 5–18). Thousand Oaks, CA: Sage.

Leach, B., & Conners, B. (1984). Pygmalion on the gridiron: The black student-athlete in a White university. In A. Shriberg & F. R. Brodzinki (Eds.), *Rethinking services for college athletes* (pp. 31–49). San Francisco: Jossey-Bass.

Lee, J. J. (2005). *Experiences and satisfaction among international students.* Paper presented at the annual meeting of the American Educational Research Association, Montreal.

Lee, J. J., & Rice, C. (2007). Welcome to America?: International student perceptions of discrimination. *Higher Education, 53*(3), 381–409.

Linder, D. E., Brewer, B. W., Van Raalte, J. L., & de Lange, N. (1991). A negative halo for athletes who consult sport psychologists: Replication and extension. *Journal of Sport and Exercise Psychology, 13*, 133–148.

MacClancy, J. (1996). Sport, identity and ethnicity. In J. MacClancy (Ed.), *Sport, identity, and ethnicity* (pp. 1–20). Herndon, VA: Berg.

Maguire, J., & Bale, J. (1994). Postscript: An agenda for research on sports labour migration. In J. Bale & J. Maguire (Eds.), *The global sports arena: Athletic talent migration in an interdependent world.* London: Frank Cass.

Marion, P. (1986). Research on foreign students at colleges and universities in the United States. In K. R. (Ed.), *Guiding the development of foreign students* (pp. 65–82). San Francisco: Jossey-Bass.

Martin, S. B., Wrisberg, C. A., Beitel, P. A., & Lounsbury, J. (1997). NCAA Division I athletes' attitudes toward seeking sport psychology consultation: The development of an objective instrument. *The Sport Psychologist, 11*(2), 201–218.

National Collegiate Athletic Association. (1996). *Guide to international academic standards for athletics eligibility.* Indianapolis, IN: Author.

Olivas, M., & Chi-Sing Li (2006). Understanding stressors of international students in higher education: What college counselors and personnel need to know. *Journal of Instructional Psychology, 33*, 217–222.

Owie, I. (1982). Social alienation among foreign students. *College Student Journal, 16*, 163–165.

Perucci, R., & Hu, H. (1995). Satisfaction with social and educational experiences among international graduate students. *Research in Higher Education, 36*(4), 491–508.

Popp, N. (2007). Do international student-athletes view collegiate sport differently than domestic student-athletes?

Pritchard, R. M. O., & Skinner, B. (2002). Cross-cultural partnerships between home and international students. *Journal of Studies in International Education, 6*(4), 323–354.

Ravizza, K. (1988). Gaining entry with athletic personnel for season-long consulting. *The Sport Psychologist, 2,* 243–254.

Richards, S., & Aries, E. (1999). The division III student-athlete: Academic performance, campus involvement, and growth. *Journal of College Student Development. 40,* 211–218.

Ridinger, L. L., & Pastore, D. L (2001). Coaches perceptions of recruiting international student-athletes. *Journal of the International Council for Health, Physical Education, Recreation, Sport, and Dance, 37*(1), 19–25.

Riley, L. (1997, February 10). Going global. *The Sporting News,* p. 21.

Sadeghi, M., Fischer, J. M., & House, S. G. (2003). Ethical dilemmas in multicultural counseling. *Journal of Multicultural Counseling & Development, 31,* 179–192.

Sander, L. (2008). For coaches, a race with no finish line. *Chronicle of Higher Education, 54*(35), 1–6.

Schram, J., & Lauver, P. (1988). Alienation in international students. *Journal of College Student Development, 29,* 146–150.

Simon, H. D., Bosworth, C., Fujita, S., & Jensen, M. (2007). The athlete stigma in higher education. *College Student Journal, 41*(2), 251–273.

Sparent, M. E. (1988, April). *The student athletes in the classroom: Developmental issues affecting college athletes and their impact on academic motivation and performance.* Paper presented at the 11th Annual Symposium on Developmental/Remedial Education, Albany, NY. (ERIC Reproduction Service No. ED 294 617)

Trice, A. G. (2004). Mixing it up: International graduate students' social interactions with American students. *Journal of College Student Development, 45*(6), 671–687.

Watkins, M. (2004). International athletes face language, culture barriers. *The Lantern,* pp. 1–3.

Watt, S. K., & Moore, J. L. (2001). Who are student athletes? *New Direction for Student Services, 93,* 7–18.

Widmeyer, W. N., Carron, A. V., & Brawley, L. R. (1993). Group cohesion in sport and exercise. In R. N. Singer, M. Murphy, & L. K. Tennant (Eds.), *Handbook of research on sport psychology* (pp. 672–691). New York: Macmillan.

Wiese-Bjornstal, D. M., & Shaffer, S. M. (1999). Psychosocial dimensions of sport injury. In R. Ray & D. M. Wiese-Bjornstal (Eds.), *Counseling in sports medicine* (pp. 23–40). Champaign, IL: Human Kinetics.

Young, K., White, P., & McTeer, W. (1994). Body talk: Male athletes reflect on sports, injury, and pain. *Sociology of Sport Journal, 11,* 175–194.

Zingg, P. J. (1982). Advising the student athlete. *Educational Record, 63,* 16–19.

PART III

CHALLENGES WHILE ENROLLED

CHAPTER 13

COLLEGE ATHLETES AND PERFORMANCE-ENHANCING SUBSTANCE USE

Richard E. Newman
Presbyterian College

For structural purposes, this chapter defines performance-enhancing substances as utilized by the American Academy of Pediatrics' Committee on Sports Medicine and Fitness in their 2005 policy statement on the *Use of Performance-Enhancing Substances*. The AAP committee defined a performance-enhancing substance as "any substance taken in nonpharmacologic doses specifically for the purposes of improving sports performance" (AAP, 2005, p. 1104). The committee further delineated that a substance enhances performance "if it benefits sports performance by increasing strength, power, speed, or endurance (ergogenic) or by altering body weight or body composition. Furthermore, substances that improve performance by causing changes in behavior, arousal level, and/or perception of pain should be considered performance enhancing" (AAP, 2005, p. 1104). The number and/or types of performance-enhancing substances are infinite, but the basic intent underlying their use by athletes is crystal clear: improved performance.

Is the following statement fact or fiction? The use of performance-enhancing substances among college athletes is pervasive in today's intercolle-

College Student-Athletes: Challenges, Opportunities, and Policy Implications, pages 183–199
Copyright © 2009 by Information Age Publishing
183

giate athletic circles. If we accept the premise of a "trickle-down" effect from professional or elite sporting venues, an immediate response might very well be fact. Virtually every day our media reports on some alleged incident of performance-enhancing drug use in the National Football League, Major League Baseball, National Hockey League, Tour de France, or among high-profile Olympic track-and-field participants. A review of current literature dealing with performance-enhancing substance use in college athletes, however, may generate rationale for a response of fiction.

Every four years, the National Collegiate Athletic Association (NCAA) conducts the "Study of Substance Use of College Student-Athletes." The 2005 inquiry revealed that public perceptions of performance-enhancing drug use in college athletes is less common than popularly thought; in fact, most college athletes do not use performance-enhancing drugs (NCAA, 2006). In addition, Dr. Frank Uryasz, president of the National Center for Drug Free Sport, questioned the impact of steroid use in professional sports on college athletes' use of steroids (Ulrich, 2008). This opinion was bolstered by a recent *Sports Illustrated* poll in which 99% of the respondents said they would not use steroids just because professional athletes do (McCullum, 2008).

Maximizing one's athletic performance capabilities is an arduous and time-consuming endeavor that involves proper hydration, adequate sleep, intelligent nutrition, moderate use of alcohol, avoidance of supplements, and quality practice and coaching. Unfortunately, some athletes do not rely on natural resources in their attempt to attain peak levels of athletic performance. They perceive a need for something that will facilitate, as well as hasten, the natural route to optimal athletic performance. Hence, they may gravitate to the use of performance-enhancing substances to attain their goal of becoming the very best athlete they can possibly be.

Minelli, Olrich, and Smith (2006) addressed the enormous breadth of performance-enhancing substances and, in so doing, provided a manageable means to examine the topic. The authors opted to divide performance-enhancing substances into two basic categories: legal performance enhancers and illegal performance enhancers. For definitive purposes, "legal performance-enhancing substances include both over-the-counter drugs and dietary supplements" (Minelli et al., 2006, p. 10). "Illegal performance-enhancing substances include anabolic-androgenic steroids (AAS), various prohormones, human growth hormone and a large variety of other drugs acquired primarily through the black market" (Minelli et al., 2006, p. 10).

ILLEGAL PERFORMANCE ENHANCERS

Thus, this chapter addresses the illegal category of performance enhancers. It is well beyond the scope of this chapter, nor is it my attempt, to address all of the performance-enhancing drugs that exist in our sporting culture. Martin, Baron, and Gold (2007) estimated that there are hundreds of performance-enhancing drugs. The task of this chapter is to focus on some of the more prevailing performance-enhancing drugs. This includes use; ways in which the substance is perceived to improve athletic performance; health and safety issues for the student-athlete; potential legal or eligibility ramifications associated with the substance use; and any current trends or projections cited in the literature relative to the most popular performance-enhancing substances.

Anabolic-Androgenic Steroids

Anabolic-androgenic steroids (AAS) remain the most commonly abused performance-enhancing drug when all categories of competitive sport are combined (Martin, Baron, & Gold, 2007). Eitzen (2006) estimated AAS usage to be 15% among male college athletes and 6% among female college athletes while the National Institute on Drug Abuse reported a range of between 1 and 6% among athletes (NIDA, 2006). The National Collegiate Athletic Association's 2005 study revealed an average usage figure of 1.13% in total (Ulrich, 2008) and the study also found that steroid use had decreased slightly from its 2001 investigation (NCAA, 2006). The decrease in use was exhibited across all three divisions. It was also interesting to note that "more than half of anabolic steroid use begins in high school" (NCAA, 2006, p. 14). This indicates that athletes are bringing their performance-enhancing drug use patterns and problems with them to college, a behavior that may be the result of either sporadic or nonexistent drug testing at the secondary school level. However, Mannie (2008) found in a recent confidential survey study of 3,200 students in grades 8–12 that those individuals who admitted to using performance-enhancing drugs (57%), "65% said they would be willing to use any type of pill, powder, etc., regardless of the effects on their health, if it guaranteed they would reach athletic stardom" (Mannie, 2008, p. 9).

When athletes engage in the use of anabolic-androgenic steroids to enhance individual performance, they anticipate experiencing an increase in muscular strength, hypertrophy or increased muscle mass, quicker recovery after high-intensity training sessions, and reduced body fat, especially among female users (Fendrich, 2005; Mangus & Miller, 2005; Minelli et al., 2006).

There is a wealth of empirical evidence and data available illustrating the short- and long-term side effects associated with steroid use. The negative health consequences can range from mild, reversible conditions like acne to severe and irreversible life-threatening conditions like liver tumors. The extent of these adverse side effects vary depending on the type and dosage of steroids used, number of steroids used if stacking and pyramiding are involved, and length of time the substance(s) have been used. Suffice it to say, using anabolic-androgenic steroids can compromise the physical, mental, and emotional health and well-being of the student-athlete. In addition, if you compound health issues with potential eligibility and legal entanglements, the cost-to-benefit ratio to play hormonal roulette for a perceived performance gain can be extremely dangerous and costly.

Wholesale accountings regarding the wide range of negative side effects associated with anabolic-androgenic steroid use and abuse can be found at the following organizations or agencies: U.S. Drug Enforcement Administration (www.dea.gov/concern/steroids.html); U.S. Anti-Doping Agency (www.usada.org/athletes/cheating_health.html); National Collegiate Athletic Association (www.drugfreesport.com/choices/drugs/steroids. html); and the National Institute on Drug Abuse (www.drugabuse.gov/ResearchReports/Steroids/Anabolicsteroids.html). In addition to these online resources, three very concise summaries detailing the negative side effects associated with anabolic-androgenic steroid abuse appeared in recent works by Gold (2007), Mannie (2004), and Petersen (2002).

Federal law placed anabolic steroids in Schedule III of the Controlled Substance Act on February 27, 1991 (Drug Enforcement Association, 2004). As such, simple possession of illicitly obtained steroids became a felony drug offense. A first offense for simple possession warrants a maximum penalty of one year in prison and a minimum $1,000 fine. In the event of a second felony possession offense, the preceding penalties double. The maximum penalties that may be imposed in a first offense for trafficking entail five years in prison and a $250,000 fine. In similar fashion to possession offenses, a second felony offense for trafficking doubles the maximum penalties. On top of federal statutes, individual states also implement their own fines and penalties for illegal use of anabolic steroids (DEA, 2004).

A second federal law, the Steroid Control Act of 2004, placed 32 additional steroids in Schedule III as well as expanded the DEA's regulatory and enforcement authority regarding steroids (DEA, 2004). This legislation was aimed at targeting substances like prohormones, precursor steroids, and designer steroids. One dietary supplement manufacturer, in fact, stated that the "era of the prohormones is over" (Minelli et al., 2006, p. 10). The implicit message was that unscrupulous biochemists will need to develop new methods to stimulate endogenous testosterone production, and the new methods may circumvent the hormonal system and trigger other internal mechanisms capable of elevating testosterone levels in the human body.

In addition to any criminal and/or legal entanglements associated with anabolic-androgenic steroid possession and usage, eligibility issues also become a significant concern for the athlete. The National Collegiate Athletic

Association enacted a drug-testing program via legislative measures at its 1986 and 1990 conventions. The program was initiated to create fair and equitable competition as well as to protect the health and safety of each and every student-athlete. Ultimately, oversight for the NCAA's year-round drug testing program was delegated to the National Center for Drug Free Sport, an organization founded in 1999 by Dr. Frank Uryasz. Uryasz is the former director of sport sciences for the NCAA and under his stewardship, "Drug Free Sport" is charged with administering a quality drug-testing system under the auspices of the NCAA vice-president for educational services (NCAA, 2005). This monitoring process includes random, periodic screenings to ensure that athletes are not using substances found on the National Collegiate Athletic Association's list of banned-drug classes. In brief, two of the banned-drug classes include stimulants and anabolic steroids (NCAA, 2005). However, a complete list of banned-drug classes, including specific examples under each banned-drug class, can be found under Bylaw 31.2.3.1 Banned Drugs (NCAA, 2005).

If an athlete is found guilty of using a substance that appears on the list of NCAA banned drugs, he or she may be declared ineligible for further participation under Bylaw 18.4.1.5.1. In essence, the athlete can lose one full year of eligibility for his or her initial positive drug test, and the balance of their remaining eligibility status after testing positive a second time.

Anabolic Steroid Precursors

The most common anabolic steroid precursors include the "infamous androstenedione," androstenediol, and dehydroeiiandrosterone or DHEA. Users of these substances are seeking similar results that have been reported with anabolic-androgenic steroid usage, namely increased muscular strength, hypertrophy, quicker recovery after intense training sessions, and enhanced body composition. These anticipated benefits are expected because anabolic steroid precursors act to increase testosterone production.

A number of potential problems exist for consumers of these performance-enhancing substances. All three are banned by the National Collegiate Athletic Association under the classification of anabolic agents. Second and minus a valid prescription, two of the agents are illegal under the DEA's Controlled Substance Act and its ensuing Steroid Control Act. Aside from jeopardizing one's eligibility and offering potential legal encounters, use of these substances present possibilities of adverse side effects plus the products may not provide users with their intended effects. For example, Brzycki (2006) has stated that DHEA is questionable for improving body composition or muscular strength. Powers (2004) is even more emphatic when he concluded that "the anabolic steroid precursors do not appear to provide any muscle or performance benefit" (Powers, 2004, p. 31).

Designer Steroids

Designer steroids are relative newcomers in the realm of performance-enhancing substances. The substances are designed to build muscle but remain invisible in terms of drug testing (Mannie, 2004).

One primary example of a designer steroid is tetrahydrogestrinone, or THG. This substance is a combination steroid consisting of trenbolone and gestrinone. It is administered as a "clear" or oral liquid and is virtually undetectable via existing drug testing protocol (Cato, 2007). Thus, it represents a clandestine attempt to manufacture a perfect performance-enhancing drug (Mannie, 2004) and, in reality, "it was developed for the sole purpose of cheating in sport" (Uryasz, 2004, p. A1).

Two major problems immediately surface regarding the use of THG for performance-enhancement purposes. THG is both an illegal substance and an NCAA banned substance. The second problem is related to health and safety. Since THG is an oral steroid, the liquid is placed under the tongue for absorption purposes. Subsequently, this administration method "makes THG 10 times more toxic on the liver than other steroids" (Cato, 2007, p. 11).

Human Growth Hormone

Intended performance-enhancing effects underlying human growth hormone (HGH) use include stimulated protein synthesis, increased muscle mass, heightened loss of body fat, elevated training intensity, improved post-training recovery, and facilitated bone growth (Brzycki, 2007; Cato, 2007; Mangus & Miller, 2005). Little is known about the safety and/or efficacy of over-the-counter HGH, but Brzycki (2007) has indicated that OTC products may not improve muscle mass. On the other hand, prescription HGH contains the potential for a number of adverse health effects (Martin et al., 2007). This would be especially true for those athletes who may be taking as much as 10 times the recommended therapeutic dosage of HGH.

According to Rush (2004), HGH may be one substance that is particularly favored by female athletes for performance-enhancement purposes. This gender preference is apparently driven by the fact that there are no perceived androgenic or masculizing effects associated with HGH.

The possession and use of human growth hormone without a valid prescription is unlawful. The substance is also banned by the NCAA under its category of peptide hormones and analogues. As a result, the use of HGH presents many of the same complications as some of the previously discussed performance-enhancing drugs. However, many athletes are opting to use HGH "because of unsubstantiated reports that it is as effective as anabolic steroids with fewer side effects" (Martin et al., 2007, p. 11). Add to these anecdotal reports the fact that HGH is easily available over the Internet and difficult to detect in drug screening tests, and it becomes apparent why athletes might choose to employ this substance to gain a competitive edge.

Erythropoietin

Erythropoietin (EPO) is to aerobic athletes what anabolic-androgenic steroids are to anaerobic athletes: endurance enhancement versus gains in strength and power. EPO stimulates the production of red blood cells, which, in turn, give the blood added oxygen-carrying capacity. This enhanced oxygen-carrying capacity then enables the blood to transport greater amounts of oxygenated blood from the lungs to the active muscle tissues. As a result, both $VO_{2\,max}$ and endurance are heightened.

The performance edge gained by the use of EPO can be significant. Rush (2004) cited one study of male athletes who displayed an 8% increase in $VO_{2max.}$ It is of interest to note that an enhanced endurance result similar to EPO's effect can be evoked by employing a natural, legal training method. Athletes electing to engage in high-altitude training trigger EPO production that seemingly yields a competitive edge when they return to lower elevation levels for competition (Foley, 2005).

The use of EPO by endurance athletes represents a demarcation from the process of "blood doping." An illegal technique itself, "blood doping" consists of withdrawing one's own blood, placing it in storage, and then reinfusing the stored blood prior to competition. The intent is to gain the benefits of an increased RBC count, but simply taking injections of EPO seems to be the current manner of obtaining a performance-enhancing endurance boost.

As with the previously mentioned substances, EPO is unlawful to use without a prescription and it is included on the National Collegiate Athletic Association's list of banned substances. Aside from the standard legal and eligibility complications associated with most other performance-enhancing drugs, EPO has emerged as one of the most deadly doping agents (Martin et al., 2007). Taken in supernatural dosages, the substance can elevate the body's hematocrit levels to the point where the blood's viscosity becomes comparable to a substance like molasses. This drastic and abnormal change in viscosity can then lend itself to seizures, strokes, and death (Cato, 2007).

Stimulants, Amphetamines, and Ephedrine

The National Collegiate Athletic Association's 2005 *Study of Substance Use of College Student-Athletes* revealed that amphetamine use has continually increased since 1997 while the use of ephedrine has remained stable since 1997, the first year its use was calculated. Interestingly, the highest percentage of amphetamine usage was found in Division III (NCAA, 2005).

The two major reasons cited for amphetamine use were treatment of attention deficit disorder followed by a desire for increased energy. Ephedrine usage was driven by weight loss and a desire for improved athletic performance (NCAA, 2005).

One final piece of statistical data from the National Collegiate Athletic Association's 2005 investigation parallels a finding relative to anabolic-androgenic steroid use. More than of 66% of amphetamine, ephedrine, and nutritional supplement use appear to start before college (NCAA, 2005). Simply stated, student-athletes are bringing their substance use and abuse behaviors with them as they matriculate to higher education settings.

Stimulants represent the final category of illegal performance-enhancing substances outlined by Minelli et al. (2006). Athletes use stimulants with the belief that the products will offer an energy boost during training or competition; aid in exercise recovery; increase arousal; suppress appetite and abet weight loss; and yield a carbohydrate sparing effect because they are believed to increase fat metabolism. In truth, stimulant use may offer either limited and/or no physiological edge to their consumers.

The National Collegiate Athletic Association's 2004–05 banned list of stimulants contained 34 substances. However, a vast majority of the literature on stimulant use in athletic populations focuses on ephedra and ephedrine. Ephedrine stimulates the sympathetic nervous system and is structurally similar to amphetamines (Powers, 2004). An updated list of the NCAA's banned-drug classes can be found at *www.ncaa.org/health-safety*.

A limited body of research concerning ephedrine and athletic performance exists, but Powers concluded that "most of the investigations do not support ergogenic claims" (Powers, 2004, p. 33). Mangus and Miller (2005) echo Powers's position. They state that "no published research definitively states that ephedrine has an ergogenic effect on performance in competitive athletes" (p. 168).

Athletes need to understand that the combination of intense exercise, insufficient hydration, extreme heat and humidity, and an ephedra-based supplement can be a lethal mixture. Stimulants increase heart rate, blood pressure, and act as a diuretic. Factor these three effects into a heart and circulatory system that are engaged in thermoregulation and intense exercise amid extreme environmental conditions, and you have a receipt for major health-related complications.

The Food and Drug Administration placed a ban on the sale of ephedra (ma huang) in April 2004. Its sale was prohibited because of severe health risks attributed to the product. In extreme cases, "studies have linked ephedra to more that 150 deaths due to heart attacks and hemorrhagic strokes" (Cato, 2007, p. 12). It should be noted, however, that the FDA's ban on sales did not make it illegal to possess or use ephedra.

In an attempt to discourage the use of stimulants by athletes, the National Collegiate Athletic Association initiated testing for ephedrine in 2002 (Uryasz, 2002). Stimulants, especially ephedrine, became subject to the NCAA's year-round drug testing protocol and procedures.

The National Collegiate Athletic Association's year-round testing for ephedrine in 2002 and the Food and Drug Administration's ban on ephedra sales in 2004 encouraged stimulant proponents to search for comparable substances. Rockwell (2008) and Cato (2007) listed synephrine, bitter orange, zhi shi, and citrus aurantium among the more popular stimulant substitutes, but all of these are prohibited by the NCAA. Some athletes have even opted to stack multiple substances in order to get a desired stimulant effect. One such example, an "ECA stack," is a mixture of ephedrine, caffeine, and aspirin (Uryasz, 2002).

Testing positive for stimulant use carries the same eligibility penalties imposed for other NCAA banned substances. Criminal sanctions may also be imposed if the substance being used is a prescription drug and no valid prescription exists by the user. As for health and safety concerns, I would reiterate the research findings indicating minimal to no performance-enhancing effects associated with ephedrine. I would also reemphasize the fact that the FDA needed solid, empirical grounds to ban the sale of ephedra in 2004. Sadly, it took a number of publicized tragedies, some in specific sport settings, before the FDA was allowed to exert its enforcement powers as a consumer protection agency.

I would now like to direction attention to the aids that Minelli et al. (2006) list under their heading of legal performance-enhancing substances. These products include caffeine, over-the-counter drugs, and dietary supplements.

Caffeine

Caffeine can be used by itself to mimic a stimulant effect or it may be combined with ephedrine and aspirin to create an ECA stack, a technique believed to heighten performance-enhancement probability. A by-product of the "stacking" process, however, is increased risk for a number of adverse side effects (Clarkson, Coleman, & Rosenbloom, 2002). Obviously, users are hopeful caffeine will yield the same benefits as other energy supplements, namely endurance, higher metabolism levels, and increased fat metabolism.

Caffeine (guarana) is on the National Collegiate Athletic Association's banned list of stimulants. A positive test for an excess level of caffeine is rendered "if the concentration in urine exceeds 15 micrograms/ml" (NCAA, 2005, p. 6). Any athlete testing positive for excessive levels of caffeine would become subject to the existing NCAA and institutional sanctions imposed for a positive drug test.

Mangus and Miller (2004) offer three distinct theories (metabolic, neurological, and muscular) as to why caffeine may have an ergogenic effect on athletic performance. Each theory is believed to offer a unique way to increase one's work output. In general, the ergogenic effects of caffeine seemingly favor endurance or aerobic athletes.

Over-the-Counter Drugs

The most common over-the-counter drugs (OTCs) used by athletes are aspirin, ibuprofen (Advil, Motril, and Nuprin) and acetaminophen (Tylenol). Each drug offers an analgesic effect while aspirin and ibuprofen are also anti-inflammatory agents.

If utilized as directed, all three drugs can combat pain and/or reduce the inflammatory response associated with sports-related injuries. On the other hand, misuse or abuse of these OTC drugs can mask pain, cause gastrointestinal problems, or foster toxic effects.

It is not atypical for an injured athlete to want to return to practice or competition as soon as possible. Many athletes, in fact, exhibit a high degree of impatience when dealing with injuries. This impatience may lead them to use abnormally high dosages of OTC drugs to speed up their injury recovery processes. An existing mindset seems to be if a little bit of an analgesic and/or anti-inflammatory medication is good, then a lot more may be better. Thus, it becomes extremely important that every athlete have a solid understanding that any drug is truly a drug! The substance can provide its intended effect if used properly, or it can be harmful or lethal if it is misused and/or abused. Perhaps this message is best illustrated by the fact that the misuse of over-the-counter drugs causes 178,000 hospitalizations annually in the United States.

Dietary Supplements

Dietary supplements represent Pandora's box when it comes to performance-enhancing substance use among college athletes. They represent a very popular path toward finding a competitive advantage, perhaps to the extent that they might be the most common manner in which athletes seek to boost their performance capabilities.

Previous survey research placed dietary supplement use as high as 98.6% among varsity athletes (Minelli et al., 2006). Another investigation placed usage figures at 20–305 in NCAA-affiliated athletes, but with a caveat that the real numbers are probably much higher (Green, 1998). Finally, research on creatine, a specific dietary supplement geared to anaerobic athletic performance, found a usage range of 28–41% in NCAA athletes (Rawson & Clarkson, 2003). The range changed from 17 to 74% when athletes of variable ages were polled (Rawson & Clarkson, 2003).

One of the daunting tasks facing all parties who have a vested interest in dietary supplements is maintaining proper vigilance over a mega industry and its constantly expanding list of products. The production of dietary supplements is estimated to be an $18 billion business, one that turns out approximately 1,000 new dietary products each year (Minelli et al., 2006). This information becomes especially troublesome when it is purported that there is very little systematic regulations in place to properly monitor a highly profitable conglomeration of supplement manufacturers.

The widespread availability of dietary supplements is due, in large measure, to the 1994 Dietary Supplement and Health Education Act, or DSHEA (Olander, 2000). This legislative initiative stipulated that dietary supplements were to be regulated as foods, not drugs. As a result, consumers were granted virtually unrestricted access to dietary and nutritional supplements. DSHEA also defined the term "dietary supplement"; curtailed some of the FDA's regulatory powers over unsafe consumer products; and, in general, deregulated the dietary supplement industry (Minelli et al., 2006; Olander, 2000). The deregulation "allowed manufactures to: a) expand marketing claims of effectiveness of supplements, and b) have greater autonomy in the development of new products" (Minelli et al., 2006, p. 10). It should also be noted that these new products "are not required to meet FDA standards for efficacy, potency, or safety before being released to the public" (Cato, 2007, p. 11).

At least one professional organization, the American College of Sports Medicine (ACSM), has voiced opposition to the 1994 DSHEA measure. ACSM leadership has suggested the FDA reexamine this piece of legislation because of its inadequacies in dealing with the safety, efficacy, and questionable ingredient issues in consumer products (AAPHERD, 1998).

Any nutritional/dietary supplement should be closely scrutinized in accordance with five fundamental criteria (Green, 1998; Powers, 2007; Roachman, 1999; Rockwell, 2008). These five criteria, presented in question format, include:

1. Is the nutritional/dietary supplement legal?
2. What is the "purity" of the nutritional/dietary supplement?
3. Does the nutritional/dietary supplement produce its desired effects?
4. Is the nutritional/dietary supplement safe?
5. Is the nutritional/dietary supplement necessary?

Each of the five criterion merit some degree of discussion.

Is the nutritional/dietary supplement legal? Some products or their chemical composition may violate the DEA's Controlled Substance Act, the use of others may be prohibited by various sport governing bodies, and some substances may present double jeopardy in terms of legal and eligibility sanctions. The National Collegiate Athletic Association and the National Drug Administration both maintain updated information on banned substances and drugs that violate provisions of the CSA statutes.

What is the "purity" status of the nutritional/dietary supplement? There are a range of issues surrounding drug purity, including getting only what is listed on the product's label, ingredients not listed on the label (banned substances that might be mixed to create other ingredients), or the potency of the product may be greater or less than advertised by its manufacturer. Investigations involving large numbers of OTC dietary supplements have consistently shown that "15 to 25 percent of products tested contain ingredients not listed on the label" (Rockwell, 2008, p. 24). A more recent study into supplement contamination levels in the U.S. market found tainted dietary supplements containing steroids as well as banned stimulants (Perez, 2007). Any contaminated product could ultimately cause a failed drug test on the part of the product's user. In such cases, the NCAA has held firm to their belief that "ignorance" is not a valid defense for testing positive to a banned substance. Consequently, any athlete who is using a nutritional/dietary supplement has an added responsibility. They must stay updated on their supplement by always seeking the most accurate and current information available.

There are some excellent resources offering athletes current and accurate information regarding nutritional and dietary supplements. Foremost among these information sources would be the Dietary Supplement Resource Exchange Center (REC), created by Drug Free Sport in 2001. It is a confidential hotline and website designed to answer questions pertaining to dietary supplements and banned substances. Many other free resources exist to help safeguard the health and safety of those athletes who have chosen to utilize a nutritional/dietary supplement for performance-enhancement purposes.

Does the nutritional/dietary supplement produce its desired effects? Unfortunately, "supplement manufacturers can legally claim that their product will improve athletic performance" (Mangus & Miller, 2005, p.191). Among their many acclaimed virtues, supplements are advertised to provide an energy boost; decrease body fat; increase lean muscle mass; and improve strength, endurance, and power. Are these claims legitimate or are they simply hyperbole designed to give false hope? Many of the claims made about the effects of a supplement are based on anecdotal reports, not on sound scientific assessments. As a result, there is no guarantee that a product will provide its intended effect and there is no promise that any supplement is safe (Clarkson et al., 2002).

Athletes need to have a bona fide reason for using any dietary supplement. What type of enhancement outcome are they hoping to gain and how will their supplement of choice play a role in improving their performance? Athletes must realize that supplements are not a substitute for high-quality training and nutrition programs. The attraction of a "magic potion" to reach the pinnacle of one's performance level is enticing, but hard work and proper diet remain the staples of getting "bigger, stronger, and faster."

Is the nutritional/dietary supplement safe? Any athlete's health and safety must be of paramount importance in programs that ascribe to an educational model of sport. Therefore, health and safety concerns become an issue with supplement use for a variety of reasons. Rockwell (2008) posited inadequate hydration, increased risk of heat stress, and harmful drug or supplement interactions among major concerns, while Cato (2007) alluded to inadequate research, quality control, and testing of performance-enhancing substances. DSHEA stipulations *advise* dietary supplement manufacturers to produce *safe* products, but "supplements do not need approval before being sold, nor do manufacturers need to submit any studies to the FDA before marketing a new product" (Brehm. 2005, p. 24). In addition, the Food and Drug Administration will only look at a product when it has received a sufficient number of consumer complaints. Even then the burden of proof rests with the agency before a product can be removed from the market (Brehm, 2005). In a nutshell, dietary supplements "do not undergo rigorous testing and screening for efficacy and safety" (Clarkson et al., 2002, p. 1).

Is the nutritional/dietary supplement necessary? A well-designed policy addressing the use of dietary supplements and a panel of knowledgeable professionals may be essential keys in answering this question. Obviously, nutritional and dietary supplements are expensive products. In many situations, it may be possible to improve performance at a fraction of the cost required to purchase supplements. Simply conducting a thorough examination of every facet underlying peak performance may prompt the need for minor changes. Once implemented, these "natural" performance-enhancing alterations may far surpass any potential effects associated with some of today's more fashionable supplements.

A "win-at-all-costs" syndrome permeates today's society. Winners are glorified and lavishly rewarded while "losers" are shunned and left to wonder how they can ever win. Nowhere is this winner-takes-all mindset more apparent than in sports. Many athletes adopt an anything-goes attitude in order to succeed. This mental approach often breeds unethical behaviors, including the use of illegal performance-enhancing drugs. A similar mental outlook is fostered by a perceived need to establish a level playing field in sports. Performance boosters may be used in this scenario to erase a perceived edge by an opponent or to keep up with a rival because they are rumored to be using chemicals to enhance their level of performance.

Because we are obsessed with winning, more and more people are willing to do anything to win! This is especially true for athletes and, according to Callahan (2004), this phenomena represents a shift from personal values to a system's value structure (i.e., a changing moral and ethical compass). Once this threshold is reached, the next step is relatively easy because help is available in the form of performance-enhancing substances. These chemical aids, especially HGH and steroids, are plentiful and easy to obtain. For example, "the amount of illegal steroids entering the United States has increased dramatically, forming an estimated 100 million dollar black market for steroids with greater than 80% manufactured in Mexico" (Martin et al., 2007, p. 10). You can even purchase your steroids at an online source like *www.legalsteroids.com* should you choose to do so.

Unquestionably, the use of performance-enhancing drugs and supplements presents major concerns in college athletic circles. The problem becomes even more problematic when sources estimate that 15 million Americans are using performance-enhancing drugs for purposes such as anti-aging, body sculpting, cosmetics, or improved quality of life (McCullum, 2008). Hence, the use of chemicals to enhance performance in sports may simply be reflective of a "mega cultural trend" in society as a whole (McCullum, 2008).

DISCUSSION

There are many different dimensions concerning performance-enhancing substance use in general, and these may provide some navigational help through the turbulent culture of performance-enhancing substance use and/or misuse. In addition, all of these dimensions may ultimately be mute points if projections of the "genetically engineered superathlete" become the norm for performance enhancement in the future (Epstein, 2008).

First, it is important to support nationwide initiatives for steroid testing and education at the high school level. We know from NCAA studies that many athletes bring their drug use behaviors with them to college. States like New Jersey, Florida, and Texas have paved the way for steroid testing while California has been a front-runner in educational programming aimed at coaches, athletes, and parents (Popke, 2005).

Second, Dr. Frank Uryasz's position is that there needs to be more collaboration in the existing NCAA drug testing program (Ulrich, 2008). Presently, only 4% of NCAA athletes are subject to drug tests each year. This number could increase if individual schools, conferences, and sports-governing bodies (NCAA, NAIA, and NJCAA) each opted to engage in testing. Encompassed with a stronger testing program would be the idea of uniformity among entities. The penalties or sanctions for infractions would be applied with uniform consistency in each and every case.

Third, the Dietary Supplement and Health Education Act of 1994 needs to be revisited and possibly amended, and the Food and Drug Administration should have more regulatory power over the dietary supplement industry. This would include responsibility on the part of supplement manufacturers to conduct rigorous testing of their products. This accountability measure would protect consumers because they would have reasonable assurance that a product works as intended, is safe, and contains only what is listed on the packaging label.

Fourth, there must be a turning-back of educational athletics moving toward a professional model of sport. Although difficult, this change is a monumental force underlying much of performance-enhancing drug use. Winning becomes the ultimate goal and the process or educational experiences become of secondary importance.

Fifth, the National Collegiate Athletic Association, as well as other sports governing bodies, needs to remain hypervigilant relative to supplements and react with legislative measures if necessary. Muscle-building supplements serve as a case in point. Because there is an unproven safety record with these types of substances, the NCAA enacted a rule stipulating that institutions "may only provide student-athletes with non-muscle-building nutritional supplements—such as those found in energy bars and sports drinks—and then only to boost calories and electrolytes" (Popke, 2000, p. 86).

Sixth, athletes themselves need to maintain a "buyer beware" position when it comes to nutritional and dietary supplements. They must realize that a majority of products are not tested for efficacy or safety. In addition, product labels can be misleading or the substance may be contaminated. Both of these circumstances could result in a failed drug test.

Seventh, inherent with use is responsibility. If athletes opt to use nutritional/dietary supplements, they need to be intelligent consumers. This would involve using appropriate resources to thoroughly investigate a supplement as well as taking most manufactures' claims with a grain of salt. Bottom line, if it sounds too good to be true, it is probably *not* true!!

And lastly, coaches, athletic administrators, and athletes need to stay abreast of the constantly changing climate surrounding performance-enhancing substances. Sound policies and uniform application of said policies become essential. In addition, open and honest communication regarding the pros and cons of performance-enhancing substances is extremely important. Ultimately, the health, safety, and general well-being of the student-athlete should be our prime concern. Consequently, we need to do everything within our powers to ensure that participants have a safe, healthy, and quality experience in their intercollegiate athletic endeavors.

REFERENCES

American Academy of Pediatrics. (2005). Policy statement: Use of performance-enhancing substances. *Pediatrics, 115*(4), 1103–1106.

AAHPERD. (1998). ACSM recommends that FDA revisit "dietary supplements." *JOPERD, 69*(9), 6.

Brehm, B. A. (2005). Understanding the dietary supplement industry. *Fitness Management, 2*(6), 24.

Brzycki, M. (2007). Pills, powders, and potions. *Coach and Athletic Director, 76*(8), 63–65.

Callahan, D. (2004). *The cheating culture: Why more Americans are doing wrong to get ahead.* New York: Harcourt.

Cato, C. (2007). Shedding light on the myths and facts of performance-enhancing substances. *Interscholastic Athletic Administration, 33*(4), 10–13.

Clarkson, P., Coleman, & Rosenbloom. (2002). Risky dietary supplements. *Sports Science Exchange Roundtable, 13* (2), 1–4.

Drug Enforcement Administration. (2004). *Anabolic steroids: Hidden dangers.* Washington, DC: Author.

Eitzen, D. S. (2006). *Fair and foul: Beyond the myths and paradoxes of sport* (3rd ed.). Lenham, MD: Rowman & Littlefield.

Epstein, D. (2008). The future. *Sports Illustrated, 108*(11), 44–47.

Fendrich, H. (2005, June 16). Trickle-down steroid use a growing concern. *The Greenville News,* p. C5.

Foley, M. (2005, September 6). The ABCs of EPO. *The Greenville News,* pp. D1, D4.

Green, G. (1998). Dietary supplements imperil eligibility, health. *The NCAA News, 35*(35), 5–6.

Mangus, B. C., & Miller, M. G. (2005). *Pharmacology application in athletic training.* Philadelphia: F. A. Davis.

Mannie, K. (2004). 'Stealth' steroids require sharper radar. *The NCAA News, 41*(5), 3, 26.

Mannie, K. (2008). Chemical conundrum: Beyond the Mitchell report. *Coach and Athletic Director, 77*(9), 6–10.

Martin, D. M., Baron, D. A., & Gold, M. S. A review of performance-enhancing drugs in professional sports and their spread to amateur athletics, adolescents, and other at-risk populations. In M. S. Gold (Ed.), *Performance-enhancing medications and drugs of abuse* (pp. 5–15). Binghampton, NY: Haworth Medical Press.

McCullum, J. (2008, March 17). The real dope: It's just not sports. *Sports Illustrated, 108*(11), 28–34.

Minelli, M., Olrich, T., & Smith, S. (2006). Performance-enhancing substances: What interscholastic athletic directors need to know. *Interscholastic Athletic Administration, 33*(1), 10–12.

National Collegiate Athletic Association. (2006). *Study of substance use of college student-athletes.* Indianapolis, IN: Author.

National Collegiate Athletic Association. (2005). *Drug-testing program 2004–05.* Indianapolis, IN: Author.

Olander, R. (2000). Supplements require regulatory measures. *The NCAA News, 37*(13), 4–5.

Perez, A. J. (2007, December 5). Study: Steroids found in supplements. *USA Today,* p. B6.

Petersen, J. A. (2002). 10 negative side effects of taking steroids. *ACSM's Health and Fitness Journal, 6*(6), 44.

Popke, M. (2000). A bitter pill? *Athletic Business, 24*(12), 75–87.

Popke, M. (2005). A growing problem. *Athletic Business, 29*(12), 116–124.

Rawson, E. S., & Clarkson, P. M. (2003). Scientifically debatable: Is creatine worth its weight? *Sports Science Exchange Roundtable, 16*(4), 1–6.

Rockwell, M. (2008). Choices . . . and more choices. *Training and Conditioning, 18*(3), 23–29.

Rush, S. (2004). Just say "no." *ACSM's Health and Fitness Journal, 8*(2), 22–24.

Ulrich, L. (2008). Safe from steroids? *Athletic Management, 20*(2), 27–33.

Uryasz, F. (2002). Ephedrine test among program upgrades. *The NCAA News, 39*(18), 4.

Uryasz, F. (2004, April 12). "Designer steroids" impact drug testing. *The NCAA News [Health & Safety Newsletter],* p. A1.

CHAPTER 14

INVOLVEMENT IN LEARNING AND ATHLETIC PARTICIPATION

Ashley Tull
University of Arkansas

This chapter addresses student-athletes' learning and participation in intercollegiate athletics. Involvement in learning activities both inside and outside of the classroom are discussed first. Particular attention is given to activities out of the classroom as they have been found to be important for the achievement of holistic outcomes in college, and then covered are the unique experiences of freshman student-athletes and their intellectual and social development as they relate to the transition to college and university life. The differences between learning and athletic participation for student-athletes in revenue- and non-revenue-producing sports and male and female student-athletes is addressed next. Services to support learning and athletic participation are addressed with regard to athletic association and institutional characteristics. Specific recommendations from the literature for campus-based services to support learning and athletic participation are provided along with balancing involvement in learning and athletic participation. This includes a discussion of maintaining eligibility while meeting

College Student-Athletes: Challenges, Opportunities, and Policy Implications, pages 201–215
Copyright © 2009 by Information Age Publishing
201

academic and other commitments as well as how academic and athletic motivation influence student-athletes' ability to persist and be successful. Finally, briefly addressed is the preparation for life beyond the classroom and playing field.

INVOLVEMENT IN LEARNING ACTIVITIES INSIDE AND OUTSIDE OF THE CLASSROOM

Involvement in learning activities both inside and outside of the classroom has been deemed important for the intellectual and social development of college students (Astin, 1993; Bok, 2006; Kuh, 1995). Research on the results of learning inside and outside of the classroom has been mixed. Some existing research on student-athletes has found a negative relationship between athletic participation and academic performance (Adler & Adler, 1985). Most research on student-athletes has focused more on academic achievement (cumulative grade point averages), rather than the overall impact of cognitive outcomes achieved while a student-athlete (Pascarella, Bohr, Nora, & Terenzini, 1995). This has made measuring intellectual development difficult. Some researchers have attributed athletic participation with poor academic performance and identified participation as exacerbating academic weaknesses and insecurities held by student-athletes (Shulman & Bowen, 2001). Others (Pascarella & Terenzini, 2005) have identified a consistent body of research suggesting student-athletes, particularly football and basketball players, may not be achieving the cognitive outcomes from college as their nonathletic peers. Heavy time commitments placed on student-athletes that may have harmful effects on academic performance have been a cause of underperformance academically (Shulman & Bowen, 2001).

Student-athletes are faced with greater demands for their time both inside and outside of the classroom. As is the case for many student-athletes, the demands placed on them outside of the classroom can be detrimental to their achieving learning outcomes (Hood, Craig, & Ferguson, 1992). Student-athletes' schedules, consisting of classes, sports related activities and homework can make for inflexible and demanding schedules (Jordan & Denson, 1990). One report by the National Collegiate Athletic Association (NCAA) found that prior to 1991, student-athletes were reporting they spent an average of more than 30 hours per week on their sport (Etzel, Ferrante, & Pinkey, 1996; Suggs, 1999). After 1991 the NCAA implemented new regulations limiting the amount of time spent on sports to no more than 4 hours per day, 20 hours per week of structured time (i.e., practice, competition, and workouts) per student-athlete (Abell, 2000).

We should not overlook the valuable learning opportunities that exist outside of the classroom for student-athletes. Researchers who examine the impact of college on students have found that the curriculum outside of the classroom (sometimes called a "hidden curriculum") can contribute greatly to the overall outcomes of college. These out-of-classroom experiences serve as a real-world laboratory, where student-athletes are able to apply knowledge acquired through formal classroom instruction (Kuh, 1995). Viewing student-athletes' out-of-classroom experiences as a real-world laboratory supports the assumption that commitment to participate in intercollegiate athletics resembles the pursuit of a vocational career. Participation has been identified as resembling a vocational career based on the psychological attachment that is developed by college student-athletes, as opposed to an economic one (Perna, Zaichkowsky, & Bocknek, 1996). Many forms of outside-of-classroom activities have been found to be important for intellectual and social development. These include not only intercollegiate athletic participation but dramatic performance and activities like fraternity or sorority membership. Each of these activities are important for practicing effective working relationships among students (Bok, 2006). In turn, students can translate their classroom experiences to activities and relationships outside of the classroom, and this has a reinforcing effect on what is learned in class (Bok, 2006).

Time commitments required for participation in intercollegiate athletics appear to affect student-athlete participation in outside-of-class activities the most. Many student-athletes appear to have little time outside of sports. When they do, many choose to spend it socializing or resting, rather than in other organized activities on campus (Adler & Adler, 1985). Researchers have found that many students, athletes or not, struggle with participation in outside-of-classroom activities. Those students with commitments in activities like newspaper production, performing arts, or part-time employment also meet challenges in maintaining these substantial commitments (Hood et al., 1992). Like athletic participation, each of these activities requires good amounts of time and energy, which student-athletes often lack. Richards and Aries (1999), for example, found that student-athletes reported greater difficulty in attending on- and off-campus activities, joining student groups, and interacting with new and different people. The learning experiences outside of the classroom vary for student-athletes based on a variety of characteristics. Student-athletes, to the degree possible, should seek out learning opportunities beyond the classroom and playing field. These will serve to make them more well rounded and satisfied with their college experience.

LEARNING ACTIVITIES OF FRESHMAN STUDENT-ATHLETES

The transition to college life inside and outside of the classroom is crucial to intellectual and social development (Oppenheimer, 1984). Freshman student-athletes arrive on campus with personal expectations about how they will perform in the classroom. Many student-athletes have commonly assumed that they would (1) put in their time by attending classes and doing homework, (2) would earn a degree, and (3) would encounter no problems with putting in their time and earning their degree (Adler & Adler, 1985). We know from examining student-athlete achievement and graduation rates that this is not always the true outcome of student-athletes' experiences on campus. The freshman year for student-athletes has been described as a period of divestment from old roles to the development of new roles, once in college. Student-athletes generally experience a sense of loss when leaving previously developed support systems, while making new adjustments once in college. Student-athletes must cope with new responsibilities in the classroom, some of which they may not be prepared for. The degree to which they are able to manage these new responsibilities will determine their success as a student-athlete (Medalie, 1981). Those student-athletes with a high internal locus of control may struggle the most with the above described disengagement process, as they will encounter difficulties that may be out of their control (Murphy, Petitpas, & Brewer, 1996). This is particularly true with inside- and outside-of-classroom learning activities.

Results vary on the degree to which intercollegiate athletic participation affects freshman student-athletes' learning. One study (Umbach & Kuh, 2004) of 12,559 student-athletes found that both first-year students and seniors were more likely to take part in active and collaborative activities on campus. First-year student-athletes were found to interact more frequently with faculty members than their nonathlete counterparts. In some cases, some student-athletes were found to report greater gains in personal and social competencies than their non-student-athlete counterparts. Additionally, some first-year student-athletes were found to have greater gains in practical competencies than their non-athlete counterparts. Another study of student-athletes at 18 institutions found that intercollegiate athletic participation had significant consequences for the cognitive development of both men and women during the freshman year (Pascarella et al., 1995). Still another study (Hood et al., 1992) found no results indicating major detriments to freshman cognitive development for revenue- or non-revenue-producing student-athletes during the freshman year. Adler and Adler (1985) found in their study that student-athletes readily acknowledged that their participation in intercollegiate athletics affected their academic performance. The transition to college life for all freshmen is critical, even more so for student-athletes. Colleges and universities should pay particular attention to the transition issues of freshman student-athletes to ensure their intellectual and social development.

DIFFERENCES BETWEEN LEARNING AND ATHLETIC PARTICIPATION BETWEEN REVENUE AND NONREVENUE STUDENT-ATHLETES

Differences for student-athletes learning both inside- and outside-of-classroom have been described in the literature with regard to revenue (i.e., football, basketball) versus nonrevenue (i.e., golf, tennis) sports. Differences exist for student-athletes in revenue and nonrevenue sports and are compounded often times based on athletic division or other institutional characteristics. Student-athletes in revenue-producing sports have been found to have performed lower at the high school level and have lower grades while in college than their non-revenue producing student-athlete counterparts (Hood et al., 1992). Hood et al. (1992) found no significant differences for academic achievement when both revenue and nonrevenue student-athletes were combined and compared to their nonathlete counterparts of similar demographics and aptitude. Pascarella et al. (1995) also confirmed the above notion. Their study results indicated similar academic performance between college student-athletes and their nonathletic counterparts when controls were used for secondary school achievement, aptitude, and other demographic characteristics. Astin (1993) found that the negative academic consequences, for freshman men, were limited to revenue-producing sports. Student-athletes in non-revenue-producing sports have been found to make fewer gains to similar student-athletes in revenue-producing sports or nonathletes (Pascarella & Terenzini, 2005). This notion might be confirmed by the fact that they come to college with greater aptitude and generally perform better once in college.

The factors contributing to why a difference exists between student-athletes in revenue- and non-revenue-producing sports are wide and varied. Generally, more support services exist for student-athletes in revenue-producing sports, often exclusive to the particular team. Richards and Aries (1999) stated that role conflict is greatest for student-athletes in revenue-producing sports as compared to non-revenue-producing sports. This does depend on association affiliation and other institutional characteristics. Some have suggested that student-athletes in revenue-producing sports can develop a false sense of security, attributed to the fact they feel others are looking out for their academic well-being. Student-athletes may feel that they have multiple chances and that they avoid paying the consequences for poor academic performance (Adler & Adler, 1985). This notion can be manifested by some student-athletes as a sense of entitlement. They may assume that members of the athletic staff will look out for them after their playing careers have come to an end. This can lead to a failure to develop career alternatives beyond their sport (Pearson & Petitpas, 1990). Still others (Pascarella et al., 1995) have suggested that the extensive time commitment or the subculture that is often developed around student-athletes (particularly football and basketball) contributes negatively to the learning experience.

Student-athlete learning experiences outside of the classroom are related to whether they are members of revenue or nonrevenue sports. Those scholarship student-athletes in sports generating the highest revenues have been found to experience the greatest amount of role conflict (Richards & Aries, 1999). Those members of revenue-producing sports teams have been found to spend at least three hours daily in practice, are expected to watch game film of other teams, participate in team meetings, and can be gone from campus from two to five days at a time. The demands on revenue-producing student-athletes also can include spending certain amounts of time with the media, attending fan events, and interacting with athletic boosters (Adler & Adler, 1985; Jordan & Denson, 1990). Organized team responsibilities (i.e., practice, games, and road trips) have been found to conflict with student-athletes' ability to complete coursework (Jordan & Denson, 1990). Additionally, the expectation to attend booster functions may not hinder academic time, but cuts into the discretionary time student-athletes might have to devote to learning in other outside-of-classroom activities (Adler & Adler, 1985). To complicate matters even more, student services programs, as is discussed later in the chapter, are generally scheduled during times when student-athletes are expected to attend practice or other conditioning activities associated with their particular sport.

When student-athletes in revenue-producing sports have time to spend on outside-of- classroom learning activities, they may be less likely to do so than those who were members of non-revenue-producing sports teams. Revenue-producing student-athletes did not attend as many on- or off-campus events or join extracurricular groups as others (Cantor & Prentice, 1996). In general, Stone and Strange (1989) found that student-athletes were less active in the performing arts, clubs, and organizations, and were less likely than their nonathletic peers to discuss something that they read with others. Student-athletes will have different opportunities to participate in learning activities outside of the classroom depending on the type of sport they participate in. All student-athletes should be encouraged to seek additional opportunities that are conducive to their particular academic and/or career choice or that are related to other outside interests.

DIFFERENCES BETWEEN LEARNING
AND ATHLETIC PARTICIPATION BETWEEN MALE
AND FEMALE STUDENT-ATHLETES

The degree to which intercollegiate athletic participation affects men and women student-athletes reviewed for this chapter identified a host of mixed results. Umbach and Kuh (2004) found that female student-athletes were more likely than male student-athletes to hold higher perceptions of their campuses supporting their academic and social needs. They also found female student-athletes to report higher levels of academic challenge and participation in enriching activities with diverse peer groups. Pascarella et al. (1995) found that participation in intercollegiate athletics by both males and females had significant consequences on cognitive development. Another study by Astin (1993) found similar results, but noted that significant consequences on cognitive development were greater for males in revenue-producing sports. Pascarella et al. (1999) found little evidence to support the notion that intercollegiate athletic participation for females affected their cognitive development on any level. They further noted that female student-athletes have significantly different levels of standardized cognitive development when compared to their nonathlete counterparts during the second and third years of college. Freshman female student-athletes in one study (Shulman & Bowen, 2001) were found to exhibit many of the characteristics of their male student-athlete counterparts. These included lower SAT scores than their nonathlete counterparts and different perceptions about their own abilities, particularly intellectual self-confidence. Pascarella and Terenzini (2005) concluded that the negative influences of intercollegiate athletic participation on cognitive development were greater for male student-athletes than for female student-athletes.

SERVICES TO SUPPORT LEARNING
AND ATHLETIC PARTICIPATION: AN ASSOCIATION
AND DIVISIONAL PERSPECTIVE

As discussed in this volume, the student-athlete learning experience can be different based on divisional and institutional characteristics. This is also true of the student support services provided to student-athletes to aid in their intellectual and social development. The ability to receive support services is often a factor in the success of student-athletes, both inside and outside of the classroom. NCAA Division I student-athletes have been found to have less opportunities to participate in the traditional college experience. They have traditionally maintained a focus on their performance and win–loss records (Watt & Moore, 2001). Some research has discovered underperformance at NCAA Division I public institutions, with more muted findings for Ivy League institutions and other co-ed liberal arts institutions (Shulman & Bowen, 2001). Student-athletes can be aided by support relationships offered by athletic departments and others on-campus. These have the effect of providing student-athletes with emotional and informational support necessary for encountering transitions that occur with college attendance and intercollegiate athletic participation (Pearson & Petitpas, 1990). The obligations of student-athletes at NCAA Division I schools are often greater than those at lower division or NAIA schools. The additional obligations held by Division I student-athletes can hinder their learning as opposed to lower division schools who often serve as models for how to maintain a scholar-athlete ideal (Shulman & Bowen, 2001). Students at these institutions are generally higher achievers academically and arrive more prepared for the academic rigors of college work.

All higher education institutions struggling to find balance between academic rigor and athletic success attempt to provide a more integrated experience for student-athletes in the college environment. This is frequently achieved at a greater level in smaller institutions where sport is deemphasized, with student-athletes playing more for the love of the sport, rather than for the trappings that come with competing at higher levels (Watt & Moore, 2001). One study of Division III student-athletes found them (1) spending more than double the amount of time on extracurricular involvements than their nonathletic counterparts, (2) graduating with GPAs that did not differ from their nonathletic counterparts, (3) involved in campus life activities as much as their nonathletic counterparts, and (4) experiencing similar levels of satisfaction with their growth and the college experience as their nonathletic counterparts (Richards & Aries, 1999). Umbach and Kuh (2004) found that Division III student-athletes reported higher levels of academic challenge and interaction with faculty members and greater gains in general education than their counterparts at Division I institutions. They also found that student-athletes at Division III and NAIA member institutions viewed their campuses as more supportive with regard to their learning experiences. Division I student-athletes may need more assistance in balancing both the internal and external challenges that come with intercollegiate athletic participation than their counterparts in Divisions II and III. This includes not only academic assistance, but also assistance in juggling the demands of coaches, the media, and their professors (Watt & Moore, 2001).

Student-athlete engagement in programs outside of the classroom can be largely determined by the type of athletic association their institution belongs to or other institutional factors. As has been discussed those student-athletes at larger institutions (i.e., NCAA Division I) and in revenue-producing sports have been afforded fewer learning opportunities for engagement outside of the classroom and have taken less advantage of those that do exist. Overall, student-athletes have been found to be as engaged or more engaged than their non-student-athlete counterparts (Umbach, Palmer, Kuh, & Hannah, n.d.).

Student services programs provided by national athletic associations are important for both the intellectual and social development of student-athletes. The NCAA, along with the Division I Athletic Directors Association, initiated the development of the CHAMPS/Life Skills Program (Challenging Athletes' Minds for Personal Success; *www.ncaa.org/wps/ncaa?ContentID=13*). This program, offered to NCAA member institutions, was first launched on 46 NCAA campuses in 1994. Since that time approximately 40 member institutions have started the program each year.

The National Association of Intercollegiate Athletics (NAIA; *www.naia.cstv.com*) was created to "promote the education and development of students through intercollegiate athletic participation. Member institutions, although varied and diverse, share a common commitment to high standards and to the principle that participation in athletics serves as an integral part of the total educational process." The NAIA, with 50,000 student-athletes from approximately 300 member institutions offers 23 championships in 13 sports (NAIA website). The NAIA, like the NCAA, offers a national program aimed at the total development of their student-athletes. Their program, Champions of Character, "seeks to create an environment in which every student-athlete, coach, official and spectator are committed to the true spirit of competition through the five core values: respect, integrity, responsibility, servant leadership and sportsmanship" (*www.naia.cstv.com*).

CAMPUS-BASED SERVICES TO SUPPORT LEARNING AND ATHLETIC PARTICIPATION

Campus-based services developed to support student-athletes' learning vary based on a variety of athletic association and institutional characteristics. There has been some agreement among both practitioners and scholars as to the types of services that should be provided to support intellectual and social development of student-athletes. Several have recommended that student-athletes work with academic advisors and counselors in the areas of eligibility, academic advising, assessment of deficiencies, tutorials and study halls, and personal and career counseling (Figler & Figler, 1984; Gunn & Eddy, 1989; Jordan & Denson, 1990). Gunn and Eddy (1989) also recommended that student-athlete support systems provide orientation programs, academic progress reports, peer mentors, and life skills workshops. Each of the above activities composes three important components important for the holistic development of student-athletes. These include personal development, career development, and academic development (Etzel et al., 1996). Carodine, Almond, and Gratto (2001) also stated that the goals of student-athlete support programs should be to assist student-athletes in academic development, athletic development, and social development. With a focus on these important elements, colleges and universities should be able to best serve the learning needs of their student-athletes, both inside and outside of the classroom.

BALANCING INVOLVEMENT IN LEARNING WITH ATHLETIC PARTICIPATION

The balance between learning activities both inside and outside of the classroom while meeting the demands of intercollegiate athletic participation and maintaining eligibility are challenging for many student-athletes. All college students are faced with new challenges while transitioning to college. Some of these include being away from home, developing new social relationships, and gaining self-discipline (Jordan & Denson, 1990). While many nonathletes struggle to meet the academic challenges that come with college work, particularly those who are actively engaged in extracurricular activities, student-athletes' likelihood of facing unique developmental issues are increased. Shulman and Bowen (2001) found that nonathletes who were involved in other extracurricular activities (i.e., newspaper production and performing arts), of equal demand to intercollegiate athletic participation, did not suffer as much academically as student-athletes. They also found that students who participated in other extracurricular activities, on the whole, finished better academically than students in general. This is said to be in large part to their identity, with an increased centeredness on athletics and the demands for higher levels of physical performance (Pearson & Petitpas, 1990). Other central challenges include balancing athletic demands and academic roles, while preparing for athletic retirement (Jordan & Denson, 1990). Those student-athletes who attend smaller institutions (i.e., lower NCAA division or NAIA schools) have more opportunities to participate in other extracurricular activities while a student. This provides greater possibilities for student leadership experience beyond the playing field through participation in student organizations, academic-related activities, and intramural sports programs.

Maintaining eligibility while fulfilling academic and other commitments as a student-athlete can be challenging, particularly for those in revenue-producing sports or those playing at the highest levels (i.e., NCAA Division I). Some student-athletes, particularly football players, have been found to spend as much as 44.8 hours a week participating in practice and training activities. Others, particularly golfers, baseball players, and softball players, have been found to spend almost equal amounts of time on activities related to their sports (Wolverton, 2008). This time in practice and related activities is above the time spent for student-athletes in the classroom or their time with other outside-of-classroom activities. Student-athletes at lower levels (i.e., NCAA Division III), unlike their counterparts at Division I, have traditionally had more time for campus life activities outside of the requirements of their sports. Some student-athletes at the Division III level have been found to be more active in campus life than their nonathletic counterparts. For many student-athletes, the challenge remains maintaining their eligibility to play their sport, with little or no interest in extracurricular activities beyond intercollegiate athletic participation. Their goal in essence is to avoid low grades and to retain their eligibility (Adler & Adler, 1985).

Academic and athletic motivation influences the degree to which student-athletes develop intellectually and socially. The conflict that can exist between these two forms of motivation can be complicated even more due to the peer culture that surrounds some student-athletes. This peer subculture can often discourage student-athletes from putting in the effort that it takes when it comes to academics. Some student-athletes have been ridiculed by their peers for taking too much of an interest in being academically successful (Adler & Adler, 1985). Gaston-Gayles (2004) found that student-athletes who were labeled as acceptors of failure (i.e., not motivated to seek academic success) were more likely to focus on being successful athletes rather than scholars. While many student-athletes enter colleges and universities optimistic about their academic experiences and possibilities of graduating, these feelings can be dashed when encountering the challenges that arise between academic and athletic motivation (Adler & Adler, 1985). These challenges can be experienced to a higher degree by black student-athletes, who have a greater desire to play sports on the professional level (Snyder, 1996). Those student-athletes with low academic motivation and higher athletic motivation (or who aspire to play professionally) are more likely to devote more of their attention, if not exclusive attention, to participation in their sport. When this occurs both their education and career preparation become less important than their desire to participate in intercollegiate athletics (Broom, 1982).

PREPARING FOR LIFE BEYOND THE CLASSROOM AND PLAYING FIELD

Many will argue that the goal for every student-athlete should be to prepare for life beyond intercollegiate athletic participation. Even for those student-athletes who go on to professional careers, they must at some point experience a retirement from athletic participation. Colleges and universities have continued to raise their academic standards for student-athletes in response to growing expectations from athletic associations, particularly the NCAA. These standards, both at the association and institutional level, have been developed to keep student-athletes on track to graduate (Wolverton, 2008). Wolverton (2008) found that one in five student-athletes said their participation in intercollegiate athletics led to their choosing the major they wanted. Some research (e.g., Gaston-Gayles, 2004) has found that the desire to play sports at the professional level may also be related to higher aspirations to obtain a college degree. Not all student-athletes share these higher aspirations as the demand of academic and career preparation have been linked to some student-athletes' inability to balance their academic work with athletic participation (Adler & Adler, 1991; Simmons, Van Rheenen, & Covington, 1999). Some researchers (e.g., Pascarella et al., 1995) have found that athletic participation may be negatively linked with overall involvement with the college experience and that career maturity and preparedness may be affected as a result. Many student-athletes lack clarity in their educational and career preparation goals. These should be the focus of support services for student-athletes, as was previously addressed in this chapter.

A number of student-athletes choose graduate studies at the completion of their collegiate athletic participation. For student-athletes who pursue graduate study, their choice of degree program, not unlike nonathletes, depended on their academic performance, aptitude, and attitudes. These could be traced to their entrance into college as freshmen (Shulman & Bowen, 2001). The rates at which student-athletes enter graduate study are not fully known, but the rate at which student-athletes go on to graduate study has been found to be consistent across institutional types, with the exception of Division I schools. These student-athletes were less likely to attend than their student-athlete counterparts at other types of institutions (Shulman & Bowen, 2001). Colleges and universities have an obligation to ensure the success of their student-athletes both inside and outside of the classroom. This includes their career and/or graduate school preparedness.

CONCLUSION

Student-athletes' learning experiences both inside and outside of the classroom are important elements of the college and university experience. As has been discussed in this chapter, the degree to which student-athletes experience learning in these settings is influenced by a variety of factors, both within and beyond their control. Student-athletes, as well as the faculty and staff who work with them, should carefully examine opportunities for learning and seek balance between time spent on the playing field and time spent preparing for a career beyond intercollegiate athletics. This involves the intentional coordination of services to support learning and athletic participation, both provided at the athletic association and institutional levels. The goal for every student-athlete should be to prepare for life beyond intercollegiate athletic participation through learning activities inside and outside of the classroom. By helping student-athletes achieve this goal each of us can contribute significantly to the holistic development of our student-athletes in meaningful ways.

REFERENCES

Abell, V. L. (2000). *2000–01 NCAA Division I Guide to Eligibility.* Indianapolis, IN: National Collegiate Athletic Association.

Adler, P., & Adler, P. A. (1985). From idealism to pragmatic detachment: The academic performance of college athletes. *Sociology of Education, 58,* 241–250.

Adler, P. A., & Adler, P. (1991). *Backboards and blackboards: College athletes and role engulfment.* New York: Columbia University Press.

Astin, A. (1993). *What matters in college?: Four critical years revisited.* San Francisco: Jossey-Bass.

Bok, D. (2006). *Our underachieving colleges: A candid look at how much students learn and why they should be learning more.* Princeton, NJ: Princeton University Press.

Broom, F. (1982). De-training and retirement from high level competition: A reaction to retirement from high level competition and career crisis in sports. In T. Orlick, J. Partington, & J. Salmela (Eds.), *Mental training: For coaches and athletes* (pp. 183–187). Ottawa, ON, Canada: Coaching Association of Canada and Sport in Perspective.

Cantor, N. E., & Prentice, D. A. (1996). The life of the modern-day student-athlete: Opportunities won and lost. In S. Richards & E. Aries (1999). The division III student-athlete: Academic performance, campus involvement, and growth. *Journal of College Student Development, 40*(3), 211–218.

Carodine, K., Almond, K. F., & Gratto, K. K. (2001). College student athlete success both in and out of the classroom. In M. F. Howard-Hamilton & S. K. Watt (Eds.), Student services for athletes. *New Directions for Student Services, 93,* 19–33.

Etzel, E. F., Ferrante, A. P., & Pickney, J. W. (Eds.). (1996). *Counseling college student athletes: Issues and interventions* (2nd ed.). Morgantown, WV: Fitness Information Technology.

Figler, S. K., & Figler, H. (1984). *The athlete's game plan for college and career.* Princeton, NJ: Peterson's Guides.

Gaston-Gayles, J. L. (2004). Examining academic and athletic motivation among student athletes at a division I university. *Journal of College Student Development, 45*(1), 75–83.

Gunn, E. L., & Eddy, J. P. (1989). Student services for intercollegiate athletes. *College Student Affairs Journal, 9,* 36–44.

Hood, A. B., Craig, A. F., & Ferguson, B. W. (1992). The impact of athletics, part-time employment, and other activities on academic achievement. *Journal of College Student Development, 33,* 447–453.

Jordan, J. M., & Denson, E. L. (1990). Student services for athletes: A model for enhancing the student-athlete experience. *Journal of Counseling and Development, 69,* 95–97.

Kuh, G. D. (1995). The other curriculum: Out-of-class experiences associated with learning and personal development. *Journal of Higher Education, 66*(2), 123–155.

Medalie, J. (1981). The college years as a mini-life cycle: Developmental tasks and adaptive options. *College Health, 30,* 75–79.

Murphy, G. M., Petitpas, A. J., & Brewer, B. W. (1996). Identity foreclosure, athletic identity, and career maturity in intercollegiate athletes. *The Sport Psychologist, 10,* 239–246.

Oppenheimer, B. T. (1984). Short-term small group intervention for college fresh-men. *Journal of Counseling Psychology, 31*(1), 45–53.

Passcarella, E. T., Bohr, L., Nora, A., & Terenzini, P. T. (1995). Intercollegiate ath-letic participation and freshmen-year cognitive outcomes. *Journal of Higher Education, 66*(4), 369–387.

Passcarella, E. T., Truckenmiller, R., Nora, A., Terenzini, P. T., Edison, M., & Hage-dorn, L. S. (1999). Cognitive impacts of intercollegiate athletic participation: Some further evidence. *Journal of Higher Education, 70*(1), 1–26.

Pascarella, E. T., & Terenzini, P. T. (2005). *How college affects students, Vol. 2. A third decade of research.* San Francisco: Jossey-Bass.

Pearson, R. E., & Petitpas, A. J. (1990). Transitions of athletes: Developmental and preventive perspectives. *Journal of Counseling and Development, 69,* 7–10.

Perna, F. M., Zaichkowsky, L., Bocknek, G. (1996). The association of mentoring with psychosocial development among male athletes at termination of college career. *Journal of Applied Sport Psychology, 8,* 76–88.

Richards, S., & Aries, E. (1999). The division III student-athlete: Academic perfor-mance, campus involvement, and growth. *Journal of College Student Development, 40*(3), 211–218.

Shulman, J. L., & Bowen, W. G. (2001). *The game of life: College sports and educational values.* Princeton, NJ: Princeton University Press.

Simmons, H. D., Van Rheenen, D., & Covington, M. V. (1999). Academic motivation and the student athlete. *Journal of College Student Development, 40,* 151–162.

Snyder, P. L. (1996). Comparative levels of expressed academic motivation among Anglo and African American university student-athletes. *Journal of Black Stud-ies, 26,* 651–667.

Stone, J. A., & Strange, C. C. (1989). Quality of student experiences of freshmen intercollegiate athletes. *Journal of College Student Development, 30,* 148–154.

Suggs, W. (1999). NCAA says it can show "direct link" in athletes' test scores and graduation rates. *Chronicle of Higher Education, 45,* A70.

Umbach, P. D., & Kuh, G. D. (2004). Disengaged jocks: Myth or reality. Wabash College: Center for Inquiry in the Liberal Arts. Retrieved May 6, 2008, from http://liberalarts.wabash.edu/cila/displayStory_print.cfm.

Umbach, P. D., Palmer, M. M., Kuh, G. D., & Hannah, S. J. (n.d.). Paper presented at 44th annual Association for Institution Research Forum, Boston.

Watt, S. K., & Moore, J. L. (2001). Who are student athletes? In M. F. Howard-Hamilton & S. K. Watt (Eds.), Student services for athletes. *New Directions for Student Services, 93,* 7–18.

Wolverton, B. (2008, January 25). Athletes' hours renew debate over college sports. *Chronicle of Higher Education, 54*(20), A1.

PART IV

INSTITUTIONAL DIMENSIONS TO STUDENT ATHLETES

CHAPTER 15

ACCOUNTABILITY TO ATHLETICS STAKEHOLDERS

Kenneth Borland
East Stroudsburg University of Pennsylvania

Richard D. Howard
University of Minnesota

Calli Theisen Sanders
Iowa State University

Thomas Gioglio
University of Pennsyvlania

What began in America's 17th century as intracollege student recreation became intercollege student-driven competition in the 19th century. Then in the 20th century, it became an object of national attention and part of regional if not American culture. Today, in the 21st century, it is a matter of significant concern to numerous college, intercollege, and external stakeholders who expect more accountability regarding it. Of course, the object of this evolution of engagement and attention is collegiate athletics.

College Student-Athletes: Challenges, Opportunities, and Policy Implications, pages 219–233
Copyright © 2009 by Information Age Publishing
All rights of reproduction in any form reserved.

Therefore, it is important to grasp the basics in regard to accountability to athletics stakeholders. What is accountability and who are stakeholders? Are there accountability and stakeholder contextual distinctions between and commonalities among NCAA divisions? Within contexts, how should one consider athletics data and reporting for greater stakeholder accountability?

ACCOUNTABILITY AND STAKEHOLDERS

Definitions

"Accountability" is increasingly common in American society, legislatures, and institutions of higher education. By definition, accountability is a willful and/or obligatory demonstration of one's or an organization's actions (including the results) and an acceptance of responsibility for those actions. Being accountable requires organization leaders to transparently and continuously demonstrate the organization's actions to stakeholders and to be responsive to their continuous input.

Stakeholders are vested organization observers and participants. The corpus of stakeholders is variegated, each individual or subgroup caring about the organization's qualitative and/or quantifiable actions and results but for a variety of reasons. John M. Bryson, in *Strategic Planning for Public and Nonprofit Organizations: A Guide to Strengthening and Sustaining Organizational Achievement*, provides a definition of a stakeholder linked to the concept of accountability and organizational success.

> A stakeholder is any person, group, or organization that can place a claim on an organization's attention, resources, or output [present and future], or is affected by that output.... [An organization's] attention to stakeholder concerns [accountability] is crucial because the key to success in public and nonprofit organizations is the satisfaction of key stakeholders. (1988, pp. 33, 55)

Historical Athletics Stakeholder Accountability

There has always been and will remain collegiate athletics stakeholder expectations for winning seasons and championships, defeating the rival, honoring and perpetuating traditions, the best facilities for preparation and competition, positive press, and so forth. Two 20th century stakeholder calls for greater collegiate athletic accountability proved to be of historic proportion, forever impacting collegiate athletics. A third call, with a potentially similar impact, is rising.

At the start of the 20th century, the Muckraker press turned public opinion against college football and contributed to calls for its reform. This fueled President Theodore Roosevelt, in 1905, to call coaches to the White House to give an account regarding brutality in the collegiate game. As a result, in 1906 the NCAA was formed and arguably became intercollegiate athletics' premier stakeholder, demanding accountability for the qualitative and quantifiable actions and results not only of intercollegiate sport but of student-athletes' collegiate education.

Title IX of the Education Amendments of 1972, written in an era of increased awareness that discrimination in educational institutions was the *status quo*, states "No person in the United States shall, on the basis of sex, be excluded from participation in, be denied the benefits of, or be subjected to discrimination under any educational program or activity receiving federal financial assistance." The government's desire for collegiate accountability, in terms of equitable participation and benefits as well as nondiscrimination, extended to the academic and has become best known within the context of the collegiate athletic venue.

These two examples of stakeholders' expected accountability challenged leaders of higher education institutions and their athletics programs from the outset, and the generations of leaders who have followed until this day.

Today's Athletics Accountability and Stakeholders

While the direct and long-term impact on intercollegiate athletics is not yet definitive, today there is a groundswell of demand for increased accountability in all of education, significantly focused on value being added to all students, and that groundswell has been operationalized by state, regional, and national entities.

Regional and professional accreditation organizations demand more data and documentation of assessment-based improvement relative to stated academic learning, human development, and resource desired outcomes. The federal government significantly engaged this demand: Note the No Child Left Behind legislation and the U.S. Department of Education's "A Test of Leadership—Charting the Future of U.S. Higher Education," known as The Spellings Report (U.S. Department of Education, 2006). Higher education institutions, notably NASULGC and ASSCU member institutions, which represent a significant population of America's public four-year institutions of higher education and students, have responded by engaging the new Voluntary System of Accountability, or VSA (Fields, 2008; Hammang, 2007).

For a compelling discussion of this press for greater accountability and achieving it in higher education today, while balancing public, academic, and market demands, see Burke and associates (2005). Also, *Change* (September/October 2007) provides valuable perspective in articles focused on accreditors and the federal government (Eaton, pp. 16–23), accountability myths (Carey, pp. 24–29), and institutional data and transparency (Kuh, pp. 31–35).

The number and variety of stakeholders has grown. There are numerous internal stakeholders and the external stakeholders have grown well beyond the NCAA and the federal government. Categories of and specific stakeholders will, depending on the institution, its charter, and mission, and relative to variations in its athletic programs. A simplistic categorization and illustrations of stakeholders follows.

Some collegiate athletics' stakeholders are external to the college or university and have constituted authority over the institution and/or its athletics program. Executive and legislative bodies within local and state government, athletics associations and conferences or leagues, regional and professional accreditors, and institutional governing boards have certain constituted authority. To these stakeholders, the organization provides direct, formal, authoritative accounts of its actions and results. However, these stakeholders' observations are also informed less directly and less formally via sources with less authority for collegiate athletics.

Some stakeholders are internal, within the institution and athletics program organizational chart. They have direct professional or performance obligations and personal interest in the success of the organization on a regular basis. These include persons from the president to the coaching staff, the registrar and faculty, fiscal and fundraising officers, and so on.

And there are athletics stakeholders, not officially associated with the institution and its program for contractual and/or extended periods of time, who have other significant intrinsic or extrinsic motivations related to athletics' actions and results. Among them are current students (including student-athletes) and their parents, alumni bases, community leaders and fans, boosters and other fans, vendors, and even the press/media may be considered significant stakeholders.

Along with these new and often powerful stakeholders' engagement and support come expressed, expected actions and results. These expressed expectations often are accompanied by significant compliance-based resource demands for time, money, property, political capital, and so on. Not to be overlooked, with each internal and external stakeholder's expressed expectations there also come significant demands for intercollegiate athletics-related information to be generated, assembled, and presented by the institution to its stakeholders. This information from data and reporting far exceeds what can be expressed in box scores.

DIVISION STAKEHOLDER AND ACCOUNTABILITY: CONTEXT COMMONALITIES AND DISTINCTIVES

When considering collegiate athletics and accountability to stakeholders, it is important to contextualize that responsibility. In this regard, accountability is akin to effective decision support, which "requires qualitative information that puts numeric information into the context of the decision to be made" (Howard & Borland, 2001, p. 109). In other words, while collegiate athletics has many commonalities between institutions, there are significant distinctives that must be considered when practicing effective accountability.

Commonalities

One set of stakeholders to which accountability is made with a high level of consistency across NCAA divisions is that of athletic associations and conferences, and the federal government. All NCAA member institutions are accountable to the Association for compliance and reporting in regard to recruitment of student-athletes, amateurism, financial aid, permissible benefits for current student-athletes, regulation of practice and competition, and so on. Most NCAA affiliate institutions belong to an athletics conference, a grouping of university or college sports teams that compete against one another regularly and are united in support of the mission and goals of their conference. Conferences develop their own mission statements, rules, and regulations and serve as significant stakeholders in the athletic programs of their member institutions. Within conferences, stakeholder accountability requirements and practices tend toward similarity.

Colleges and universities that receive federal aid are accountable to the federal government for compliance with Title IX of the Education Amendments Act of 1972, a statute prohibiting gender discrimination in all educational programs. Collegiate athletics programs have been the highest profile and most controversial of programs examined under this law. All athletics programs are required to submit an annual report, the Equity in Athletics Disclosure Act (EADA), to detail intercollegiate athletic program revenues and expenditures, and athletic participation opportunities for students.

Athletics is accountable to its campus community. While not everyone in a campus community will appreciate the value and place of intercollegiate athletics in their institution, athletics programs are a vital part of higher education institutions. Therefore, internal athletics stakeholders (even those in the campus community who are not supportive) need to be made aware, through accountability, of the many characteristics and necessities that make athletics unique to other campus departments. One poignant example of the need to be accountable to campus community stakeholders is the search for a coach. At the highest level of competition (Division I-FBS institutions), coaching searches are conducted much differently than searches for new faculty, often quietly and quickly, and high-profile sport coaches are paid substantially more than their direct supervisors. In many cases they can be paid more than the institution's president. Campus community management, without a higher level of accountability from athletics, can sometimes hinder the ability of athletic departments to operate in their unique yet responsible fashion or fail to have information upon which to build support for athletics. Nevertheless, the athletic department is part of the university, bound to follow its policies and procedures, and is advantaged when it gives account to the campus.

The media plays a key role in shaping public stakeholder opinion about athletic programs on all NCAA levels and can itself be considered a significant stakeholder eligible for certain levels of accountability. The department of athletics is best served by being responsive to and communicating regularly with the press. Today's media market includes the Internet and countless official and unofficial blogs. Many stakeholders who are fans do not hesitate to express their opinions about the athletic program, often disseminating information that has no basis in fact.

When everything is going well for an athletic department, the media can be a tremendous asset. After all, the department of athletics, considered by some to be the "front porch of the institution," is the only department on campus with its own section in local, regional, and national newspapers. On the other hand, if there are real or perceived problems within the athletic department, this type of news can easily end up on the front page of the newspaper and often reflect negatively on the institution. It is critical for there to be good-quality communication between the department of athletics and the university's public relations office in order to effectively manage such a crisis situation. This type of situation also validates the belief that it is essential for the director of athletics to have a direct line to the president. Because of the high-profile nature and ability of the department of athletics to impact the image of the entire institution, the director of athletics is accountable to these external stakeholders.

The intercollegiate athletic committee (IAC) is an internal stakeholder to which athletics may be accountable on respective campuses. The IAC usually represents a variety of campus constituents including faculty, staff, administrators, and students who act as an advisory board to the university president in regard to intercollegiate athletics. They ensure that all policies, procedures, and operations of the program adhere to the philosophy and guiding principles as stated in official university and athletic department documents. The more accountability athletics provides to the IAC, the better the IAC can advise the president.

Where the director of athletics is positioned in the institution's organizational structure or direct reporting line can be a strong indicator of the importance that an institution places on its intercollegiate sports program, its athletics philosophy, a factor defining a context for stakeholder accountability. The director of athletics will directly report to one of a variety of administrators, with no or potentially several persons between him- or herself and the institution's president. The number and type of campus community stakeholders and the level of accountability to each person between the director and the president can vary and will shape the context for stakeholder accountability.

Distinctives

Accountability to stakeholders is best practiced when conducted in a defined context because distinctives shape internal and external stakeholder accountability expectations, requirements, and practices. One useful framework for defining contextual distinctives, utilized below, is that of the several NCAA divisions.

Division I-FBS. Several factors create a different context for stakeholder accountability in the NCAA Division I Football Bowl Subdivision (I-FBS; formerly I-A). These institutions sponsor the highest level of intercollegiate football and have a commitment to provide resources to compete on the national level. Also, there is a minimum paid attendance criterion in order to be classified as Division I-FBS. Thus, having a strong, consistent fan base is essential to competing at this level.

Both factors define the level of accountability and stakeholders. The Division I-FBS Philosophy statement illustrates accountability to various stakeholders:

> ... (c) Recognizes the dual objective in its athletics program of serving both the university or college community (participants, student body, faculty-staff, alumni) and the general public (community, area, state, nation); ... (e) Sponsors at the highest feasible level of intercollegiate competition one or both of the traditional spectator-oriented, income-producing sports of football and basketball ... (g) Strives to finance its athletics program insofar as possible from revenues generated by the program itself ... (NCAA Division I Manual, 2007, p. 324)

I-FBS athletic programs receive widespread exposure, which invites extensive scrutiny, and directors of athletics tend to report directly to the president. They are usually considered senior campus administrators charged to provide a great deal of accountability to many external stakeholders. The department of athletics relies on substantial income from a variety of outside resources including but not limited to ticket sales, television contracts, corporate sponsorships, booster club memberships, and charitable donations. This financial revenue assists the institution's department of athletics with its daily operation, capital projects such as new facilities or upgrades to existing venues, and the funding of student-athlete scholarships.

There is a high level of media interest in I-FBS athletics, a significant stakeholder accountability factor. Football, basketball, and other sports are often televised regionally or nationally, comparatively giving exponentially greater exposure to athletics in this division. The institution and department of athletics garner direct financial benefits by earning revenue through television contracts and publicity agreements. Indirect benefits through television coverage include an increased pool of talented recruits and greater revenues through private donations and corporate sponsorships. Even though there is no organizational accountability to the television industry or to boosters and corporations, athletic departments consider these entities as tremendous stakeholders to the institution and offer certain levels of accountability to them.

Fans and boosters who contribute to the athletic department on any level are significant stakeholders and pay close attention to the activities of the athletic program. They have a keen interest in the on-field and on-court success of the program as well as the student-athlete's academics, citizenship, and service to the community. The successes or failures of the athletic program in any of these areas can be considered a form of accountability relative to these stakeholders' support, and enhance or lessen donations. An athletic program where monetary support is significant is accountable to the contributors.

Divisions I-FCS and I. NCAA Division I Football Championship Subdivision (I-FCS; formerly I-AA) institutions have a stakeholder accountability context similar to Division I-FBS institutions. Most of the division criteria are similar to those for I-FBS institutions, but I-FCS institutions offer fewer scholarships and have less scheduling restrictions.

Division I-FCS institutions and Division I institutions (those that do not sponsor football; formerly I-AAA) have struggled with their identity over the years. Their athletic programs tend to have similar pressure, being accountable to many of the same stakeholders and media exposure as those at the I-FBS level. However, they do so with fewer operational resources.

The most common reporting structure for Division I-FCS athletic directors is a direct report to the university president, but there is a substantial number of directors that demonstrate stakeholder accountability and report directly to the chief student affairs officer. Those who report to a student affairs officer remain accountable to external entities such as donors and the media, but have more of an internal stakeholder accountability focus.

A reporting structure to a student affairs official likely indicates that the institution views its intercollegiate athletic program in a similar fashion to other campus student affairs entities. Athletics is considered to be an additional educational experience and more of a service to students and the community as opposed to a revenue generator and, therefore, is less accountable to external constituencies. Ironically, the expectation that revenues be increased and there be no unfavorable media or fan attention to the program is still extremely high. This helps explain why Division I directors of athletics who do not report directly to the university president are less satisfied with their reporting structure than those with a direct line to the CEO. Athletics directors at Division I-FCS and Division I institutions without football teams have the shortest tenure in their positions compared to all other NCAA divisions. This may be related to director concerns about whether the stakeholder accountability level is consistent with their level of access to the university president (Sanders, 2004).

Divisions II and III. When compared to their NCAA Division I counterparts, which have larger alumni counts and more extensive national exposure, Division II and III institutions have very different contexts for stakeholder accountability. However, the contextual difference is better understood philosophically, then numerically.

The philosophical underpinnings of Division II athletic programs are described in the NCAA Division II Strategic Positioning Platform.

> Life in the Balance. Higher education has lasting importance on an individual's future success. For this reason, the emphasis for the student-athlete experience in Division II is a comprehensive program of learning and development in a personal setting. The Division II approach provides growth opportunities through academic achievement, learning in high-level athletic competition and development of positive societal attitudes in service to community. The balance and integration of these different areas of learning opportunity provide Division II student-athletes a path to graduation while cultivating a variety of skills and knowledge for life ahead. (NCAA, 2008)

Similarly, the overall educational experience is the highest priority for Division III athletic programs. The Division III platform as stated in the 2007–08 NCAA Manual best describes its primary interest:

> Colleges and universities in Division III place highest priority on the overall quality of the educational experience and on the successful completion of all students' academic programs. They seek to establish and maintain an environment in which a student-athlete's athletics activities are conducted as an integral part of the student-athlete's educational experience, and in which coaches play a significant role as educators. They also seek to establish and maintain an environment that values cultural diversity and gender equity among their student-athletes and athletics staff. To achieve this end, Division

III institutions: (a) Place special importance on the impact of athletics on the participants rather than on the spectators and place greater emphasis on the internal constituency (students, alumni, institutional personnel) than on the general public and its entertainment needs. (NCAA, 2007)

These institutions are not permitted to offer scholarships based on athletic ability and consider athletic activities an integral part of the student-athlete's educational experience.

Membership in Division II requires a less significant institutional financial commitment, requires a lower number of sponsored sports, and offers fewer scholarships than Division I institutions. Division II member institutions differ in student body size, educational mission, and reporting structure, so too stakeholder accountability of Division II is also very diverse across institutions. An athletic program where there is an expectation of athletics-related revenues being increased will have a higher level of external stakeholder accountability. If there is no expectation to generate greater or any athletics-related revenue, the intercollegiate athletic program will be expected to operate as other student affairs entities on campus and, therefore, will focus more on internal stakeholder accountability.

Each Division II institution's philosophy will dictate to whom the director of athletics reports, but it is usually the university president or the chief student affairs officer. The most common reporting structure for Division III athletics is to the Office of Student Affairs, the next most common is to the President, and that is closely followed by a direct line to an Academic Dean or Department Chair (Sanders, 2004).

The Vice President for Academic Affairs is another administrator in Division III that frequently oversees the athletic program. With this reporting structure, the department of athletics serves as a recruitment strategy for the institution and is accountable for the enrollment of students to the campus. The institution, therefore, makes decisions regarding extracurricular offerings based on which sports give the institution the best opportunity for enticing prospective high school graduates to their campuses. This stakeholder accountability reaches internal academic and fiscal constituents as well as external stakeholders such as prospective students and their parents.

DATA AND REPORTING

In higher education we regularly generate and disseminate information via teaching, scholarship, and service, and increasingly stakeholders are holding private and public colleges and universities accountable for those actions and the results. Governing bodies, students, parents, accreditation associations, faculty, funding agencies, alumni, voters, the press, and many other internal and external stakeholders are currently pressing for higher levels of college and university accountability. These stakeholders want data-informed reports, couched in the context(s) of concern to specific stakeholders, as a basis for institutional *and* athletics accountability.

Data Needs

To provide athletics stakeholder accountability, one must grasp the need for collection and management of the data that are necessary to meet external accountability mandates and those needed internally to monitor and support student-athlete academic success.

External demands for data typically reflect mandates for accountability. These stakeholders tend to be interested in summary data that reflect the overall academic progress and academic success or graduation rates of student-athletes, usually presented by sport, gender, and race. The primary stakeholders here are the NCAA or other national athletic association, conference governing bodies, and institutional governing boards. In general, the focus of their concern is at the institution and specific sport levels, not the individual athletes. These stakeholders tend to be interested in the overall academic performance of the student-athletes related to that of the general student body and to compare that performance across race and gender. These comparisons are conducted across all sports and within each sport. These reports are usually episodic and reflect a snapshot of the status of student-athletes' academic performance at a given time each year or reporting period.

These same statistics are of interest within the institution, as they provide the base data for analyses of patterns over time that might reflect either gender or racial biases, or if the academic progress and success of student-athletes are consistently below par within a specific sport. These types of analyses are typically conducted at the same time or before the accountability reports described above are developed.

In addition, each semester the academic progress of each student-athlete is reviewed and based on his or her academic standing and each student-athlete is certified as eligible to participate or not. To support this process, specific data reflecting semester course grades and overall academic standing (usually the cumulative grade point average) for each student must be available. These reviews are typically conducted by a faculty member and/or a faculty-based committee with the "faculty representative" signing off on each student's eligibility to participate.

While the timing for each of these activities tends to be different and at times contradictory, the base data required for each activity are the same. To complete any of the accountability reports for external reporting, to conduct the trend analyses, and to certify student eligibility, unit record data, or data about each student-athlete, must be up-to-date, accurate, and available.

Data and Their Sources

The data necessary for the reporting and analyses described above are typically collected by, and the responsibility of, four units:

1. Registrar: Academic standing and progress data are collected and maintained by the registrar. These data reflect grades for individual courses, major, and academic standing. At many institutions, the registrar also maintains systems that provide students and advisors the ability to monitor at any given point the academic progress that has been made by a student toward a specific degree.
2. Admissions: During the admissions process, data about the student's gender and race are collected.
3. Financial Aid: Financial aid data are created and maintained by the financial aid office and typically maintained in a specially designed database.
4. Athletics Department: The Athletics Department is responsible for providing the information about those students that are participating and the related sport information.

Successful institutional reporting and analyses requires that the data from each of these four sources be integrated and available to meet reporting deadlines. In general, integration of data from the financial aid files, the admissions' files, and the registrar are easily done using student IDs. While complex systems, these systems are related to each other through the use of a unique common identifier for each student that is created when the student enrolls. This identifier is then used as the primary starting point for building subsequent databases where academic, financial aid, and other student-specific data are collected and stored.

The data from the Athletics Department is, however, normally collected and stored in a related database that is centrally accessible. Generally, each coach is responsible for providing a list of the students who are participating in his or her particular sport. At some institutions, these lists are maintained in a standalone database in the Athletics Department and, at other institutions, systems have been built and added to the Registrar's databases in which the coach's rosters are maintained. And, in some instances, coaches are asked to generate the rosters at the time the data are needed for generating the reports. How rosters are collected and then maintained is institutionally specific. When there is not a centralized system in which these data are maintained, documented processes for collecting and entering the data, defined responsibilities, and time frames for entering the data, meeting institutional responsibilities for external accountability reporting is at risk.

Issues

The final notion in the above paragraph is important. As outlined above, academic data for all students at an institution are stored on a student records system that is maintained by the registrar. Other demographic data may be kept on files maintained by the admissions office. In addition, data related to financial aid will be kept on still another system and managed by the financial aid officer. Because all of these systems support the operations of these different offices, they tend to be current (i.e., the real-time academic status of any student can be ascertained using the data in these files).

Maintaining data related to athletic participation, the coach's rosters, typically are not a component of the coach's activities associated with preparing students to compete. However, they are the single source of this information, without which analyses and reporting cannot occur.

External reporting (accountability) is driven by time frames that are set by the external stakeholder—primarily the NCAA. Often, these reporting deadlines are inconsistent with the calendars various athletic programs have for recruiting and building a complete roster of participants. Not setting and requiring a specific date on which all participating student-athletes are identified can lead to delays in getting the needed data as coaches are often not sure of their rosters early in the academic year.

Another timing issue is defining when degree recipients are counted. On most campuses, grades are often submitted to the registrar late. Many times, faculty will give students additional time to get work submitted, and students are often given time to make up missed work. In these cases, when the degree files for other (IPEDS) reporting mandates are closed these students often are not counted as they have not completed all requirements for the degree. Shortly after the file is closed, the student completes his or her work and the degree is considered completed by the institution. Athletics directors and coaches invariably want to maximize the number of graduates counted as this is the number that is used to calculate their graduation rates. As such there is often pressure applied to include these late completers. This results in two problems: (1) processing of the data becomes more complicated and often results in delays in getting the reports out; and (2) reports sent to various external agencies reflect inconsistent graduation statistics for the institution. In the second case, questions often arise about the actual number of graduates and the institution's graduation rate.

Organizing and developing guidelines and procedures for the collection and maintenance of athletic participation data can be difficult. However, it is critical if the institution is to be able to develop valid and reliable information about their athletic programs and the academic progress of their student-athletes. It is critical for achieving an appreciated and effective level of internal and external stakeholder accountability.

CONCLUSION

Today, collegiate athletics is a matter of significant concern to numerous college, intercollege, and external stakeholders who expect more accountability regarding athletics. Therefore, it is important to grasp the basics in regard to accountability to athletics stakeholders. The person who would lead or otherwise professionally engage college athletics must understand the nature and work of accountability and who the stakeholders are within and beyond the institution. An awareness of NCAA division contextual commonalities and distinctives will further inform the increasingly necessary work of college athletics stakeholder accountability. And, couched in the context(s) of concern to specific stakeholders, the professional must also intelligently consider athletics data and reporting to achieve appreciated and effective internal and external stakeholder accountability.

REFERENCES

Burke, J., & Associates. (2005). *Achieving accountability in higher education: Balancing public, academic, and market demands.* Sand Francisco: Jossey-Bass.

Carey, K. (2007, September/October). Truth without action: The myth of higher-education accountability. *Change,* pp. 24–29.

Eaton, J. (2007, September/October). Institutions, accreditors, and the federal government: Redefiing their "appropriate relationship." *Change,* pp. 16–23.

Fields, C. (2008, February/March). Transparency and accountability: "College Portrait" project wins eearly praise. *Public Purpose,* pp. 2–6.

Hammang, J. (2007, September/October). Truth in learning: Accountability project nears completion. *Change,* pp. 6–7.

Howard, R., & Borland, K. (Eds.). (2001). *Balancing qualitative and quantitative information for effective decision support.* San Francisco: Jossey-Bass.

Kuh, G. (2007, September/October). Risky business: Promises and pitfalls of institutional transparency. *Change,* pp. 31–35.

National Collegiate Athletic Association. (2007). *Division I Manual.* Indianapolis, IN: NCAA Publishing.

National Collegiate Athletic Association. (2008a). *NCAA Division II Strategic Positioning Statement.* Retrieved August 7, 2008, from www.ncaa.org/.../resources/file/eb4a004f51bd332/SP%20Platform—In%20Color—Two-Sided-8.5X11.pdf?MOD=AJPERES.

National Collegiate Athletic Association. (2008b). *NCAA Division III Philosophy Statement.* Retrieved August 7, 2008, from http://www1.ncaa.org/membership/governance/division_III/d3_philosophy_stmt.

Sanders, C. (2004). *The Administrative Reporting Structure of Athletics Directors in NCAA Divisions I, II, and III Intercollegiate Athletics.* Unpublished doctoral dissertation, Montana State University.

U.S. Department of Education. (2006). *A test of leadership: Charting the future of U.S. higher education.* Washington, DC: Author.

CHAPTER 16

POLICY IMPLICATIONS OF COLLEGE STUDENT-ATHLETES

More than Campus Discussion

Michael T. Miller
University of Arkansas

Daniel P. Nadler
Eastern Illinois University

As outlined throughout this book, college student-athletes face a number of typical and atypical student challenges. They make institutional selections based on rational and irrational criteria, much like the mainstream college student population, and they are filled with emotion and hope as they arrive on campus. They face real-life problems, academic successes and challenges, and career and identity crises upon arriving on campus, and throughout their entire collegiate experience. They represent their institution in competition that can bring fame, fortune, publicity, embarrassment, and prestige to the faculty and public perception of the institution's quality (Cornelius, 1995; Engstrom & Sedlacek, 1989). The potential

College Student-Athletes: Challenges, Opportunities, and Policy Implications, pages 235–241
Copyright © 2009 by Information Age Publishing
All rights of reproduction in any form reserved.

impact of athletics on all types of institutions, ranging from rural community colleges to large, urban graduate-focused institutions is so extreme that college presidents become actively involved in fashioning the policy and practical implementation of athletic programs. The result is an increasingly regulated environment for athletic competition, where rules and regulations have become so dominant that armies of compliance officers and academic support counselors have grown up in many institutions.

The idea of regulating athletic programs has a 100-year history in the United States, dating to Roosevelt's involvement in creating the NCAA (Newman, 1994). The regulation by the NCAA and increasing congressional oversight, accompanied by landmark gender-equity Title IX rulings, have produced environments in athletic offices that are far removed from individual psychosocial or intellectual development, and at times, driven by the profit-potential of athletic programs. Institutions have subsequently turned their attention to what has become called the "athletic arms race" to build newer, more sophisticated athletic facilities and venues in the hopes of swaying athletes to decisions to enroll and to allow for greater economic incentives for ticket prices, advertising, and in selling corporate sponsorships through luxury seats, suites, and skyboxes.

The cumulative effect of attempting to regulate collegiate athletic enterprises is that there is a general failure to agree on the fundamental principles that guide college sports. There is no philosophical discussion to frame what athletic competitions should encompass, and the surprisingly narrow and shallow approach to regulation formation is based largely on short-term problem solving. In 2007, for example, the NCAA eliminated the ability of college coaches to send text messages to student-athletes that they are recruiting. The NCAA, and college leaders, failed to look at the underlying concern about how much contact is healthy and appropriate for college coaches and high school athletes and the resulting pressure, as highlighted by Paul Hewitt in Chapter 4 (this volume), and instead, focused on one small processual aspect of recruiting.

The business of college athletics, entirely reliant on the human capital of student-athletes, is on a collision course with calls for concern about the well-being of student-athletes. There are a number of policy areas that impact this debate and this future, and outlined in this chapter are several domains of policy that need to be considered: institutional policy, agency policy, and federal policy. The chapter concludes with a brief examination of where all of these often divergent policies are leading the academy's effort to allow sport as a central function of student life.

INSTITUTIONAL POLICY

Higher education policy formation is typically seen as a legislative process of consensus development and coalition building. This representative process results in coalitions that rise and fall based primarily on issues and challenges, as compared to tightly defined special interest groups. In NCAA Division I and often II institutions, athletic divisions or departments of intercollegiate athletic programs have become silos and are often hidden from the decision making of the larger institution. The NCAA has additionally focused the interreliance of athletic departments by mandating one faculty member to serve as a "Faculty Athletic Representative." At many institutions with over 1,000 faculty members (or even over 100 faculty members), the notion that one individual can represent the ideals of academic rigor and student interests is highly problematic.

Institutions have a responsibility, however, to provide all students with equal rights and responsibilities once enrolled on-campus. Institutions must enforce codes of conduct, honor codes, and judicial matters with student-athletes as they do with all students. The resultant issues range from policies on how many class sessions can be missed in one semester to living arrangements and hours of outside required work. At many land-grant universities (NCAA Division I institutions), for example, graduate students are restricted in their teaching or research assignments to 20 hours per week. The Council on Graduate Schools similarly enforces the 20 hours per week of work for full-time graduate students. Yet, student-athletes can be required to participate in over 30 hours of participation in training, practices, and gaming. This duplicity is problematic on many levels, including exploitation, but primarily because it represents a lack of understanding or insight on the part of institutions about the responsibility for the primacy of the welfare of students. Similarly, faculty members may be implicated if they ask students to participate in out-of-class activities, yet coaches routinely require summer training of their athletes, claiming "summer conditioning is voluntary, but so is being on the team." Such veiled threats would not be tolerated of faculty or other administrators, but are routinely allowed for coaches.

A similar example is provided when considering an institution's code of student conduct. A nonathlete, for example, is often brought before an honor council or similar judicial board for public fighting or taunting fellow students. Yet student-athletes are encouraged to engage in a certain level of taunting during competitions and gaming. Even fights between student-athletes, however minor, would be brought before most institutions' honor councils, yet are readily tolerated by athletic divisions and even celebrated by frenzied spectators. Such duplicity is partially the result of inconsistent policy implementation, but is also representative of institutional control and consistent poor leadership on the athletic question at many institutions.

A broader discussion on institutional policy includes factors beyond those considered the "letter of the law," meaning what is intended to be good and acceptable. Institutions have an informal curriculum or culture that encourages students to engage in a variety of activities, collaborate with other students in multiple disciplines, and to even collaborate with faculty members in areas of pure and applied scholarship. Yet, institutions have a tendency to restrict the activities and movement of student-athletes on scholarship, in direct contradiction to their treatment of nonathlete students. The policy implication is that at all levels of institutions, there has emerged a class-system that recognizes and exploits those who can bring fortune and fame to an institution, while holding a double standard for other students.

AGENCY AND STATE POLICY

With the wide variety of public and private institutions that participate in intercollegiate athletics, there are few state policies that have universal impact on college-level sports. There are policies that call for the disclosure of public employee compensation and typically gifts or benefits, and these are sporadically enforced with athletic personnel. Some institutions have found loopholes in state regulatory guidelines by paying coaches or administrators two salaries, one from public coffers and one from private sources. Although this would not be allowed for other state employees, it is a readily acceptable process for paying major athletic program coaches salaries.

For private institutions with little or no state oversight, there are relatively few state policies or regulatory questions that impact athletics. There are common codifications of nonprofit behavior related to disclosure and accounting and fair employment, but little to influence how athletes are treated.

The primary policy that influences athletic programs is considered "agency" policy, where institutions voluntarily subscribe to one body's oversight and regulation. Although there are a number of bodies that offer regulation, as illustrated in the chapter on community college athletics, the primary body is the National Collegiate Athletic Association (NCAA). The NCAA is a nonprofit organization that regulates the composition and competition among colleges and universities. As such, the guidelines they develop and oversee regulate the entire process of how and when athletes are recruited, how they are transitioned to an institution, and what kinds of supports can be provided to these athletes. NCAA regulation is extreme and impacts all facets of intercollegiate athletic sports. However, as a regulatory body, they are more concerned with the regulations themselves and less concerned about the philosophical and guiding questions that influence sports.

Grumblings among different factions in the public over the past decade have begun to make headway with the NCAA, but these measures have done nothing substantial to remove the lucrative financial gains the NCAA realizes for nonpaid performers (athletes). Other bodies would have difficulty with the American Civil Liberties Union or organized labor, where those who are in arguable unpaid apprenticeships produce massive profits for institutions have no monetary or financial share of performance. Furthermore, the NCAA, by claiming to be entirely voluntary, avoids antitrust-like behavior even when they authorize institutions to annually renew, or not renew, scholarships to athletes who may not be performing as recruiting coaches might have anticipated. So although the NCAA has policy authority to regulate athletes and athletic programs, they have failed to do so in a manner that supports students or higher education, and instead have gravitated to regulatory behavior void of policy direction.

Another layer of agency policy that may impact athletic programs and student-athletes specifically are conference policies. Conferences are voluntary associations of institutions who agree to compete against each other. Conferences such as the Patriot, Pioneer, and Ivy League have found success as peer groups because they fundamentally believe that by restricting the temptation for "more is better" thinking, they are able to trust each other's actions and treat sports as an extension of the overall learning experience.

FEDERAL POLICY QUESTIONS

There are a substantial and growing number of federal policies that are impacting colleges and universities, including FERPA (protecting educational records), Title IV (gender equity), and HIPAA (protection of medical records). Additionally, congressional inquiries into the ethical behavior of athletic personnel and the fairness of profiting from noncompensated labor have piqued the interest of several key congressional leaders. The overarching federal concern for higher education, as highlighted by Margaret Spelling's commission report, *A Test of Leadership* (U.S. Department of Education, 2006), is on the accountability of higher education to do or produce something. Presumably, and as argued by Hersh and Merrow (2005), higher education has become distinctly tied to job preparation with a deemphasis on learning. Federal involvement, through the regional accrediting bodies, has in turn demanded that institutions be able to document that courses and degree programs demonstrate student learning outcomes and that these outcomes are measurable. Recognizing the interest in account-ability, the consistent message from Washington will be the regulation and involvement of oversight measures that better protect student-athletes.

As with all political decision making, there are temptations and coali-tions opposed to change. These coalitions often unite around the so-called pageantry of big-time sports combined with lucrative financial deals made available through television and radio contracts. In reality, fewer than a third of all major college sports programs are self-sustaining and can sup-port themselves without using student fee or tuition monies. Worse, the ele-gant pageantry often alluded to is replete with alcohol abuse and is typically unrelated to student learning, campus climate or culture, or even alumni networking for the purpose of fundraising. In the popular book, *Rammer Jammer Yello Hammer* (St. John, 2004), these types of abuses are portrayed as glamorous, as mature adults leave work, abandon their responsibilities, and caravan around the southeastern United States to party and refer to 18-year-old student-athletes as warriors of the gridiron.

As long as there is the temptation of easy money, garnered through tele-vision contracts that now offer football and basketball virtually any night of the week, the NCAA and sports will not regulate themselves. These athletic dons should heed these early warnings from Washington that the future may in fact be radically different.

THE FUTURE OF COLLEGE STUDENT-ATHLETES

The NCAA has consistently proven itself to be an organization that operates for the benefit of its member institutions, as perhaps it should, and to that end the NCAA has been highly successful. Yet, an ends-driven organization can have problems, and change is largely inevitable. Change could come from any number of fronts, either forward-thinking college presidents such as Gorden Gee and Scott Cowan who have tried to put athletics to a defined place in their institutions, or it could come from the federal government by demanding that institutions be accountable for their actions. Regardless of the source, many of the abuses occurring too frequently on today's college campuses cannot, and must not, continue.

For the most part, NAIA and NCAA Division III athletic programs have been successful at self-regulation, and lacking the temptation of easy money, have been able to hold sports within a respectful dominion at their institu-tions. In these settings, athletes are heralded and fans still cheer, but at the end of the season, coaches teach and students give their full attention to the classroom (to the extent that any student does or will). But in the large Division I institutions, athletics have at times become a disgraceful example of chasing money and anti-intellectual behavior. Changing the mentality that "greed is good" is highly desired by faculty and the public, but hugely problematic. What to do with a 90,000-seat football stadium?

As critical as much of this volume has been about the state and practice of college athletics, there is still much to be optimistic about. Medical facilities and the training of medical and athletic personnel is at an unmatched level in the history of sports, and training facilities are among those that are the most efficient ever built.

The underlying problem is that college sports have become a big entertainment industry that gives little to nothing back to the performers (athletes). This cannot continue unchecked, and the college athletic enterprise of 15 or 20 years from now will in all likelihood look significantly different. The difference will be the reconciliation between student-athlete expectations and figurative compensation. This volume intended to initiate a discussion about college student-athletes from the perspective of students first, athletes second, and introduce significant points to the conversation about the physical, mental, and academic welfare of athletes. Ultimately, the question of student-athletes must be broached from a philosophical perspective that demands that institutions become insightful and intentional in their offering of entertainment activities, such as sports.

REFERENCES

Cornelius, A. (1995). The relationship between athletic identity, peer and faculty socialization, and college student development. *Journal of College Student Development, 36,* 560–573.

Hersh, R. H., & Merrow, J. (Eds.). (2005). *Declining by degrees: Higher education at risk.* New York: Palgrave.

Newman, R. E. (1994). *Attitudes of high school personnel toward NCAA academic integrity reform measures and proposals.* Unpublished doctoral dissertation, University of Nebraska–Lincoln.

St. John, W. (2004). *Rammer jammer yellow hammer: A road trip into the heart of fan mania.* New York: Crown.

United States Department of Education. (2006). *A test of leadership charting the future of US higher education.* Washington, DC: Author.

Made in the USA
San Bernardino, CA
18 September 2015